The Psychological Covert War on Hip Hop

By Professor Griff

I

This is where the covert war begins on a very subconscious level, in the spirit of a people who have been robbed and spoiled. Robbed of the classical spiritual teachings of our ancestors and spoiled by trading our god for the enemies' wealth. More discussions about the soul are in my book **"The Meta-Physical God-Estry of the Soul of Hip Hop."** These definitions have further altered the true meaning. In actual practice, modern psychology deals almost exclusively with physiology (brain chemistry, neurology, genetics) and the behavior of the biological organism (stimulus-response), completely disregarding and ignoring the mind (man's inner self, and more to the point, man's true and vital self). The dictionaries will sooner or later remove the concept of "mind" completely from the definition following the lead of "official" psychology as taught in western universities and colleges.

Professor Griff teaching a class in Baltimore at Habesha
A Tafari "Nuzulu" Melisizwe Photo at HABESHA in Baltimore, MD in 2011

"We want to raise the level of consciousness of the people to the degree where we can connect with like minded people around the globe to put in place an infrastructure to lay the bases for a new reality, intergrated but separate from thinking our hand picked leading blacks. e need a **L.I.F.E** curriculum," we need a "GOD" centered education. **-- Professor Griff**

First edition-first printing February 2011
All rights reserved copyright © 2011
by: Professor Griff aka Kavon Shah

Published by Heirz To The Shah
ISBN# 0977124290

Kavon Shah
P.O. Box 11902
Atlanta GA 30355
Pka Professor Griff

COVER DESIGN BY:
Marcus "Society" Effinger
Saddiqq Bey
societyprod@aol.com

PHOTOGRAPHY

Tafari "Nuzulu" Melisizwe
kmtvsns@gmail.com

Carolyn Grady
Rhythm Of Life Entertainment
www.RhythmOfLifeEnt.com
Rhythmic Images Photography
www.RhythmicImages.blog.com

Dwayne gross
dwayne@thosecomputergeeks.com
registered@thosecomputergeeks.com

Carolyn Ferrari
http://www.carolynferrarijewelry.com
diamondancer@yahoo.com
carolynferrari@yahoo.com

"Angel" Arlisha Sims
angelmichelle1919@gmail.com

Khalil Amir (A DJ Named Khalil)

Carolyn "Diamond" Ferrari Photo taken at the Charles Wright Museum in Detroit in 2009

This is dedicated to those that are dedicated.

———— Phil Valentine

Art is mind, and mind does not at all need to feel itself obligated to the community, to society, it may not, in my view, for the sake of its freedom, its nobility. An art that goes in unto the folk, which makes her own the needs of the crowd, of the little man, of small minds, arrives at wretchedness, and to make it her duty is the worst small -- mindedness, and the murder of mind and spirit. And it is my conviction that mind, in its most audacious, unrestrained advance and researches, can, however unsuited to the masses, be certain in some indirect way to serve man in the long run.

-----Excerpt from Thomas Mann's Doctor Faustus

Acknowledgements

Master Fard Muhammad, The Most Honorable Elijah Muhammad, The Honorable Minister Louis Farrakhan, my Public Enemy family, Jason Orr, Corey Johnson, Marcus 3x Williams, Otim Larib, Brother Bo, Steve Cokely, Mwalimu Bomani Baruti,"Yaa" and "Nana Mawati"and the Akoben Institute, Kamou Kabon and Nana Mawati, and the Blacknificent Book Store, The Black Dot, Mutwase, Cynthia McKinney, Minister Paul Scott, Davey D, Bro Cedric Muhammad, Del Jones, Professor Leonard Jefferies, Professor Smalls, Professor Simmons, Temple #7 in New York, Mr. Earle Holder and wife Mariland Holder, Nissa Shabazz, Arlisha "Angel" Sims, Kalonji Jama Changa, the Griffin family, Juana Williams, my souljahs Richard Shabazz, Sadiqi Bakari, "KB" The Ghetto Shaman,Martin Muhammad,Lashanda Presley and family.

Chuck D for the vast levels of music history and facts. For the endless ability to see the value of notes that don't fit into a measure of time and corporate plan. Jason Orr for the discussions that push my warrior spirit to the end and then the scholar aspect of the souljah has to show and prove and offer its (Maat) balance and order. Earle Holder – our political discussions kept me in the know about current events and gave me a degree of insight as to the future of Black people plight in America. Minister Paul Scott – thanxz for keeping me abreast on the matter of hip hop as it relates to the African Diaspora. From No Warning Shot Fired, Khalid El-Hakim and the Black History 101mobile museum Tasleem "Taz" El-Hakim and Omari "King Wise" Barksdale, your poetic lyrical vibrations mean a lot in the entire scheme of things...trust me, they do. Rahssan Robinson, if I had a chance to present all of what you have given me, I would more than likely be on the enemy's hit list. WHERE DO YOU GET THIS STUFF FROM? Calvin Benjamen, the deep degree of info right in our faces can only be sent from a scientist with a knack for getting the information that the daily news won't give us. Dr. Scott Whitiker, I am healthier because of you and Dr. Llaila O. Afrika, Jahi Muhammad, we rolled with nothing – imagine if we had a nickel or a dime. Pam Africa, "I know you know that I know." Shahid M. Allah, Anthony "A-Tone" Muhammad, Philip Muhammad, Davey D, Rahiem DeVaughn, Cannibus, Red Pill and Blue Pill. Opio Lumumba Sokoni and family.

Pre-Translating and Editing
Lisa Manley
Anjanette LaCreshia Joell "Jan The Man"
Tasha Hampton Moffett

Translating and Editing done by:
Donna Shannon

Special thanxz to the Publisher of
BlackElectorate.com

http://www.blackelectorate.com/**Cedric Muhammad**

LIVING SACRIFICE

An Angel Sims photo taken in 2010 in Atlanta GA

Romans 12:1 – I urge you therefore, brethren, by the mercies of God, to present your bodies a living sacrifice, holy and acceptable to God, which is your rational (or intelligent) service

KJV: BIBLE

"In the end, we will remember not the words of our enemies but the silence of our friends."

Dr. Martin Luther King Jr.

Forward

"Taking the lowest essence of what the culture has to offer and giving it maximum exposure"
Black Dot, author of Hip Hop Decoded

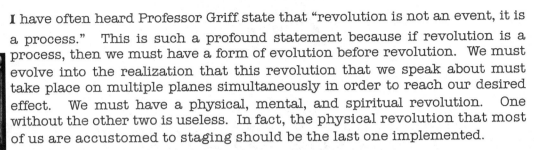

I have often heard Professor Griff state that "revolution is not an event, it is a process." This is such a profound statement because if revolution is a process, then we must have a form of evolution before revolution. We must evolve into the realization that this revolution that we speak about must take place on multiple planes simultaneously in order to reach our desired effect. We must have a physical, mental, and spiritual revolution. One without the other two is useless. In fact, the physical revolution that most of us are accustomed to staging should be the last one implemented.

If we physically take over the "system" without the mental capacity to sustain it and the spiritual knowledge of our existence, then the leftover residue of the Willie Lynch Syndrome will be prevalent in the minds of every Black man and woman in this country. The end result will be brothers and sisters acting like niggers, hoes, pimps, hustlers, and players. Oh, pardon me, that's the way that we act now. Can you imagine how we would act if we had the power, freedom, and resources of a sovereign people?

Hip Hop was supposed to be that vehicle that brought about a revolution on all fronts. It was something in which we physically partook; it mentally put us in tune with our glorious past via the lyrics and images of us as kings and queens, warriors and great builders. And it had potential to bring about a spiritual awakening as well. It is the culmination of all music forms. No genre of music other than hip hop can be credited with uniting people on a global scale no matter what color, religion, or creed as Hip Hop has done. Hip Hop is the new religion. But just like most major religions, after a while, the scripture becomes tainted, misconstrued, and tampered with. This has undoubtedly led the people astray. Hip Hop has become a tool of power used by those who control it.

Can anyone deny that this is exactly what has happened to Hip Hop? There is barely a trace of Hip Hop's true essence alive today. This is no accident. This was purposely done to bring about a divide amongst those who practice the true religion of Hip Hop which encompasses all of the elements, and those who practice rap as a way of life. And just as most major religions have an esoteric teaching which is reserved for a chosen few who understand the religion's true meaning and an exoteric teaching for the masses; Hip Hop has an esoteric and exoteric teaching as well. Those who control Hip Hop control the minds of millions worldwide, so it must die so that it can be reborn again on a higher frequency. We must all become born again Hip Hoppas. Those of us who practice Hip Hop esoterically already know this. Those who are against this rebirth will fight to keep you looking on the outside (exoteric) of yourself for what Hip Hop is really all about, as opposed to finding the true essence of Hip Hop within one's self.

In my humble opinion, that's what this covert war on Hip Hop is really about. It's not about cars, jewelry, gangsta rappers, and poppin' bottles. Those are just the distractions. It's about the realization that we are spiritual beings having a human experience and we can utilize anything at our disposal to bridge the gap between the physical and the spiritual. In the last days, we chose Hip Hop as that bridge, but how many are ready to cross it?

Ask yourself: is Hip Hop all about degrading women? Does BET really entertain me? Why is every rap video filled with half naked women? Is the repetitiveness of songs played a form of brainwashing?

"If you feel that there is nothing wrong with Hip Hop, then this book is not for you. If you feel that gangsta rap, rolling on 20's, violence, drugs and videos with half naked women in them has elevated hip hop as an art form, then this book is definitely not for you. But if, on the other hand, you feel that turning on the radio and listening to the same rap songs that are laced with negative lyrics over and over, watching soft porn or graphically violent videos while reading glossy Hip Hop magazines that endorse this way of life has shaped the minds of our youth, and are collectively being used as part of a mind control operation to mentally and spiritually enslave our future generations, then welcome to: HIP HOP DECODED."

Preface

"Sound Check 1, 2"

This book was not written for the sole purpose, but the soul purpose of educating people about racism, white supremacy and freeing the minds of a generation of young people who will, if they have not already, un-expectantly become victims of this cultural war on their God frequency that is a war on Black people for the purpose of white genetic survival.

I wrote this book to help return Hip Hop to its origin and its original intent. The origin of this work was sparked by three beautiful people to whom I will forever be indebted. The work of the Black Dot, Cedric Muhammad and Congresswoman Cynthia McKinney (D-Georgia) has moved me in such a way where I was convinced that we are under attack, by a people and a government that are about the business of GENOCIDE.

The content of this book is a compilation of life experiences and deep research. This book is a product of being under the tutelage of Minister Louis Farrakhan, Khalid Muhammad and Steve Cokely, learning how to connect the dots and doing the research necessary to unravel the lies in order to present the truth to our people.

This book was written to bring about an understanding of whom and what the enemy is and how the enemy is destroying us as a people. We need to know how racism (white supremacy) and the genocidal program works, who the ones are pulling the strings, making the rules and the laws. We have to unravel this complex web of lies that have gotten Black people into such a poor cultural state. There exist in America 50 to 70 million Black people and millions throughout the world in need of divine intervention in their lives. When we get to the point where our enemy has taken the war to our doorsteps and is tearing away at the very fabric that keeps us bonded one to another, then we can collectively determine it is time to defend ourselves. If not, may the earth reject our bodies. "A courageous man dies but one death, but a coward dies a thousand."

The term "ghetto" is not specifically for Black African people who were brought here for the purpose of enriching the lives of White people who created the most profitable business the world as ever known... Slavery. We as revolutionaries are left with the responsibility of raising the consciousness level.

"You are fishers of men," is what I've been told. The reason why we pour libation is to demonstrate our determination to please the ancestors by our deeds by our conscious behavior.
I would encourage Black people to get knowledge of self. Maybe in some small way, this book can serve as a tool to help educate the human family to the level of the God frequency.

-- Professor Griff

The Rules of Engagement

(Excerpts from the Teachings of the Messenger)

The Most Honorable Elijah Muhammad taught us in our lessons, "The Supreme Wisdom" which are the Original Rules of Instruction to the Laborers of Islam and the title of Muslim given by our savior before his Departure, with a Footnote of a few words of Explanation to lay Pressure Upon their Minds of their many Errors in the Past and Present, that they may see the Light and Walk therein.

The Dumb must speak Plainly. The Stammering Tongue is speaking Clearly. NO man can be Successful in Teaching a People that cannot speak, Clearly, the People's Language.

We are asked the question...and taught to learn the answer verbatim. **If a civilized person does not perform his Duty, what must be done?** If a civilized person does not perform his Duty, which is Teaching civilization to others, they should be punished with a severe punishment. **(Ezekiel - Chapter 3, 18th verse; St. Luke - Chapter 12, 47th verse).**

Ezekiel 3:18
When I say unto the wicked, Thou shalt surely die; and thou givest him not warning, nor speakest to warn the wicked from his wicked way, to save his life; the same wicked man shall die in his iniquity; but his blood will I require at thine hand.

Luke 12:47
And that servant, which knew his lord's will, and prepared not himself, neither did according to his will, shall be beaten with many stripes.

Who are the 10%? A question given to us by the Most Honorable Elijah Muhammad.

ANSWER: The rich; the slave-makers of the poor, who teach the poor lies – to believe that the Almighty, True and Living God, is a spook and cannot be seen by the physical eye.

Otherwise known as: The Blood-Suckers of the Poor. And in the research given to us by Steve Cokely, we have learned to connect the dots. The 10% blood suckers of the poor **are the 13 Bloodlines of the Illuminati.**

Table of Contents

Introduction

The "Ology" of the Mind, Controlled vs. The Study of the "Psyche" Freed

Professor Griff

The definition of "psychology" given to us in an article by Gene Zimmer at **www.sntp.net/ psychology_definition.htm** is a prime example of the theft of African consciousness. The word "psychology" is the combination of two terms – study (ology) and soul (psyche), or mind. The derivation of the word from Latin gives it this clear and obvious meaning: The study of the soul is more accurate. This definition is coming from Black people in ancient Kemet (Egypt).

The study of the soul or mind as traditionally taught in western class rooms is very misleading. **"The mind is not the soul (psyche)."** This meaning has been altered over the years until today; this is not what the word means at all. The subject of psychology, as studied in colleges and universities, currently has very little to do with the mind, and absolutely nothing to do with the soul or spirit. It is important to understand that words and ideas are supposed to refer to something. The realm of mind is an actual realm that can be experienced, and at one time there were words that accurately referred to this realm.

Most of us would agree we have a "psyche" per the above definition in the sense of mind, thought, and emotions. Most would also agree they have a "soul" per the second definition above relating to man's mental, moral or emotional nature. But, according to the history of the known world via the textbooks written by the conquerors, we are taught we were without a soul and had to be rescued and saved from ourselves. So we were enslaved and re-written in the scripture as servants and hewers of wood to justify their enslavement.

The mind control programs they are presently using to control the masses of the people are seen in the genre of music called Hip Hop and in the entertainment industry as a whole. Here are a few covert operations to give you an idea of what is going on in hip hop music today. These covert operations are designed to kill the voice of the voiceless...Hip Hop, not just rap music.

Black people were the original creators of the Arts and Sciences. Bringing "Hip Hop" forward from the genetic code from African spiritual concepts resonated with it from the very beginning because it was the Christ child, the Messiah, "the Messianic Vibration" we were waiting for.

'Your vision will become clear only when you look into your heart... Who looks outside, dreams. Who looks inside, awakens.'

Carl Jung wrote much of his work in German. Difficulties for translation arise because the German word "seele" means both psyche and soul. Jung was careful to define what he meant by psyche and by soul."I have been compelled, in my investigations into the structure of the unconscious, to make a conceptual distinction between soul and psyche. By psyche, I understand the totality of all psychic processes, conscious as well as unconscious. By soul, on the other hand, I understand a clearly demarcated functional complex that can best be described as a "personality." (Jung, 1971: Def. 48 par. 797)"

A "scream" is always just that - a noise and not music,All the works of man have their origin in creative fantasy. What right have we then to depreciate imagination.
Children are educated by what the grown-up is and not by his talk. Every form of addiction is bad, no matter whether the narcotic be alcohol or morphine or idealism.Man's task is to become conscious of the contents that press upward from the unconscious.Read more:http://www.brainyquote.com/quotes/authors/c/carl_jung_2.html#ixzz1bKncCwqJ

"The Study of the mind in western psychology is a lot different from the study of the soul."

. Dr Richard King considers the presence of melanin to be a key agent in heightening psychic sensitivity in the human organism. Melanin in the brain increases from the lower primates and reaches its peak in the BLACK HUMAN.

"All humans possess this Black internal brain evidence of their common Black Afrikan Origin. The All Black neuromelanin nerve tract of the brain is profound proof that the human race is a Black race, with many variations of Black, from Black-Black to White-Black, all internally rooted in a vast sea of Brain Blackness."
    -- Dr. Richard King, African Origin of Biological Psychiatry

Melanin is found everywhere, throughout nature... in animals, plants (that's why raisins and banana bruises are brown), the soil, waters of creeks, lakes, seas, and even in comets! Concentrations vary from parts per million to parts per billion, and it is soluble in liquid phases. Melanin is necessary for humans to reproduce!
Melanin is abundantly present at the inception of life: a melanin sheath covers both the sperm and the egg! In the human embryo, the melanocytes (skin pigment cells), the brain, and the nerve cells all originate from the same place, the neural crest. Melanocytes resemble nerve cells and are essential for conveying energy. When the presence of melanin is missing or insufficient in the ectoderm, this causes the mother to lose her baby; in the case of all whites, a defective baby is produced. Melanin is the major organizing molecule in living systems.

"We are at WAR." **-- Sister Souljah**

The Father of Spin: Edward L. Bernays and the Birth of PR

The Century of the Self: The Untold History of Controlling the Masses through the Manipulation of Unconscious Desires

It is impossible to fundamentally grasp the social, political, economic and cultural developments of the past 100 years without some understanding of Bernays and his professional heirs in the public relations industry. PR is a 20th century phenomenon, and Bernays -- widely eulogized as the "father of public relations" at the time of his death in 1995 -- played a major role in defining the industry's philosophy and methods. Characteristically (and again, paradoxically), Bernays was remarkably candid about his manipulative intent. "If we understand the mechanisms and motives of the group mind, it is now possible to control and regiment the masses according to our will without their knowing it," he argued in *Propaganda,* one of his first books. In a later book, he coined the term "engineering of consent" to describe his technique for controlling the masses. http://www.prwatch.org/prwissues/1999Q2/bernays.html

"The conscious and intelligent manipulation of the organized habits and opinions of the masses is an important element in democratic society," Bernays argued. "Those who manipulate this unseen mechanism of society constitute an invisible government which is the true ruling power of our country. . . In almost every act of our daily lives, whether in the sphere of politics or business, in our social conduct or our ethical thinking, we are dominated by the relatively small number of persons . . . who understand the mental processes and social patterns of the masses. It is they who pull the wires which control the public mind."

Communication professionals should have at least a cursory understanding of Edward Bernays' work. Along with Ivy Lee, he's considered one of the fathers of the field of Public Relations. He may have actually coined the term. Edward Bernays was the nephew of Sigmund Freud, but I'll let the video [posted below] explain that.

"If we understand the mechanism and motives of the group mind, is it not possible to control and regiment the masses according to our will without their knowing about it? The recent practice of propaganda has proved that it is possible, at least up to a certain point and within certain limits."
— Edward Bernays (*Propaganda*, 2005 ed., p. 71)

He called this practice of persuasion the "engineering of consent."

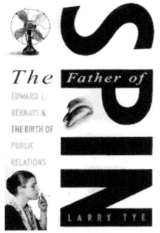

The *Father of* SPIN

EDWARD L. BERNAYS & THE BIRTH OF PUBLIC RELATIONS

LARRY TYE

http://typedesk.com/2009/05/14/the-work-of-edward-bernays/

"If we understand the mechanism and motives of the group mind, is it not possible to control and regiment the masses according to our will without their knowing about it? The recent practice of propaganda has proved that it is possible, at least up to a certain point and within certain limits."

"We are governed, our minds are molded, our tastes formed, our ideas suggested, largely by men we have never heard of. This is a logical result of the way in which our democratic society is organized."

(Edward Bernays, *Propaganda*, 2005 ed., p. 71) He called this practice of persuasion the "engineering of consent."

Edward Bernays and Sigmund Freud are the main characters. It is the first of a four part BBC documentary *The Century of the Self* directed by Adam Curtis. This definition of "democratic society" is itself a contradiction in terms -- a theoretical attempt to reconcile rule by the few with the democratic system which threatened (and still threatens) the privileges and powers of the governing elite. On occasion, Bernays himself recoiled from the anti-democratic implications of his theory. During Bernays' lifetime and since, propaganda has usually had dirty connotations, loaded and identified with the evils of Nazi PR genius Joseph Goebbels, or the oafish efforts of the Soviet Communists. In his memoirs, Bernays wrote that he was "shocked" to discover that Goebbels kept copies of Bernays' writings in his own personal library, and that his theories were therefore helping to "engineer" the rise of the Third Reich.Information Control For Social Manipulation

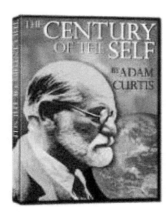

Propaganda Minister Dr. Joseph Goebbels was arguably the most brilliant, fanatical figure in the Third Reich.

The news and entertainment we consume, and thus our thoughts and opinions, are shaped not just by the media and entertainment corporations but by governments, their agencies and the military-industrial complex.

-- David B. Deserano, MS

1ˢᵗ DEGREE

Rap vs Hip Hop.
The Hip Hop Revolution Conceived or Deceived. Racism and The Reality of a Mind Revolution Beyond the 21ˢᵗ Century.

In June 1948, National Security Council Directive 10/2 defined **covert operations** as actions conducted by the United States against foreign states "which are so planned and executed that any U.S. Government responsibility for them is not evident to unauthorized persons and that if uncovered the U.S. Government can plausibly disclaim any responsibility for them." It then authorized the Central Intelligence Agency (CIA) to undertake clandestine activities including "propaganda, economic warfare; preventive direct action including sabotage, anti-sabotage, demolition and evacuation measures; subversion against hostile states, including assistance to underground resistance movements, guerrillas and refugee liberations groups, and support of indigenous anti-communist elements in threatened countries of the free world."

**http://
www.intmensorg.info/
cia.htm**

Read more: http://www.answers.com/topic/covert-operation-2#ixzz1BakzITYu

The presidency of <u>Dwight D. Eisenhower</u> (1953–61) marked the "golden age" of covert operations. More than any other chief executive in the postwar era, Eisenhower made covert action a major part of his foreign policy. The CIA, led by <u>Allen Welsh Dulles</u>, undertook a variety of clandestine activities at presidential direction, including the successful overthrow of unfriendly governments in <u>Iran</u> and <u>Guatemala</u>, and a failed attempt to topple the government of Indonesia. During the Eisenhower–Dulles era, clandestine collection and covert action accounted for 54 percent of the CIA's total annual budget.

Read more: http://www.answers.com/topic/covert-operation-2#ixzz1BakU3Ghl

Cuban leader Fidel Castro, lower right, watched the CIA-funded Bay of Pigs invasion from inside a tank near Playa Giron, Cuba, on April 17, 1961. (Canadian press file, 1961) Read more: http://www.miamiherald.com/multimedia/news/castro/bay.html#ixzz1cV9vQkfO

Although the disastrous attempt to invade Cuba at the Bay of Pigs in 1961 painfully revealed the limits of the CIA's capability for cover paramilitary action and led to the dismissal of Dulles, presidents during the 1960s continued to utilize covert operations with undiminished enthusiasm, most notably in the Caribbean, Africa, and Southeast Asia. Read more: http://www.answers.com/topic/covert-operation-2#ixzz1BakFyefi

"Human progress is neither automatic nor inevitable... Every step toward the goal of justice requires sacrifice, suffering, and struggle; the tireless exertions and passionate concern of dedicated individuals."

-- **Martin Luther King, Jr.**

THE SECRET COVERT WAR ON BLACK AMERICA!

http://africanpress.wordpress.com/2010/08/11/the-secret-covert-war-on-black-america/

The US government's intelligence divisions have developed advances in the studies of behavioral psychology that have given them much more control over its population. It initially used these advancements to develop psychological warfare programs used to manipulate foreign populations, but it was eventually decided that this same method of psychological warfare could be used domestically as a tool to manipulate public opinion.

Today to control and produce uniformity among the masses, the U.S. government disseminates propaganda domestically among its own citizens. The main sources that it uses to spread its propaganda are the Press, the Cinema, Education and the Radio.

This psychosocial program uses propaganda to adversely manipulate and shapes the minds and collective perceptions of Americas Black population by subjecting them to seeing only the fraudulent worst in themselves.

Fred Hampton, Sr.

The U.S. Government has an extensive history of conducting planned campaigns of extensive strategic psychological operations through the national media to domestically direct the perceptions and climate of the nation towards its governmental objectives. Information given through the media can greatly influence every facet of our lives.

"You can kill a revolutionary but you can never kill the revolution"

When these propaganda programs are directed at particular targeted groups, they can be effectively used as psychological manipulation tools while implying that they admire, respect, and trust only Whites. It is designed to break down African Americans sense of racial unity and allegiance, mold the character of self-hatred, self-doubt, self-loath, and distrust among their group. This program conditions Black people to accept white dominance over their lives by misleading them to believe that they are now themselves their own worst enemies.

Through totally white controlled media outlets African Americans are seeing themselves through lenses that have been deliberately assigned to them by white mass media manipulation experts. It is a covert and sophisticated method of control that ensures the continuance of America's white racial hierarchy by manipulating and shaping the minds and collective perceptions of its Black population. This insidious, yet very sophisticated, mass manipulation program works by using the science of psychology.

Bob Woodward, the best investigative reporter in the country, spent six years examining the CIA using hundreds of inside sources and secret documents to paint a picture of the world's largest espionage apparatus

(Left to right- Bobby Seale, Huey P. Newton, Eldridge Cleaver, Fred Hampton Sr)

Kennie Anderson's must-read book, "Land of Hypocrisy," a political, non-fiction book that covers American infrastructures from a perspective not commonly presented, serves as a comprehensive guide to American foreign policy.

Read more: http://blogcritics.org/politics/article/why-it-feels-so-good-to/
#ixzz1WveSstyp

United States of America has been at the top of the charts for quite some time. This top spot has not been challenged by any other government to date. The following is a partial list of America's Greatest Hits, these are some of the atrocities, massacres, murders, and injuries in recent history for which the United States is solely responsible: This list was compiled by Kennie Anderson, "Land of Hypocrisy."

50,000 Haitians killed when the US military destroyed a peasant uprising in 1915.
Between 4,000 and 5,000 Haitians killed in the early 1990s by US-established forces.
45,000 people killed in South Lebanon since 1982 by Israel, always armed and supported by the US.
Hundreds of Black Panther supporters and American Indians framed, beaten, or murdered by the FBI and its cohorts in the late 60's and early 70's.
1,500,000 killed between 1980 and 1988 in southern Africa by the US-armed South Africa.
? Thousands of people in Pacific islands, Puerto Rico, Utah, California, Nevada, Washington, New Mexico, and various other places killed, infected, or harmed as a result of US weapon experiments (especially nuclear weapons and weapons using depleted uranium).
? Hundreds of civil rights activists beaten, tortured, framed, and killed in the US by government agencies in recent history.

As America moves toward a third world war, here is a document from John Stockwell in 1987 which gives you a prime example of how 6 million people were killed in CIA secret wars against third world countries. John Stockwell, former CIA Station Chief in Angola in 1976, worked for then Director of the CIA, George Bush. He spent 13 years in the agency. He gives a short history of CIA covert operations. He is a very compelling speaker and the highest level CIA officer to testify to the Congress about his actions. He estimates that over 6 million people have died in CIA covert actions, and this was in the late 1980's.

SECRET WARS OF THE CIA: by John Stockwell

A lecture given in October, 1987

For research purposes, here is a list of mind control projects that have been exposed over the years:

http://www.informationclearinghouse.info/article4068.htm
http://www.informationclearinghouse.info/article4069.htm

CHAPTER – In 1947, the Navy conducted the first known post-war mind control program, Project CHAPTER, which continued the drug experiments. Decades later, journalists and investigators still haven't uncovered much information about this project - or, indeed, about any of the military's other excursions into this field. We know that the Army eventually founded operations THIRD CHANCE and DERBY HAT; other project names remain mysterious, though the existence of these programs is unquestionable.

CHATTER - 1951 Project CHATTER, a highly classified Navy program to search for a truth drug, began. They were looking for a way to make someone talk "fast" in the event of a security emergency. These experiments used barbiturates, amphetamines, and heroin. The drugs were supplied by the Bureau of Narcotics and pharmaceutical companies. Some of the experimental subjects included the scientists themselves, and mostly students. 1953 Project CHATTER was abandoned by the Navy.

ARTICHOKE – 1951 Project BLUEBIRD was renamed Project ARTICHOKE. The CIA director approved a liaison with the Army and Navy who were interested in finding a truth drug. Another liaison was formed with the Air Force who wanted to study interrogation techniques. Information was also exchanged with the Canadian and British governments. Some of Project ARTICHOKE's experimental subjects included: suspected agents, suspected double agents, people who "had a known reason for deception," American college students (supposedly for more benign testing), and foreigners (since the CIA was more likely to try certain procedures out on them rather than American citizens.) "Terminal" or "to the death" experiments were usually carried out in other countries. According to Bowart, the control method used on two agents involved drugs and hypnosis (narco-hypnosis). The subjects were hypnotically regressed and made to relive past experiences. Posthypnotic suggestions were given to induce total amnesia of their interrogations. The CIA called this experiment "very successful."

BLUEBIRD – 1950 Project BLUEBIRD was approved by the first CIA Director, Roscoe Hillenkoetter. He also approved the use of unvouchered funds to pay for its sensitive areas. This began the CIA's first structured behavioral control program. Their goals consisted of "controlling an individual to the point where he will do our bidding against his will and even against such fundamental laws of nature as self-preservation." Some of their experimental subjects included North Korean prisoners of war and suspected double agents.

The newly-formed CIA plunged into this cesspool in 1950 with Project BLUEBIRD, re-christened **ARTICHOKE** in 1951. To establish a "cover story" for this research, the CIA funded a propaganda effort designed to convince the world that the Communist Bloc had devised insidious new methods of re-shaping the human will; the CIA's own efforts could therefore, if exposed, be explained as an attempt to "catch up" with Soviet and Chinese work. The primary promoter of this "line" was one Edward Hunter, a CIA contract employee operating undercover as a journalist and, later, a prominent member of the John Birch society. (Hunter was an OSS veteran of the China theatre - the same spawning grounds which produced Richard Helms, Howard Hunt, Mitch WerBell, Fred Chrisman, Paul Helliwell and a host of other note worthies who came to dominate that strange land where the worlds of intelligence and right-wing extremism meet.) Hunter offered "brainwashing" as the explanation for the numerous confessions signed by American prisoners of war during the Korean War and (generally) UN-recanted upon the prisoners' repatriation. These confessions alleged that the United States used germ warfare in the Korean conflict, a claim which the American public of the time found impossible to accept.

Many years later, however, investigative reporters discovered that Japan's germ warfare specialists (who had wreaked incalculable terror on the conquered Chinese during WWII) had been mustered into the American national security apparatus - and that the knowledge gleaned from Japan's horrifying germ warfare experiments probably WAS used in Korea, just as the "brainwashed" soldiers had indicated. Thus, we now know that the entire brainwashing scare of the 1950s constituted a CIA hoax perpetrated upon the American public: CIA deputy director Richard Helms admitted as much when, in 1963, he told the Warren Commission that Soviet mind control research consistently lagged years behind American efforts.

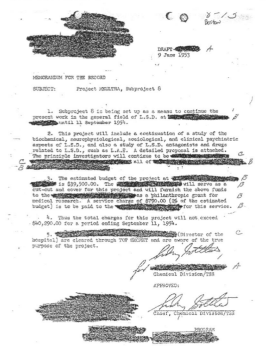

Members of **the Warren Commission** on September 23, 1964.

Mengele's research served as a basis for the covert, illegal
CIA human research program named MK-ULTRA

"Trauma-based mind control programming can be defined as systematic torture that blocks the victim's capacity for conscious processing (through pain, terror, drugs, illusion, sensory deprivation, sensory over-stimulation, oxygen deprivation, cold, heat, spinning, brain stimulation, and often, near-death), and then employs suggestion and/or classical and operant conditioning (consistent with well-established behavioral modification principles) to implant thoughts, directives, and perceptions in the unconscious mind, often in newly-formed trauma-induced dissociated identities, that force the victim to do, feel, think, or perceive things for the purposes of the programmer. The objective is for the victim to follow directives with no conscious awareness, including execution of acts in clear violation of the victim's moral principles, spiritual convictions, and volition.

Dissociative Identity Disorder is a trauma disorder. It is most often the result of experiencing repeated traumas especially early in life prior to age 6

CASTIGATE – 1952 Project CASTIGATE began when the Navy and the CIA teamed up to test a "secret potion" that consisted of a depressant, a stimulant, and the active ingredient in marijuana. The drugs were to be administered over a three-day period. The experiment was carried out in Germany at a secret CIA base on a military installation. Experimental subjects included one known double agent, one suspected double agent and three defectors. Project CASTIGATE was considered a failure.

MKNAOMI – 1952 MKNAOMI (Pronounced M-K NAOMI with M-K standing for mind control.) TSS's agreement with the Special Operations Division of the Army's biological research center at Fort Detrick, Maryland. SOD's job was to produce germ weapons for the CIA's use.

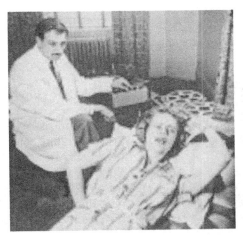

MK-Ultra Dr. Donald Ewan Cameron w/ torture victim

MKULTRA – 1953 MKULTRA, a CIA program for the covert use of biological and chemical weapons began. Bowart states, "According to CIA documents, MKULTRA was 'an umbrella project for funding sensitive projects and covered policy and procedures for the use of biochemicals in clandestine operations.' MKULTRA was exempted from normal CIA financial controls and allowed TSS to begin research projects without contracts or written agreements." TSS stands for Technical Services Staff and was an agency referred to as "the Gadget Wizards," similar to what "Q" is to James Bond. As usual, MKDELTA and MKNAOMI had already been set up prior to the CIA being given official permission for MKULTRA. MKDELTA became the operational side of MKULTRA.

The victim/survivor is called a *"slave"* by the programmer/handler, who in turn is perceived as *"master"* or *"god."* About 75% are female, since they possess a higher tolerance for pain and tend to dissociate more easily than males. Monarch handlers seek the compartmentalization of their subject's psyche in multiple and separate alter personas using trauma to cause dissociation

I noticed the heavy influence of the mind control programs going on in the hip hop community, i see it in the video's and i hear it in the songs. I see more and more artist are pushing the half human half robot agenda. it reminds me of what rage against the machine as been telling us. Below are a few movies to watch to understand the agenda.

The Manchurian Candidate❓: All-American Conspiracy

Real Life All-American Conspiracy ripped from yesterdays headlines makes The Manchurian Candidate a quick course in How the Real World Really Works. Mind control. Microchip implants. Global slush funds. Programmed assassins and patsies. Phony wars for corporate profits. Stage-managed political conventions. Its all there. You know - just like real life. So here are the Real World analogues --

- Mind control - The CIAs MK-Ultra, Project Monarch, and other black (covert) projects recounted by survivors of trauma-based mind control, including Annie McKenna (and Arizona Wilder.Microchip implants - Verichip manufactured by Applied Digital Solutions (Florida) and recently implanted in Mexico's Attorney General office staff for security.Manchurian Global - Read Carlyle Group, a global slush fund masquerading as a private equity fund, employing politicos and world class criminals like former President-CIA Director George Herbert Walker Bush.

  Programmed assassin-patsies - Lee Harvey Oswald (John F. Kennedy murder), Sirhan Sirhan (Robert Kennedy murder), Mark David Chapman (John Lennon murder), Timothy McVeigh (Oklahoma City Bombing) et al

  Phony wars for corporate profits - World War II, Vietnam War, Gulf War, War on Iraq, War on Terrorism, War on Drugs (you could call them the War on American Citizens)

  Phony stage-managed political conventions - Republican Party-Bush, Democratic Party-Kerry (each so-called party selecting a member of Yale's Order of Skull and Bones secret society as candidates for the US Presidential election; by the way, there are only 800 members of the Order world-wide).

It's time to wake up... and get a life. We live in a 3-dimensional world. Until now, the world of computing has been a flat world, consisting of 2-dimensional imagery. Now, through the use of exclusive breakthrough technology, ARC has made it possible for you to get a life. A-Life, where we can work and play in a lifelike world of 3-dimensional reality. A-Life, the living monitor.

.when the chips are down, when the pressure is on, every creature on the face of the Earth is interested in one thing and one thing only.Its own survival.

Somebody got into our heads with big steel-toe boots, cable cutters and a chainsaw and they went to town. Neurons got got got exposed and circuits got rewired. Our brain cells got obliterated, Raymond.

"Universal Mind Control"
MIND CONTROL

Afrika Bambaataa and Kool Herc

Describe the social climate during the 70's during the birth of Hip Hop. Was Hip Hop a product of the social & economical struggle within NYC?

The Social Climate during the 70's were Revolutionary Groups, The Black Panthers, The Nation of Islam, The Young Lords Party, SNCC, The Ansaaru Allah Community, Street gangs, The Ku Klux Klan, The Weathermen, Soul Train, Fania All Stars, Funk, Rock, Salsa, Salsoul, Soca, Calypso, Hard workers in the communities, Drugs, Crime, Police, Police Brutality, Politicians, Pimps, Fires, Block Parties, Concerts, TV Shows like Batman, Dark Shadows, Green Hornet, Soap Operas, American Bandstand, Wolfman Jack, Frankie Crocker, The Midnight Special, Soul, The Bill Cosby Show, The Jefferson's, Room 222, Welcome Back Kotter, Kojack, Death wish with Charles Bronson, Blacula, Abby, Superfly, Hell Up In Harlem, Black Cesar, Slaughter, The Price is Right, Lets Make a Deal, The Ed Sullivan Show, Johnny Carson, Five on The Black Hand Side, Putney Slope, Five Fingers of Death, Karate Movies, & the list goes on

Grandmaster Flash

Afrika Bambaataa

My thoughts on revolution in the realm of hip hop should be understood in the context of waging war on the weakness of self (self being "higher" and "lower" self). On one level, we should begin with the steps of bringing about a physical change for us as a people by battling those inner demons. We must truly begin to do as our ancient ancestors have taught us. "Know Thy Self." All of those revolutionaries that came to bring about a change in the minds and hearts of the people have all said the same thing. We must begin to remove ourselves from the wicked un-civilized nation as the scripture teaches us here is excerpt from the Honorable Minister Louis Farrakhan's address on the occasion of the 12th Anniversary of the Million Man March, delivered from the Atlanta Civic Center on Tuesday, October 16, 2007:

I want to talk to you today, about that voice in the 18th chapter of Revelations, a voice from heaven saying, "Come out of her my people, that you be not partakers of her sins and her plagues, for her sins have reached unto heaven." This means that the deviation, the abomination and filth of this world permeates America and it has even reached the holy people. Jerusalem is no longer a holy city except in name, for the filth and abomination of this Mystery Babylon has reached Jerusalem. It has reached Mecca, it has reached Medina, and if Rome, as the seat of Christendom where the Pope as the vicegerent of Christ resides, the filth and abomination of Satan's world has reached Rome and The Vatican.

In other words, the sin of this world has reached the height and the degree where God, Himself, is angry and is now sending plagues that reflect His absolute displeasure with the degree of sin and the abominations that have engulfed God's people and the world that is ruled by Satan. Even the Holy Qur'an, which is the Book of scripture of Muslims, says in these words, "Set your face for religion, being upright." The Honorible **Minister Louis Farrakhan**

Inside of the word revolution we have the word "re" meaning to go back to, and we also have the word "evolve" and "evolution" In the word revolution we have re-evolve in order to bring about the desired results.

Dr. Khalid Abdul Muhammad said to me that "revolution is complete, constructive, conscious, cosmic change." As I studied the revolutions that have taken place throughout the world of indigenous people's right to exist, I noticed a common factor: we were all fighting the same enemy. I open here with Malcolm X's voice in my head when he said, "You write revolution off as though you made one." In a meditative state, I often try to synthesize revolutionary ideologies to bring about a quick solution to a vast and complex problem. Then Steve Biko offers an answer that I must respect so that I don't get burnt out. "Revolution is not an event, it's a process." Revolution is not about love, it's about survival.

There's no such thing as a non-violent revolution. There's no such thing as a peaceful revolution. Revolution is bloody and knows no compromise. The revolutionary will kill because death threatens him; the government kills because life threatens them. I am not committed to nonviolence in the face of the most violent race of people known to man. Then my Christian revolutionary brother interjects the teachings of Dr. Martin Luther King Jr., "Those who make peaceful revolution impossible, make violent revolution inevitable. Violence in the context of revolution is not good or evil, it is necessary." As I pray, I often think of the idea of "Desperate times call for desperate measures" and I ask myself, am I willing to pay the ultimate price to advance Black people's cause for liberation and freedom? I am quickly reminded that there are no spectators in this fight for freedom, justice and equality. Malcolm X often is in my head. I hear him as clearly as you hear me, "Revolution is not a spectacle, there are no spectators. Everyone participates. Whether you know it or know it not."

It's a matter of life as an oppressed, kidnapped slave destined for jail or the grave or both, or death as a revolutionary freedom fighter. Frederick Douglas said, "We may not get all that we pay for in life, but we sure pay for everything we get."

Rap, as I understood it, is only one part of a four-part foundational structure which serves as a basic foundation for a sub-culture called hip hop. Hip Hop as explained to us by minister server from KRS ONE's temple of hip hop was an acronym which stood for **H**igher **I**nfinite **P**ower **H**ealing **O**ur **P**eople. The other three elements – breakin', MC'ing, and DJ'ing as given to us by our forefathers - coincide with the four elements of the universe, earth, air, fire and water. On the cover of **Hip Hop Decoded (from its ancient origins to its modern day matrix**) written by The Blackdot, we are given a perfectly deep illustrated picture of hip hop and the theft of hip hop by the culture bandits. Here we find the Kaballah, which is the tree of life sitting over the Medu Ntr (the divine writings) paralled by the matrix of hip hop (a parallel universe).

On top of that is a Black man who represents the GOD standing over his black dot (his pineal gland, third eye) as Dr. Richard King teaches us, displaying the four elements earth (Graffiti), Air (the DJ), Water (B-Boy), Fire (Emcee). From alpha to omega, beginning to the end, showing that we were always here and we will always be here. From its ancient origin and now its modern day matrix, NIGGERS to GODS, in which the matrix turned us from GODS to Niggers.**http://da.ish.free.fr/English/Hip_hop_culture.html**

Graffman which paints a subway train

DJ behind its vinyl platinums

young b-boy dancing in the street

Here are a few simple questions I had the pleasure of getting answered from my brother Chuck D from public enemy. Dealing with Rap vs. the hip hop revolution, a revolution conceived or deceived, as it relates to a mind revolution. I have sent these questions to my brother Chuck D to get some insight on where we are today in this war for the minds and hearts of our people.

Prof. Griff: Was, is, or will there ever be a Hip Hop Revolution? If so, what kind of revolution will it be? If not were we deceived?

"During times of universal deceit, telling the truth is revolutionary."
-- **George Orwell**

A Conversation / Interview with Chuck D

Chuck D: There will not be any HIP HOP Revolution until the architect is respected. Hip Hop is an evolution, not a revolution. The elements evolved from black culture which was heavily paramount in North America because it was the main expression of black people throughout slavery, Jim Crow and afterwards. Black art had started as code, love music to lookout and let those who felt that language know what was coming and happening. Thus, in Black folks' music there was and is a closer attachment to it.

Hip Hop's elements did not start in the 1970s; they were just modified and re-termed. For example, EMCEEing is Vocalization – you can compare NAS, Billie Holiday and a griot on a similar scale. TURNTABILISM is musicianship, whether it's Grandmaster Flash on 2 turntables or jazz pianist Art Tatum. BREAKDANCING is dance originating to the beginning of time, and GRAFFITI goes beyond hieroglyphics.

The deception is that hip hop started from nowhere, out of nothing. Without its foundation of history and legacy, revolution of change from it will be designed, predictable and probably against the people it came from.

Prof. Griff: Is the reality of a Hip Hop mind revolution, will you see it in your time?

Chuck D: Geography is an important, necessary and essential tool for freedom. Most Americans **period** know little of either, thus they are chained to their birth-rock. The Hip Hop mind revolution can be possible with real things and realities in place. If the culture does not reconnect itself to the Diaspora, it will continue to recycle slave rhetoric, rebellion and dependency like a dirty wash. Not knowing where you from and where you are will keep one spinning in circles just like the 45s, 12 inches and CDs that DJs used to spin. Thus, that without History AND geography, that will be the only revolution in circles.

Prof. Griff: Are we still in the musical age of black music, white business?

Chuck D: Since the 1920s we have had black music, white business. This is because we have never really been on the end that gets the music past the musician or the instrument. The musician has always been performance art. The industrial age came along to sink its hooks into the business of communications -- radio, television, pressing of sounds into discs, players to play them, record players, transistors, walkmans, tape recorders, CD players, mp3 iPods and cell phones.

For years it was a standoff, and a rip-off business wise.   Standoff because regardless of whatever technology was invented, they couldn't emulate a people's soul. Once it was the main thing Black folk had. It disappears like the polar caps every decade from 'global warning'. Now in the new century, the business is more 'white' than ever, or maybe non-black in America because of lack of knowledge of self in turn makes it also clueless to whom, what and how it was created. Now "black music" is a term that rings hollow. "Urban" has replaced the term, which means you can have a black face of course, but the ownership, accountability and responsibility from where it came from is forsaken. It is a reduction and transition of a musical age into a product age of image.

Prof. Griff: Your open letter to hip hop, what did you want to accomplish as your overall goal?

Chuck D: Creating an accountable infrastructure from a 'pimpastructure'. Everything circling and hovering around the artists I wanted to confront and address.   There's an imbalance of varied topic existed in the projection of hip hop. I didn't 'go in' on any artists per se; I went for their masters. There's an imbalance of accountable people who surround and govern HIP HOP as a selling culture. My point is that worldwide it is more than that, and not simply product for product's sake.

And I wasn't simply pointing at a white executive who just profited off the genre and was oblivious to the fact of the music and community's call and goal to re-connect the human family at its best, while disregarding the faces he was behind. I was also pointing at the laziness in DJs, the clichés, the individualism, the manipulation of women's images, the distancing of the art form away from the youth, and the rest of the earth's HIP HOP homage and respect to the fundamentals and the legacy of the history.

The goal was to make American HIP HOP cats wake up and recognize a world that hasn't just caught up, but surpassed in thought, style, commitment, and skill.

Prof. Griff: Has the Black overseas African Diaspora felt the effect of this demonic paradigm in black music?

Chuck D: Yes, and I encouraged the hip hop community in South Africa and Nigeria to NOT follow the USA. That they are superior in the commitment to the legacy of people and the craft of latter culture such as hip hop, it might have to be the other way around. I warned that companies like VIACOM sting up MTV in Africa had an agenda of turning Africans into Americans by trying to impress them with the same false materialist B.S. that unbalanced HIP HOP in the USA.

The cell phone companies setting up to carry content could be used against Africans through the portal of RAP music with some men pushing buttons in a New York or Los Angeles boardroom. I told many that the cell phone, while being a great innovative tool for communication, also is a double edged sword, a human remote so to speak, if humans don't stay on top of these apparatuses rather than stoop to their glitz and bling.

In fact I had to reinforce history and legacy to many people they call 'born free' as they were born post-apartheid in South Africa and have been directed in such a way to not look back. There were many Public Enemy supporters in South Africa that co-signed this re-enforcement of values to the media. And this was different from the USA.

Prof. Griff: Is there a psychological covert war on hip hop?

Chuck D: Yes, because communication is a two-way street. It goes in and out. Hip Hop is a cultural communicative force. The technology and devices that allow sight, sound, and text seem to ride the hip hop wave today in a way very few past cultures have done. Sight, sound, and text are the key tools in propaganda, thus mind control. Mind control is the elemental basis in slavery. The body and the soul will follow. The powers that be have understood this for centuries and now people volunteer for this new slavery through the guise of entertainment.

It's easy for the corporate financial powers that be to say that hip hop is the biggest music today when it actually isn't. It's propaganda, and actually there has been a grass roots initiative against its negativity for years. This is obscured by the fact of popular culture fabricating numbers with little meaning.

How big can hip hop be with the disappearance of women in the scope?
How big can hip hop be with the disappearance of groups?
How big can hip hop be with the exclusion of the more dominant international scene?

The psychological war spawns from its business based re-definition from people who look and feel differently than the people they project and exploit.

Never have so many been pimped by so few. Since the music has so much power, and image has become everything to the point that it can dictate the direction of a person in their life, it is my mission now to really become a "freedom fighter" and stop this radiation. With Jay-Z and others who, for years would faint their worth, the statement of "with great power comes great responsibility," is truer. Words are powerful and they can both start wars and bring peace. This cannot be taken lightly. It's important for the words to be body with the community. If not one dime of $250 million doesn't benefit the people who contribute to it, then why does that warrant coverage above the will and effort of many in the music who have done great things.

[Note: Chuck D wrote this essay as a letter to Chuck "Jigsaw" Creekmur (AllHipHop.com) and Davey D (DaveyD.com). With permission, the message by the Public Enemy leader, has been edited slightly into a scathing editorial about the media, Hip-Hop and the how the culture has been pimped by a mere few.]

Chuck D: Open Letter to Hip Hop

I really don't know what constitutes for "relevant" coverage in HIP-HOP news in America these days, but I really want to give you all a heads up. As you know, I've been through three passports, 76 countries on the regular in the name of Hip-Hop since 1987 and in 2010, although I've never stopped traveling the earth this year, I've seen, heard and felt some new things.

As far as RAP and HIP-HOP, it's like USA Olympic basketball, the world has parity now and has surpassed the USA in ALL of the basic fundamentals of HIP-HOP – TURNTABLISM, BREAKING, GRAFFITI, and now EMCEEING with succinct mission, meaning and skill. Skill-wise rappers spitting three languages have created super rappers to move the crowd with intensity and passion. The "arrogant" American comes in blackface, but if there was a HIP-HOP or Rap Olympics, I really don't think the United States would get Gold, Silver or Brass or even ass for that sake.

Personally, Public Enemy has been setting records in a record book that doesn't really exist. The 20th year anniversary of FEAR OF A BLACK PLANET has become into a year and a half celebration of eights legs and five continents. All the while, looking at a HIP-HOP Planet across 25 countries while still somewhat supportive of American rap, the rest of the world has surpassed the U.S. in skill, in fundamentals and commitment to their communities. Public Enemy's mission is to set the path, pave the road for cats to do their thing for a long time as long as they do it right.

Because of the lack of support from local radio, television and community in the United States, the ability for "local" acts to thrive in their own radius has killed the ability to connect and grow into a proper development as a performer, entertainer and artist. Rappers trying to get put on to a national contract hustle from a NEW YORK or LOS ANGELES corporation has caused the art-form to atrophy from the bottom, while never getting signed to a top echelon that really doesn't exist, but to a very few.

HIP-HOP NEWS spreads like any other mainstream NEWS in America. The garbage that's unfit to print has now floated on websites and blogs like sh*t. For example, a rapper working in the community gets obscured while if that same rapper robbed a gas station he'd get top coverage and be label a "rapper" while getting his upcoming or current music somewhat put on blast, regardless of its quality which of course is subjective like any other art. RAP sites and blogs are mimicking the New York POST.

This is not mere complaint, this is truth and it's coming down on Americans like rain without a raincoat with cats screaming how they ain't wet. This is real. The other night upon finishing groundbreaking concert performances in Johannesburg, we followed a special free concert in Soweto. To make a point that our agenda was to "show" and encourage the Hip-Hop community to be comfortable in its mind and skin without chasing valueless American values.

Never have so many been pimped by so few.

It does the people of the planet little good to hear that an artist is famous and rich, will wear expensive jewelry straight from the mines, show it off, stay it the hotel, ride in limos, do the VIP with chilled champagne in the Clubs, ape and monkey the chicks (meaning not even talking) and keep the dudes away with slave paid bodyguards when real people come close. The mimic of the VIACOM-sanctioned video has run tired, because it shows off, does NOT inspire and it says NOTHING.

Here in South Africa PUBLIC ENEMY has done crucial groundbreaking performances. It's the same level of smashing the house that we've done this year in Moscow, New York, Paris, London, Chicago and other places this year. This is not news; we are not trying to prove any point other than to show that a classic work is timeless and doesn't have a demographic per se. The Rolling Stones and U2 are NOT measured by mere tracks; they are measured by the all-around event they present. The art of the performance has left Hip-Hop whereas somebody has led artists to do more performing off the stage than on it. The agenda here is to create artist exchange.

This serves as a call to the infrastructure-less Hip-Hop game in America. We know what your hustle is, but what is your work and job here? Faking it until making it runs its course in a recession, which is a depression for Black folks who are increasingly becoming more skill-less as they become jobless.

Never have so many been pimped by so few.

Since the music has so much power, and image has become everything to the point that it can dictate the direction of a person in their life, it is my mission now to really become a "freedom fighter" and stop this radiation. With Jay-Z and others who, for years would faint their worth, the statement of "with great power comes great responsibility," is truer. Words are powerful and they can both start wars and bring peace. This cannot be taken lightly. It's important for the words to be body with the community. If not one dime of $250 million doesn't benefit the people who contribute to it, then why does that warrant coverage above the will and effort of many in the music who have done great things.

Picture from the camera of Griff in San Francisco at Yoshi's
January of 2011

"You don't have to sell out to sell out."
-- Chuck D

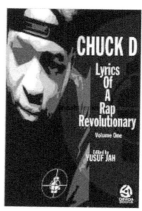

Never have so many been pimped by so few.

I turned 50 this year. Every day I get the question what's up with Hip-Hop today. If nothing was wrong, the question wouldn't be the dominating question I get. I do massive interviews worldwide. I'm covered from varied aspects - Hip-Hop, Public Enemy, social issues, musicology in general. So, my interactive world dialogue is deeper and more present than 140 characters. Never have so many been pimped by so few.

I am tired of the silence of people that know better. There is nothing worse than a person that knows better and does worse. Or says nothing. And makes excuses for bulls**t.

You know damn well HIP-HOP in the USA has fell way the f**k off as the American dollar and much of America itself. Held up and dictated by White business lawyers, accountants in New York, and Los Angeles offices.

To dictate to a community and not even live or be with the people is offensive. VIACOM's reach into Africa to turn HIP-HOP in to America, which is as exploitative as those slave-makers who carried us across on boats. The decisions made in a boardroom in New York City while these cats scurry to their high rises, and suburban mansions from cultural profiteering must stop. And I'm going to do something about it.

Never have so many been pimped by so few.

My agenda of Hip-Hop around the world is in line with its creators, who followed Black Music. The music had the people's back. It has never been my personal agenda. Americans arrogantly have no back. Hip-Hop has followed this. I am disturbed by the fact that I tell artists that doing work in their community will get them little or no buzz for their effort, but in the same sense if they robbed or shot someone or did a bid they would get national and sometimes international attention.

Never have so many been pimped by so few.

So many of your favorite people suck up to the NBA and NFL, because it has order and when you make the game look bad David Stern or Robert Goddell is kicking their asses out . They are the indisputable HWIC, and Negroes are in line and silenced. But here in Hip-Hop the dysfunctionality reward makes the money that puts food on many tables.

Its time, because I hear too many excuses. I won't allow what's in the USA f**k up what I and others worked hard to instill. I drive a '94 Montero, a '97 Acura, and have no expensive jewelry. There is nothing on this planet materially that is better than myself. This is what I instill in many doing Hip-Hop that nothing is greater than what is given. These games of people doing anything to get things have seeped into my way so therefore witness some radical virtual things coming from me in protecting the art-form of Hip-Hop.

Never have so many been pimped by so few. So, I'm going after the few. I'm tired of it.

-- Chuck D from Cape Town, South Africa. Public Enemy's 71st Tour 6th Leg of a Fear of a Black Planet Tour

The Arena – Interview with Professor Griff on Blog Talk Radio

Interview date: December 20, 2010 At 9:30 EST on the Podcast, the Arena Host comes in....

PG: Um, yes I can, as a matter of fact, in dealing with racism/white supremacy, as taught to us by Neely Fuller in his book, 'United Independent Compensatory Code System and Concepts A textbook/workbook for Thought, Speech and/or Action for Victims of Racism (white supremacy)', along with Dr. Frances Cress Welsing's book, 'The Isis Papers', they teach us that (?) it's a global, local and global power system and dynamic structured by persons that classify themselves as white people, but the key thing is here, is whether the consciously or unconscious or subconsciously-determined, pardon me, that we have this way that we assist racism/white supremacy, but if you go back to Neely Fuller's book, he broke it down in such a way that Ray Charles and Stevie Wonder can see it. He said there are 4 basic stages of racism/white supremacy; the establishment, the maintenance, the expansion, and the refinement. And a lot of us that are conducting ourselves in the way that we are conducting ourselves,the enemy of self, we gonna talk about that in a minute, are helping to, not establish because racism/white supremacy is already established, but in maintaining and expanding and refining racism/white supremacy, and they don't even know it.

Dr. Frances Cress Welsing's

PG: Our goal is to eradicate racism/white supremacy and bring justice on the planet Earth. Among the human family. And sadly enough, a lot of people listening, you may not think that includes white people, but it does. So, let's just get that straight from the root, from the beginning. Because, white people need to be taught also.

DJ: I mean we as black people, don't understand that the European is functioning from a different dynamic then we are. He's is fighting for his survival on the planet and we cannot lose sight of that.

There was a counterintelligence program headed by J Edgar Hoover, I believe in the 50's and the 60's, and the main purpose of the counterintelligence program , their goals and objectives were to prevent the rise of a Black Messiah. And that they said they can never have someone that would lead black people that would electrify the masses of black people. When I started doing my lecture "The Pacify Antidote', which lead into 'The Psychological Covert War on Hip Hop', that's the very exact thing I was saying. I said, you see, COINTELPRO is now the Patriot Act 1 and 2, and Hip Hop became, Hip Hop was the voice of the voiceless. When I say Hip Hop, I'm talking about '**H**igher **I**nfinite **P**ower **H**ealing **O**ur **P**eople', which is a phrase given to us by our good Brother, Minista Serva, out of The Temple of Hip Hop, KRS One's camp, are you following me?

DJ: Exactly.

PG: So, the COINTELPRO never died. It's a counterintelligence program still at work. So I studied Cedric Muhammad's work, dealing with www.blackelectorate.com, where he talked about the rap co-intel pro. And when I got the call from Cynthia McKinney, she said it's still alive. Then when I started studying further, I seen how they were doing surveillance on Hip Hop artists. I seen how they were making up stories, causing crew to fight one another, the same ol' damn dirty tricks that they always been doing, are you following me?

You can go pick up any book on the CIA dirty tricks and you'll see the same damn tricks played on us today in 2010, in and outside of Hip Hop

You see, Elijah Muhammad taught us about these people, they're called blood-suckers of the poor. Are you following me? This is 10 percent element that Elijah Muhammad warned us about. He said that 85 percent are the blind, deaf and dumb, he said the 5 percent are the poor righteous teachers of the planet Earth. But when it got down to that 10 percent, which are the rich slave-makers of the poor, are you following me? And these are the ones that teach the people lies on a massive scale. Study the media – m-e-d-i-a, **M**ulti **E**thnic **D**estrunction **I**n **A**merica or **M**aniac **E**uropean **D**evils **I**n **A**ction. These are these people who are called the 10 percent and are called the blood-suckers of the poor, this is exactly who the Illuminati is. This is where this is coming from – Professor Griff was making progress with young people in the hood, and they seen this. Because the evidence was Youtube and other websites and people calling and energy is being generated now, are you following me? And people are asking questions about the Illuminati and we're moving closer to the goal, where we're understanding this particular dynamic.

Now, they were forced to put it on t.v., with Jesse Ventura every Friday evening. Now they are making television shows about it. Are you following me? So, now it's cool, it's fashionable now to mention the Illuminati. A minute ago, no one knew what this was. But they said, we have to slow Professor Griff down. So, they got one of their little imps, their little agents like Lenon Honors, and they said well damn, we don't have anything on him; he don't drink, he don't smoke, he don't screw white women, so damn, what can we possibly say about him? Ahh! We'll say that he's gay, that he's a homo, he's a fag and maybe that will slow him down. We already sent someone to blow up his house, to burn his house down. We already sent people to shoot at him, you understand what I'm saying. We already sent people to move on him physically and that didn't slow him down, so now we'll pull some other tricks out of the bag and we'll say he's a homosexual. We'll have this agent, Lenon Honors go public and basically say to discredit Professor Griff, and actually I called it, 'The Assassination of Professor Griff and the Blueprint of a Non-Rap COINTEL Operative called Lenon Honors', with this madness entitled 'The Hip Hop Hidden Hand and The Degradation of the Black Masculinity'. Chuck D said, "Every Brother ain't a Brother". And we have to understand that and the only one that hollers, Malcolm X said it – if you throw a rock in a crowd of dogs, the only one that will holler is the one that get hit. And this dude is barking real loud.

In the global scheme of things, we must keep in the front of our minds that racism (white supremacy) is still intact and forever working to maintain racism (white supremacy). Neely Fuller Jr. teaches us that if you do not understand (racism) white supremacy, what it is, how it works - everything else that you think you understand will only confuse you.

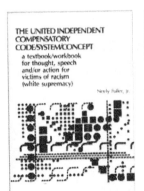

-- Francis Cress Welsing MD

"Racism (White Supremacy) is the local and global power system and dynamic, structured and maintained by persons who classify themselves as White, whether consciously or subconsciously determined, which consists of patterns of perception, logic, symbol formation, thought, speech, action and emotional response, as conducted simultaneously in all areas of people's activity (economics, education, entertainment, labor, law, politics, religion, sex and war), for the ultimate purpose of White genetic survival and to prevent White genetic annihilation on planet Earth – a planet upon which the vast majority of people are classified as nonwhite (Black, Brown, Red and Yellow) by white-skinned people, and all of the nonwhite people are genetically dominant (in terms of skin coloration) compared to the genetically recessive white-skinned people.

"The system of Racism (White Supremacy) utililizes deceit and violence (inclusive of chemical warfare, biological warfare and psychological warfare), indeed Any Means Necessary, to achieve its ultimate goal objective of White genetic survival and to prevent White genetic annihilation on planet Earth. In the existing system of Racism (White Supremacy) when the term is undefined and poorly understood, there is general confusion and chaos on the part of the victims of that system (local, national and global). It then becomes impossible for the victims of Racism (White Supremacy) to effectively counter the global system of Racism (White Supremacy). The African enslavement, imperialism, colonialism, neo-colonialism, fascism, etc., are all dimensions and aspects of Racism (White Supremacy)."

Black Eyed Peas: Sellouts in Post-Sellout World

To give you an example of this mind numbing counter culture mind controlled covert operation, is more visable when you see a relative good "black" rap group like the Black Eye Peas will inject a white woman (Fergie)into the group and the they are seen as "sellout" by black people in the hoods from which they come. At this point they have to justify making such a bold move. There desire to want to perform in front of black audiences are quickly deminished because white promoters do not promote to black audiences for there white clubs.as a result of this on going trick by the "Industry" The white woman will go off to become a mega star and then the black rap group will have to compitulate to the control of the "Music Industry" as we "don't" know it.

and then people like Seth Stevenson can make the following statements against The black eyed peas. It is still possible for a musician to "sell out" in this hyper-commercialized world. "we as a culture must reserve our right to shower disdain on the Black Eyed Peas."

The Peas aren't an unknown band eager to "gain national exposure quickly,", "These insatiable revenue-bots are just raking in more coin." Stevenson admits that "when the music's this bad it's sort of beyond the point,"

Lets look into this and other mind control tricks and schemes that have been a very successful practice in the misic industry.

Huey: Vision? What do you know about my vision? My vision would turn your world upside-down, tear asunder your illusions and the sanctuary of your own ignorance crashing down around you. Ask yourself... are you really ready to see that vision?

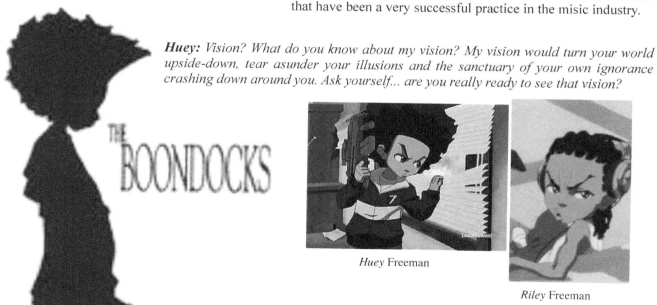

Huey Freeman

Riley Freeman

Capture their minds, and their hearts and souls will follow.
-- Author Unknown

2ⁿᵈ DEGREE

Hip Hop s Co-In-Tel- Pro Files, Rap Sheets and the Hip Hop Cop

Power is the ability to define reality and to convince other people that it is their own definition.
-- Dr. Wade Nobles

Congresswoman Cynthia McKinney's CBC Brain Trust:
"Countering Culture: COINTELPRO Attacks On Political Musicians"

As many may know, Congresswoman McKinney has been the foremost member of Congress to explore, investigate, and educate the public regarding the FBI's Counter Intelligence Program (COINTELPRO) infamously run by former FBI head J. Edgar Hoover, and for the past five years Black Electorate "The COINTELPRO is in full effect Patriot act 1 & 2."

COINTELPRO is an acronym for a series of FBI counter intelligence programs designed to neutralize political dissidents. Although covert operations have been employed throughout FBI history, the formal COINTELPRO's of 1956-1971 were broadly targeted against radical political organizations. In the early 1950s, the Communist Party was illegal in the United States. The Senate and House of Representatives each set up investigating committees to prosecute communists and publicly expose them. (The House Committee on Un-American Activities and the Senate Internal Security Subcommittee, led by Senator Joseph McCarthy). When a series of Supreme Court rulings in 1956 and 1957 challenged these committees and questioned the constitutionality of Smith Act prosecutions and Subversive Activities Control Board hearings, the FBI's response was COINTELPRO, a program designed to "neutralize" those who could no longer be prosecuted. Over the years, similar programs were created to neutralize civil rights, anti-war, and many other groups, many of which were said to be "communist front organizations," as J. Edgar Hoover, longtime Director of the FBI put it.

The forces which are most anxious to weaken our internal security are not always easy to identify. Communists have been trained in deceit and secretly work toward the day when they hope to replace our American way of life with a Communist dictatorship. They utilize cleverly camouflaged movements, such as peace groups and civil rights groups to achieve their sinister purposes. While they as individuals are difficult to identify, the Communist party line is clear. Its first concern is the advancement of Soviet Russia and the godless Communist cause. It is important to learn to know the enemies of the American way of life.

The FBI conducted more than 2000 COINTELPRO operations before the programs were officially discontinued in April of 1971, after public exposure, in order to "afford additional security to [their] sensitive techniques and operations."

Black Nationalist Hate Groups "prevent the rise of a Black Messiah." Use of Jewish Defense League against, use of La Cosa Nostra against, cartoons, "Blackboard," Rabbi Kahane, William O'Neal, and numerous victims including: Southern Christian Leadership Conference, Revolutionary Action Movement, the Deacons for Defense and Justice, Congress of Racial Equality, SNCC, Nation of Islam, Poor People's Campaign, Republic of New Africa, US organization, Black Liberators, Martin Luther King, Malcolm X, Stokely Carmichael, H. "Rap" Brown, Elijah Muhammad, Maxwell Stanford, Dick Gregory, Huey Newton, David Hilliard, Ron Karenga, Charles Koen, Sylvester Bell, Bobby Seale, Eldridge Cleaver, Fred Hampton, Mark Clark, Geronimo Pratt, John William Washington, Richard Henry, Muhammed Kenyatta, Jeff Fort.

NAMES of TYPES of DISINFORMATION AGENTS

The intelligence agencies have their own lingo for the types of disinformation agents they send against everyone else. So far, we have named only double & sleeper agents. Here are some of their disinformation agents:

AGENT OF INFLUENCE--These agents can be unwitting, under mind-control, or ideologically motivated to use their positions of influence to sway the minds of others. Examples of Agents of Influence are anchor men on TV, journalists, labor leaders, TV commentators, academics quoted by the media, & some politicians.

CONFUSION AGENT--An agent whose job is to produce confusion by disseminating confounding information.

CONTRACT AGENT--These are the rogue agents, such as the mob, who the CIA get to do particular jobs on contract. Their connections can be denied.

DEEP COVER AGENT--A sleeper agent (often a programmed multiple or person with mind-control programming) who has been a long term sleeper agent.

DISINFORMATION AGENT--This is a highly placed agent who passes disinformation to other governments.

NOTIONAL AGENT--A fictitious non-existent "agent" which is created with a real-looking identity to mislead.

PROVOCATION AGENT--An agent sent in to provoke and destabilize the target group to do foolish things.

If I had found that the FBI didn't have any dossier on me, it would have been tremendously embarrassing and I wouldn't have been able to face my friends.

SPOON-FEEDER AGENT--

Someone who dribbles out legitimate information, this is often done to build up a person's credentials (bona fides). Lots of the people who are pretending to expose the NWO are spoon-feeder agents who provide a little new information, tons of already known secrets, and sprinkle in a measure of disinformation for added fun. Generally, spoon-feeders increase their percentage of disinformation once they gain respectability. There are very few people really exposing anything of consequence about the NWO. This author has endured the loss of several of the really legitimate whistle blowers who were friends being assassinated since he began writing exposes.

At the moment, the system is set up so that the perpetrators of the mind-control are in control of the credentialing process, so that they can provide their stooges/and agents with the best credentials. As the reader can see, the roots of power behind the mind-control go deep.

'I WAS ABOUT TO SAY THAT IF OL' J. EDGAR WAS STILL RUNNING THINGS, WE WOULDN'T BE HAVING THIS BIG IMAGE PROBLEM... BUT LET IT PASS.'

COINTELPRO is an acronym for a series

of FBI counterintelligence programs designed to neutralize political dissidents. Although covert operations have been employed throughout FBI history, the formal COINTELPRO's of 1956-1971 were broadly targeted against radical political organizations. In the early 1950s, the Communist Party was illegal in the United States. The Senate and House of Representatives each set up investigating committees to prosecute communists and publicly expose them. (The House Committee on Un-American Activities and the Senate Internal Security Subcommittee, led by Senator Joseph McCarthy). When a series of Supreme Court rulings in 1956 and 1957 challenged these committees and questioned the constitutionality of Smith Act prosecutions and Subversive Activities Control Board hearings, the FBI's response was COINTELPRO, a program designed to "neutralize" those who could no longer be prosecuted. Over the years, similar programs were created to neutralize civil rights, anti-war, and many other groups, many of which were said to be "communist front organizations." As J. Edgar Hoover, longtime Director of the FBI, put it

The forces which are most anxious to weaken our internal security are not always easy to identify. Communists have been trained in deceit and secretly work toward the day when they hope to replace our American way of life with a Communist dictatorship. They utilize cleverly camouflaged movements, such as peace groups and civil rights groups to achieve their sinister purposes. While they as individuals are difficult to identify, the Communist party line is clear. Its first concern is the advancement of Soviet Russia and the godless Communist cause. It is important to learn to know the enemies of the American way of life.

The FBI conducted more than 2000 COINTELPRO operations before the the programs were officially discontinued in April of 1971, after public exposure, in order to "*afford additional security to [their] sensitive techniques and operations.*"

All propaganda has to be popular and has to adapt its spiritual level to the perception of the least intelligent of those towards whom it intends to direct itself.
-- Adolf Hitler, Mein Kampf ("My Struggle"), Vol. I

Adolf **Hitler** giving the Nazi salute during a rally in 1939.

Adolf Hitler, Mein Kampf ("My Struggle"),

What this means is that agents for groups that do mind-control may: have been sleepers for many years and look very legitimately innocent, they may give good correct information to our side, they may say all the right things and try to get us motivated to do more than we would want, they may talk about other friends who are giving them information who do not even exist. It takes discernment to spot people who are not on our side. Unfortunately, such discernment seems to be fundamentally lacking within the public at large. For instance, I have seen people choose obvious NWO agents over this author as a source of "information" (which is in reality disinformation). Most people have bought so much disinformation during their lifetime, perhaps it's unrealistic to expect them to purge out all the junk they've accepted. Just as people in the world need to toss out their worldly thinking, people in the church need to toss out all the indoctrination they've gotten from the numerous kinds of harlot churches.

Hip Hop and the New World Order by: Keidi Obi Awadu (The Conscious Rasta)

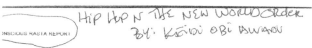

Word was on the street, and it was evident within his music, that towards the end of his life Eazy E was involved in a Satanic cult and one could suspect that this *devil business* may have been related to whatever turned his fellow band-mates off to the situation there at Ruthless. I'll have much more to say about Eazy E and Ruthless Records later in this report.

The following excerpt is from a declassified document which emerged from the FBI's infamous COINTELPRO campaign — an illegal campaign against militant Blacks which targeted black leadership for "neutralization" to include spying, provocateur acts of sabotage against dozens of black organizations, and ultimately included the most drastic form of neutralization — assassination. Please study the following carefully

TO: DIRECTOR, FBI (100-448006)

FROM: SAC, SAN FRANCISCO (157-601) - P

RE: COUNTERINTELLIGENCE PROGRAM BLACK NATIONALIST-HATE GROUPS RACIAL   INTELLIGENCE

SA RAYMOND N. BYERS is assigned to coordinate this program within the San Francisco Division.

B. "The Negro wants and needs something to be proud of. The Negro youth and moderate must be made to understand that if they succumb to revolutionary teaching, they will be dead revolutionaries. Is it not better to be a sports hero, a well paid professional athlete or entertainer, a regularly paid white or blue collar worker, a peaceful human being with a family, or a person who at least is being accepted, than a Negro who may have got even with the establishment by burning it down, but who along with this, burned down his own home and gained for him and all his people the hatred and distrust of the whites for years to come?" [emphasis added]

Orders from FBI Headquarters:

Instructions for Operations – Selected "Enemy" Were To Be
1) Exposed; 2) disrupted; 3) neutralized.

Credibility is a condition of persuasion. Before you can make a man do what you say, you must make him believe what you say. A necessary condition for gaining his credence is that you do not permit him to catch you in lies. Hence, the constraint upon all propagandists to accurate reporting of matters which are subject to verification by the audience. Propaganda, to be effective, must be not only factually true, but credible.

-- Sykewar, Daniel Lerner, George W. Stewart, NY, 1949

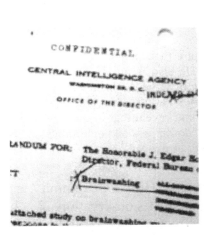

The coverage of the 9/11 attacks ensured a global impact zone, making it an effective act

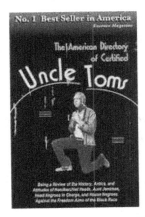

The American Directory of Certified UNCLE TOMS."
This book being a review of the History, Antics and attitudes of
Handkerchief heads, Aunt Jemima's, Head Negroes in Charge,
and House Negroes Against the Freedom Aims of the Black Race.

236   The American Directory

nation of FBI sabotage (COINTELPRO), white liberal deception, and Uncle Tom duplicity. As the Black youth culture developed its own forms of expression—unsupported by any of the traditional institutions of school and church—it developed its own leadership, whose varied motivations bore little philosophical resemblance to the civil rights agenda: Initially, the Black Power messages of community empowerment and nationalism dominated rap lyrics, along with heavy dosages of "party hard" themes. But soon the trail blazers of what came to be known as hip hop developed their own style and identity, operated independently, and became the *de facto* leaders in the community of Black youth.

The Uncle Toms that haunt the middle echelons of the music business had the first opportunity to nurture and develop the new original sounds emerging from their own youth and to guide rap's evolution as a positive force. They, instead, rejected the whole hip-hop movement as strongly as the youth embraced it. They ignored its urban appeal and, true to their own middle-class acculturation, sought their talent from artists whose styles were of the Lionel Ritchie/Michael Jackson "crossover" mode.

"The Negro child...will be presented with an insulting picture of the Negro as dirty, shiftless, lazy, happy-go-lucky, stupid, ignorant, treacherous, superstitious, and cowardly, and he may find himself expected to live up to this."
Gertrude F. Kern,
The Negro Personality

Consequently, a new generation of white businessmen moved in. They had heeded the advice of their forbears in the entertainment business, who'd always adhered strictly to their industry's most profitable commandment: "Go Black, young man." With their cash and superior industry position, these white entrepreneurs installed a new leadership over the hip-hop movement, and began to promote a nefarious "niggerization" of rap music. *The Vibe History of Hip Hop* is very explicit about the roots of this ominous new trend, warning that "acting like a nigger was about to become more lucrative than ever." They point out that as rappers KRS-One and Public Enemy became strong positive forces for Black youth, a group called NWA (Niggaz With Attitudes) emerged with an explicitly opposite point of view. The group's founder, Andre Young, a.k.a. Dr. Dre, expressed his philosophy thus:

I wanted to make people go, "I can't believe he saying that shit...I wanted to go all the way left. Everybody trying to do this black power and shit, so I was like, let's give 'em an alternative, "niggerniggerniggernigger fuck this

46 See Ronin Ro, *Gangsta* (New York: St. Martin's Press, 1996), pp. 6-7 and passim. Also, Chuck D., *Fight the Power: Rap, Race and Reality* (New York: Delacorte, 1997), pp. 2-9. See also Robert Scoop Jackson, *The Last Black Mecca: Hip Hop* (Chicago: Research Associates, 1994).
49 Nelson George, *Hip Hop America* (New York: Penguin Books, 1998), p. 59.

The Covert War Against Rock: What You Don't Know About the Deaths of Jim Morrison, Tupac Shakur, Michael Hutchence, Brian Jones, Jimi Hendrix, Phil Ochs, ... Tosh, John Lennon, and The Notorious B.I.G.

Many have been led to believe that the survelience of rap artists by police started in New York the birthplace of Hip Hop. Ground zero is actually in Utah with a black officer who once infiltrated the Ku Klux Klan. This is an incredible story that will blow you away... The Hip Hop Police-pt1 (Orgins [...]

The Hiphop Cop A Tale of NYPD's Rap Intelligence Unit

By Dasun Allah

Damon Dash, longtime partner of rap icon Jay-Z, is the CEO of a Hiphop empire that includes the brands Roc-a-Fella and Roc-a-Wear, and produces music, films, clothing, and vodka. He also is a man known to travel with an entourage of family and friends, the kind of company police rap intelligence has been watching and documenting in recent years. Interviews with former detective first grade Derrick Parker, who claims to be the founder and architect of the New York Police Department's rap intelligence unit, reveal that in the 1990s Parker thought it was important to monitor people who were starting to "latch on" to rappers and entertainers, some of whom, Parker says, may have been known to him as "a shooter, or a strong-arm guy."

Benjamin Chavis-Muhammad, head of Simmons' Hip-Hop Summit Action Network (HSAN), likened the surveillance to the FBI's observation of Rev. Martin Luther King, Jr. and said that HSAN is exploring the possibility of filing lawsuits in any jurisdiction where these rap-intelligence units operate. "A very dangerous precedent has been set. It needs to be exposed, and we're going to take legal action against these police departments for violating the constitutional rights of hiphop artists."

Cedric Muhammad Publisher BlackElectorate.com
http://www.blackelectorate.com/

Has a "cover story" been written to justify a war against Hip-Hop and Black youth, in such a way that civil rights violations, mistreatment and even the killing of young Black and Latino youth could take place and the majority of Americans or the majority of the world would think that such actions were warranted? Has rap music been a battlefield for this larger initiative, if it exists? Some might say that such a plan is unthinkable today. But is it a stretch or unreasonable to believe that the more brutally honest or negative aspects (depending upon whom you speak to) of rap music lyrics and videos have been projected domestically and abroad in such a way that it has enabled an unattractive image of Black youth - males in particular - to dominate the opinions of many people who might not regularly interact with Black Americans? Consider this from an article from the November 16, 2003 issue of the New York Times written by a Black American Muslim traveling in Egypt:

NYPD Admits to Rap Intelligence Unit
A look inside the NYPD's secret "Hip-hop Task Force"

Dasun Allah

"We have an intelligence division and we have detectives that monitor the music industry and any incidents regarding the music industry," says Officer Doris Garcia, an NYPD spokesperson. "And in regards to Miami P.D., we did exchange information, and that's it."

In recent reports the Miami PD has been catching a lot of heat for their alleged surveillance and profiling of rappers. This practice was started with help and information from the NYPD, who has been rumored to have it's own rap intellegence unit.

The First
Hip Hop Cop is
Ron Stallworth
who comes
Straight Outta Utah
& Not New York

Due to the uncovering of Miami's little secret, New York City Police department officials acknowledge that they did exchange information with the Miami Police department, but still denied the existence of a team assigned to keep track of rappers activities.

According to the Village Voice, a two month investigation into the existence of such a team produced proof that there is such a division within the NYPD.

Retired detective Dereck Parker says he was the founder and architect of the intelligence operation. Parker, says the basis of this unit was his personal expertise, initiative, and an assignment starting in the 1990s to be a one-man shop keeping tabs on any and all incidents involving rappers or their crews. NYPD attention to rappers really came to a head, according to Parker, after the 1997 murder of rapper Biggie Smalls.

Someone is Always Watching & Listening...
The Orgins &
Evolution
of the
Hip Hop Police
-Breakdown FM-

Parker was also the officer that the NYPD sent to "exchange information" with the Miami PD.

NYPD had this to say about the so called "Hip Hop Task Force":

"We have an intelligence division and we have detectives that monitor the music industry and any incidents regarding the music industry," says Officer Doris Garcia, an NYPD spokesperson. "And in regards to Miami P.D. we did exchange information, and that's it."

Several leaders have spoken out against this type of police activity including hip hop music heavyweight Russell Simmons. "They don't follow around every rock and roll outlaw. They should be following around all these drug dealers that are real obvious," he says. "You know who the drug dealers are. You know all of their names. Why are you wasting your police force energy on singers?"

Benjamin Chavis-Muhammad, head of the Hip-Hop Summit Action Network (HSAN), said, "A very dangerous precedent has been set. It needs to be exposed, and we're going to take legal action against these police departments for violating the constitutional rights of hiphop artists."

As for Parker, he defends the actions of the unit, "We prevented certain crimes because when you started talking to rappers and you knew they had hits on them and you were on to them, people wouldn't go and shoot them or rob them if they knew you were around. . . Most of the time, it's not the rappers, it's the guys in their entourages that cause the problems."

Military scholars recognize that a new form of soldier, with no allegiance to the nation-state, is developing in much of the non-Western world. Major Ralph Peters, U.S. Army, who is responsible for evaluating emerging threats for the Office of the Deputy Chief of Staff for Intelligence, terms this threat, The New Warrior Class. It is being taken seriously enough by the U.S. Army to be included in its perceptions of early 21st-century Army operations. This type of soldier, which has developed as an outcome of a breakdown in social organization in many failed nation-states, operates in subnational groups such as armed bands, private armies, crime networks and terrorist organizations. Debate in professional U.S. military and affiliated journals over the past two years has dealt with concerns that this new form of soldier may be developing within the United States. Street gangs would be one logical source from which this new form of soldier could emerge in this country. These gangs have developed in failed inner cities, where poverty and crime run rampant and family social structures have been severely eroded.

A California congressman blasted the Federal Bureau of Investigation forviolating its charter after the bureau took an official position on the controversial rap song "Fuck the Police", by NWA (Niggers With Attitudes), agroup from Compton, California. The congressman's move came in the wake ofan FBI letter sent to NWA's label, Priority Records, that condemned the songfor "advocating violence and assault" against police."This smacks of censorship, and the FBI shouldnt be in the business ofcensorship", said Congressman Don Edwards, Democrat of San Jose, California, who is chairman of a House subcommittee that monitors the bureau's activities. Edwards -- a former G-man himself -- contacted the FBI on October 10th, objecting to its letter about NWA and demanding a fullexplanation. In addition, the American Civil Liberties Union in Washington,DC, protested the FBI's action and called on the Justice Department toretract the letter. Members of NWA would not comment on the issue, although group member and songwriter Ice Cube previously called the track a "revenge fantasy" stemmingFrom what NWA views as repeated police harassment of young blacks. Priority-More-- Records chief Bryan Turner said, "We dont advocate violence in any way, shape or form, but we do advocate freedom of speech." Turner recently returned from the Soviet Union, where he lined up a Russian distribution deal forPriority albums that could include "Straight Outta Compton", which contains the inflammatory tune.

The FBI's letter, signed by assistant director and bureau spokesman Milton Ahlerich, claimed the angry rap number "encourages violence against and disrespect for the law enforcement officer", describing the "unprecendented" surge in violent crime and detailing statistics of police murders during 1988. Concluding that "music plays a significant role in society", the letter ended on an ominous note, warning Priority "to be aware of the FBI's position relative to this song and its message."Earlier this year, the song became subject of an intense fax campaign among local police departments, with the lyrics transmitted to cops in cities where NWA toured. The number was deliberately excluded from the tour's regular set list, but when a few lines of "Fuck the Police" were chanted at a Detroit concert, a scuffle broke out, and group members were later briefly detained by local authorities.

- Jeffrey Ressner, Rolling Stone Magazine

• N.W.A. Urged To Stop Recording By F.B.I.

Federal agents officially asked rap pioneers N.W.A. to stop recording after receiving a slew of complaints about their expletive-laden lyrics. In an essay written for America's Flaunt magazine, group co-founder Arabian Prince reveals he and bandmates Ice Cube and Eazy-E received letters from F.B.I. officials asking them to stop releasing hardcore rap music. Prince - real name Mik Lezan - recalls, "(They told us) to stop recording such music... Upon our arrival at every airport terminal, we received a visit from the police reminding us not to use profanity onstage in their town, or face going to jail." But the Straight Outta Compton rap supergroup refused to acknowledge the threat against them - because they felt they were on a free-speech mission. The rapper writes, "N.W.A. is best known for the fight for freedom of speech and expression."

From the Book, "Behold A Pale Horse", written, by William Cooper a former Naval Intelligence Officer, in regards to a document concerning the American Public:

Diversion Is The primary Strategy. The Simplest Method For Securing Silent Weapons & Gaining Control Of The Public Is To Keep The Public Undisciplined And Ignorant Of Basic Systems Principles While Keeping Them Confused, Disorganized And Distracted With Matters Of No Real Importance.

Whereas, The Media Keeps The Adult Population's Attention Diverted From The Real Social Issues, And Captivated By Matters Of No Real Importance; The Schools Keep The Young Public Ignorant Of Real Mathematics, Real Economics, Real Law, And Real History. Entertainment Is Kept Below The Sixth Grade Level. The Public Is Kept Busy Working And The Result Is No Time to Think.

Question: Who is willing to pick up their Responsibilities & Work on this problem in their Personal & Private Lives, as well as in the Public.....Let the Best among you be a servant".

Those Lawyers and accountants who control the Hip Hop industry at behest of there handlers cause distractions all on any and all levels to keep the masses pre-occupied with "Matters of no real importants" in this excerpt from william coopers book we clearly see that the programing of VH1,MTV and BET networks with there mindless shows that dumb down and insult the intelligence of the people have made there mark and have establish themselves as main stream TV.

MTV- Music TeleVision. An American cable station that's central goal is to brainwash America's youth. instead of playing music, it plays "reality" shows that tells teens and kids to be spoiled, make fun of smart people, exploit overweight people, marry only for money, that having the vocabulary of a 3rd grader is ok, be prejudice toward people of different races and sexual orientations, dress like a slut or a gangster, always be concerned about what others think of you, to be promiscuous, the only way to be thin is to throw up your lunch, neglect people who don't listen to rap music, people who aren't rich are worthless scum, and to make anyone who has a sense of individuality an outcast of society. This is the reason why modern music is on the verge of extinction.

Why todays youth are so stupid and ignorant. MTV told them rap and punk "music" are cool. MTV told them being "ghetto" is cool. MTV brainwashes everyone too young to understand just what corporations are trying to do. Look in any high school in america. MTV tells kids to have sex at a rediculously young age, drink large amounts of alcohol, and talk shit about everyone the second they turn around, also the reason so many teens do drugs and drink alcohol. Makes teens think they are tough when they roll up in their shitty cars blasting "fiddy" or whatever is cool that week. Makes "being cool" the most important thing/ MTV says if your not cool you should be dead. Also, has resulted in the popularity of stupid internet accesories such as AIM napster and myspace, why? because having a lot of "friends" is "cool" and you dont want to be "uncool"? do you? MTV is also the leading cause behind teen pregnancy.

By the way, im a teenager and im not a punk or ghetto fag or anything shitty like that im REAL (unlike the real world). Some people need to wake up and smell the crap

43

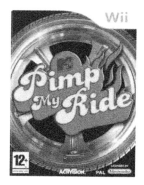

I was 14 years old when I was forced into prostitution. Like many teens at that age, finding my own identity and defying my parents were top on my list. So when a man came into my life and showered me with attention and listened to me when I complained about my parents, I did not think twice that he was ten years my senior. After all, he said I was mature for my age and told me I understood him better than anyone his own age. Little did I know, he was laying down the seeds of manipulation. It did not matter what my parents said, to me they did not understand me and he was the only one that "got me". After six months, I thought I loved him, at least that is what he told me, so I did what I thought my heart was telling me and ran away to be with him. We ended up in Cleveland, Ohio. He told me we were going to meet the rest of the family.

I had no idea the "family" meant myself and three other girls. After I was introduced to the "family," I was told what my role would be. I would go out to "work" that night and bring him back the money. How else would we build our dream home? He assured me he would always love me no matter what, but he needed to know how much I loved him by making sure I would do anything for him. The pimps who are trafficking young women and girls on the street have a great marketing tool: the media. You can turn on the TV now and see pimps glamorized in TV shows, music videos, and movies. Young people use "pimp" in everyday conversation: "my ride is pimped out," "your clothes are pimping." They do not understand the reality behind the term.Enslaved in America: Sex Trafficking in the United States.......... *Source: By Tina Frundt*

In the book The FBI War on Tupac Shakur and Black Leaders: U.S. Intelligence's Murderous Targeting of Tupac, MLK, Malcolm, The Panthers, Hendrix, Marley, Rappers & Linked Ethnic Leftists, it is claimed that Death Row Records was a front for the FBI in order to subvert black activism.

Columbia University graduate John Potash, the book's author, says his research shows that the FBI deliberately target Tupac Shakur due to his influence in the African-American community through Hip Hop.

"What I think it was was that he had become the most influential black man in the black community in the country," Potash, a Baltimore native, told The Baltimore City Paper. "The CIA and U.S. intelligence, what they have to do is win the hearts and minds of the people.

They don't want to control us by force, they want us to control ourselves by having us believe in a certain way—that we don't need national health care, for example. And here, Tupac was threatening to win over the hearts and minds of people, he was able to counter so much of the propaganda in the black community."

The book includes the results of ten years of research, court testimony, FBI documents, and numerous documents from The Black Panthers provided to Potash.

"I believe that Death Row Records, which included dozens and dozens of police officers at all levels, according to a high-level police officer that investigated them, was a front company and was trying to continue penal coercion and mess up [Tupac Shakur's] head," added Potash. A research documentary is paired with the book, which is in stores now.

Rap CO-IN-TEL-PRO: Subverting the power of Hip-Hop
One-on-One with BlackElectorate.com's Cedric Muhammad

'Why, if the FBI was following my son the night he was murdered, why don't they know who is responsible for the murder?'
—*Voleta Wallace, mother of Christopher Wallace (Notorious B.I.G.)* By FinalCall.com News

'I believe I began writing on the murders of Biggie and 2PAC, because of two very simple facts that I think are glossed over and those facts are: that at the very time of their murders, in the case of Biggie in particular, but in the last days and weeks of their lives it is a documented fact, it has been reported that both 2PAC and Biggie were under government surveillance by federal agencies.'**In the last days and weeks of their lives... it has been reported that both 2PAC and Biggie were under government surveillance by federal agencies.** http://www.blackelectorate.com/articles.asp?ID=1123

Puffy Combs, who now calls himself P. Diddy, remains the head of Bad Boy Entertainment. In 1998, he branched off into men's fashion with his Sean John collection. In 2003, he donated $2 million to the "children of New York City" for their "health and educational needs."

Pop Matters today publishes an essay, "Watching Rap," which starts like this:

In March of 2008, the LA Times published an article that implicated Sean "Diddy" Combs and his associates in the 1994 shooting of Tupac Shakur at Quad Recording Studios in New York. A few days later, the Times retracted the article once it became apparent that the author, Chuck Phillips, had relied on fabricated documents and less-than-credible sources. Nevertheless, despite the quick (and embarrassing) retraction, the story got nearly one million hits on latimes.com, more than any other story for the year, and as a result, the story-within-the-story became the overwhelming public interest in the shooting, even 14 years after the fact.

Puff is Free!
Can He Stay Free of
Trouble? by - Davey D
3/19/01

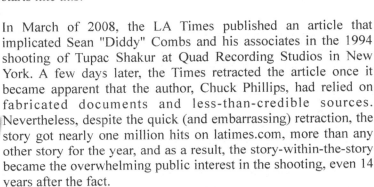

Well I'm still processing Friday's verdict which acquitted **Sean Puffy Combs** of all charges and left **Shyne** holding the bag while looking at anywhere from 12-20 years jail time. He gets officially sentenced on **April 16th**..On one hand I'm happy that Puff got off...but something don't sit right.. Something just don't sit right and I can't figure out what it is

Hip-Hop Homicide"Worth More Dead Than Alive

"By Anthony Bruno

But the most sinister theory fingers Knight for both murders. Before his death, Tupac Shakur was becoming a problem for Knight. The star was questioning Death Row's method of bookkeeping, which indicated that Shakur owed the company $4.9 million even though he had earned the company $60 million in record sales. Unhappy with his Death Row contract, Shakur was rumored to be looking for a new label once he'd completed his three-album obligation. Shakur also had a burgeoning acting career after having appeared in several movies, including *Juice, Above the Rim,* and *Gridlock'd*. Shakur's allegiance to Death Row might have been slipping, but Death Row possessed tapes of 200 unreleased songs recorded by Shakur, raw material for future albums. In the record business, death has a way of increasing public interest in an artist. As Cathy Scott quotes one unnamed record industry insider: Tupac was "'worth more dead than alive.'"

According to this theory, the killing of Notorious B.I.G. was a cover for Tupac Shakur's murder, meant to make both killings appear to be the products of the East Coast-West Coast feud. The fate of 19-year-old Yafeu "Kadafi" Fula appears to add some credence to this theory

So who did kill Shakur and B.I.G.? Police in Las Vegas and Los Angeles continue their investigations, but the cases have grown cold. Unless a surprise witness comes forward, the prospects of solving these crimes grow dimmer as the years go by. Nevertheless, Notorious B.I.G.'s mother, Voletta Wallace, is determined to find out who killed her son, and she has filed lawsuits against the City of Los Angeles and the LAPD in her quest to get answers. Tupac Shakur's mother, Afeni Shakur, also wants answers, and she rejects the theory that her son's murder was simply gang retaliation for the beating of Crip Orlando Anderson

In a taped confession given to the L.A. Weekly, Keffe D says, "[Combs] took me downstairs and he's like, 'Man, I want to get rid of them dudes.' ... I was like, 'We'll wipe their ass out, quick. It's nothing.' ... We wanted a million."

Despite Tupac dating Quincy Jones' daughter Kidada, at first, Quincy didn't like Tupac because Tupac made the following remark to "Source," magazine: "Interracial couples. Quincy Jones is disgusting. All he does is stick his d**k in white b**ches and make fucked up kids."

This made Quincy mad and two white readers responded to "Source," by saying, "If you don't like white people, what about when you hung with us in San Francisco?"

Tupac would later apologize to Kidada, "I didn't mean that about your dad or you."

Kidada says, "We started dating steadily and one night Tupac and I were sitting in a booth at Jerry's Deli in L.A. and two hands slammed down on Tupac's shoulders from behind."

"We jumped up, and there was my father standing there. He said to Tupac, "I need to kick it with you for a minute." This was the first time they'd met, so he took Tupac to a booth and they sat and talked for a long time. Then, they stood up and hugged when it was over and they got along fine from then on."

According to information from the dvd "Tupac Breaking The Oath" sexual advances were made toward tupac

by Quincey Jones

with her close friend
Kidada Jones,
daughter of the great
Quincy Jones

Kidada Jones and Tupac

It can't be understated the degree to which this surveillance is weird and threatening and, relative to the amount of crime that actually takes place in the (narrowly-defined) rap community, completely disproportionate. Hip-hop cops are, as Nielson points out, a naked throwback to "the COINTELPRO days of the '50s and '60s, when black artists and activists were routinely monitored by the FBI and other law enforcement agencies"--except these days, the New Yorker writes bemused profiles about the cops involved. I have yet to read an even remotely convincing justification for their existence, although Ian Frazier did give it a shot in that New Yorker piece: Fabolous shouts out Street Fam, which is in fact a criminal gang, all the time; Vibe reported on Young Jeezy's ties to the "ATL street crew" Black Mafia Family. So yes, these dudes knew/grew up with/are still friends with criminals.

This ain't no threat, this is real, man. We're gonna ostracize him. You're not allowed to come among us as black people. Anywhere you find this idiot, we got to deal with him. I sent out an order, to the Brothers in the street and the Brothers in the prisons – he's not allowed to come among us. You can't go to the east coast and do a lecture nowhere – we will find you , we will mobilize and we will shut you down, man. You not gonna disrespect us and disrespect Hip Hop and think you just gonna walk freely among us, like everything is everything. Brother, let me give you a bit of history – do you remember this trick called Eugenia Sells in Grenada? Working for the CIA, I believe she set up Michael Manly. Right after she set up Michael Manly,they invaded Grenada. Remember this other trick,

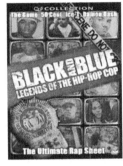

Notorious C.O.P. is an opinionated firsthand account of the side of hip-hop you hide from your mother. Charged with the daunting task of standing up to New York's flyest, Derrick Parker spent 20 years combing the streets of Gotham for anyone flashing a mic and a handgun. The self-proclaimed "hip-hop cop" was raised a B-boy in Hollis, Queens, before joining the force and rising up the New York Police Department ranks, eventually heading the first special-force unit focused on rap-related crime. Hip-hop in the 1990s was a bloody sport, and really, who shot Big? Parker had his hand in all, and C.O.P. is his time to beat his chest and do some bragging, even if it's about his mundane escapades with J.Lo. Top-notch detective or not, this egocentric sleuth should stray far from the pen, as clichéd terminology and a knack for the typographical error run rampant in this stream-of-conscious tell-all that will leave you yearning for an abridged copy.

In March of 2008, the LA Times published an article that implicated Sean "Diddy" Combs and his associates in the 1994 shooting of Tupac Shakur at Quad Recording Studios in New York. A few days later, the Times retracted the article once it became apparent that the author, Chuck Phillips, had relied on fabricated documents and less-than-credible sources. Nevertheless, despite the quick (and embarrassing) retraction, the story got nearly one million hits on latimes.com, more than any other story for the year, and as a result, the story-within-the-story became the overwhelming public interest in the shooting, even 14 years after the fact.

I'm being nice about it, nurse rivers, that worked with the doctor down in Tuskegee? Syphilis experiment – and they passed on syphilis to 400 black men and then they moved to Atlanta and they walked among us, freely like everything was everything – not today, man. Not on Professor Griff's watch. That's never going to happen again, not as long as I am breathing. And if I don't do anything, may the goddamn earth reject my goddamn body, man and I'm serious. That's never going to happen to us again. People like him can not walk among us, people. At the peak of my five to seven years of putting the information out to the hip hop community i have received numerous threats and attacks. These books and dvd's will give you a hint into what is going on in hip hop.

And, after a kind of survey of why one million people would care about this story--the fact the deaths remain unsolved, the allegations of police involvement in Pac's death, the rise of so-called hip-hop cops, and so on--the piece's author, Erik Nielson, winds up here: "This recent mainstream interest in the subject may suggest that these kinds of surveillance tactics are new, but the existence of the "hip-hop cops" is really just further evidence of a long-standing tradition of institutional surveillance of rap as a whole--a tradition that has been so pervasive that in many ways it has become intrinsic to the genre as we know it." So far--great.

Hip hop & law enforcement have a strained relationship, but it?s hard to imagine one without the other. But has it gone so far that there are special divisions of the FBI, the DEA, & the New York & Los Angeles police departments devoted to investigating artists like Jay-Z, 50 Cent, & Keith Murray? This documentary by Don Sikorski asks that question & interviews both sides to see where reality & paranoia meet. Major names in the industry such as Russell Simons, Kanye West, Snoop Dog, & a host of other important members of the hip-hop community are interviewed in this expose. Sikorski uncovered hours of surveillance footage & massive files on the personal lives & activities of the artists who may have been treated like key players in a Mafia sting operation rather than entertainers. Rap Sheet, Hip Hop & the Cops Documentary.

Don Sikorski

All of this information and more were made readily available to "Don Sikorski", the dvd Rap Sheets was made.

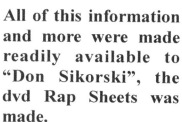

JAM MASTER JAY MURDER LINKED TO GOTTI ASSOCIATE?: McGriff may have targeted deejay for working with 50 Cent, affidavit reveals.
courtesy of www.eurweb.com

*The feds are looking into whether Queens drug kingpin Kenneth (Supreme) McGriff is behind the death of Jam Master Jay because the deejay ignored an industry blacklistof 50 Cent.

The information, obtained by the Smoking Gun web site, appeared in a 2003 affidavit used by federal agents to obtain a search warrant for the offices of record label Murder Inc., founded by McGriffs longtime associate Irving (Irv Gotti) Lorenzo. The document eveals that McGriff had been keeping tabs on 50s whereabouts with the ultimate plan of his shooting death. Beef between the two reportedly began in 2000, when Fif released a song called "Ghetto Koran" that included details about McGriff's "Supreme Team" drug gang.
Jam Master Jay, 37, was shot and killed by masked gunmen who burst into his 24-7 recording studio in downtown Jamaica. His murder is still unsolved.

Kenneth (Supreme) McGriff

50 Cent — Ghetto Qu'ran (Forgive Me) Lyrics

[Talking]
Uh huh, uh huh, uh huh
Southside, what y'all niggas know about the dirty south? One time

[Chorus]
Lord forgive me, for I've sinned
Over and over again, just to stay on top
I recall memories, filled with sin
Over and over again, and again

Yo, when you hear talk of the southside, you hear talk of the team
See niggas feared Prince and respected Preme
For all you slow muthafuckas I'm a break it down iller
See Preme was a business man and Prince was the killer
Remember, he used to push the bulletproof BM, uh huh
This here get ya seasick, I sat back and peeped shit
The roll with Easy Rider and they ain't get blunted
Had the whole projects workin for fifty on five-hundred
As a youth, all I ever did was sell crack

I used to idolize cat
Heart me in my heart to hear that nigga snitched on Pat, how he go out like that?

That first verse is just a dose of the shit that I'm on
Consider this the first chapter in the ghetto's Quran
I know a lot of niggas that get dough like Remmy and Joe
And Prince and Rightous from Hillside with the mole on his nose

49

The industry would like us to think that 50cent had something to do with the death of jam master jam but no evidence points to this.

Rap legend Jam Master Jay was carrying a gun the night he was murdered - but trusted his killer so much he never went for it when the man entered his studio, a witness told the Daily News.

Read more: http://www.nydailynews.com/news/ny_crime/
2007/11/25/2007-11-25_breaking_silence_witness_says_jam_master.html#ixzz1bA8RhsNy

"The Hip-Hop community gotta be more vocal."

Anatomy of the shooting
Witness to shooting: Rincon says the gunmen entered the studio as he was reaching for his cell phone, and he only saw the shooter's back after the murder

Uriel (Tony) Rincon was shot in his left leg as he was reaching for cell phone

Jasea (Jam Master Jay) Mizell

Storage room

Control room
Randy Allen and Mike B. were in the control room with a wanna-be singer

Lydia High, Mizell's assistant

Gunman

Rapper's gun

Vocal booth

Front door

Gunman

Hallway

Run DMC (l. to r.) Mizell, Darryl McDaniels and Joseph Simmons.

'Hip-Hop Cop' to Release Tell-All Book

by Kenny Rodriguez

D-J DOWN

NT ACCOUNTING SCANDALS [Fox] CITIGROUP TO NAS RUT UNCH

Fox News Shows Jam Master Jay Body Bag

For some reason the Fox News Network was repeatedly showing the body bag of Run-DMC DJ Jam Master Jay being removed from the New York Recording studio where he was gunned down on Wednesday. Read on to check out a couple video captures of the disturbing scene. http://rapdirt.com/fox-news-shows-jam-master-jay-body-bag/2826/

The police-backed 'war on hip-hop' is no longer an urban legend, at least according to former detective Derrick Parker. He should know. In the 1980s, he was dubbed the 'hip-hop cop,' and in his upcoming book titled "Notorious C.O.P.," he talks in great detail about how he was assigned to monitor hundreds of rappers.During his 20 years on the force, the New York detective investigated the unsolved murders of Tupac Shakur, Notorious B.I.G., and Jam Master Jay, as well as the ongoing Busta Rhymes and Lil' Kim cases. But in 2001, Parker was assigned to create "the Binder" – a database detailing the criminal associations and arrests of hundreds of rappers, including Sean 'P. Diddy' Combs, 50 Cent and Jay-Z. When the dossier was leaked to the American Civil Liberties Union, Parker writes, "I was suddenly public enemy number one." Parker also describes run-ins with several crooked cops, including a crack addicted officer who stole paychecks from his precinct.

Hip Hop's first cop Ron Stallworth has written 4 books on Gangsta Rap

He also details an all-cop "cocaine fiesta" in the Bronx, where a female sergeant offered him "a shoebox full of cocaine" after snorting some herself. Parker reported the incident to his commanding officer the next day. The hip-hop loving author, whose book hits stores in July, insists rappers were lucky they were on his beat. "The cultural ignorance of my fellow officers made them assume that all rappers were evil criminals," Parker says, explaining that officers under Mayor Rudy Giuliani's administration labeled them as "young, black, rich and angry.""...Because they know if the rappers get a revolutionary message, that if the rappers start to clean up their act and rap revolutionary rap, the game is over. The enemy, and those who control the distribution of rap, shut down revolutionary rap and would only fund gangster rap after [the 1992 L.A. rebellion against police brutality.] We saw an extreme rise in gangster rap and the elimination of revolutionary rap. ... I say to Brother Russell Simmons and the other rappers:

Davey D's Hip Hop Corner-(The Blog)

The World from a Hip Hop Perspective

Davey D

Yes indeed Snitching is big business in more ways than you can possible know. Its just a shame that 60 Minutes got Cam'ron to talk about such a serious issue, cause from what they showed, he definitely didn't break it down the way he should've. Well don't fret 'cause we break the whole thing down in this eye opening interview on Hard Knock Radio
http://www.kpfa.org/archives/index.php?arch=19554

Cam'ron

Be Warned Snitching Is Big Business

by Davey D

Busta Rhymes

BUSTA JACKED FOR HIS BLING BY AN ORGANIZED CREW OF THIEVES:

The following caption currently appears in our "Hip Hop Gallery Gossip" column: In the book "Notorious C.O.P." by Derrick Parker, one chapter focuses on a crew from Bed-Stuy named, "The Commission." They were known to rob rappers of their bling and sell the diamonds to a celebrity jeweler for meltdown. All the rappers were unknowingly set-up by members of their road crew. Rapper Busta Rhymes was once robbed by "The Commission." The crew robbed Busta of $100,000 dollars worth of bling and one of the crew members, Da Kommander was so brazen, he would wear Busta's laser emerald earrings that were stolen in the robbery. "The Commission" still operate and are suspected in the recent robbery of a athlete who got into an altercation with a Fabolous crew member. http://panachereport.com/channels/hip%20hop%20gallery/Rapclassified.htm

51

DJ Drama Arrested In Atlanta Mixtape Raid

Aphilliate Music Group partner Don Cannon, 17 others also taken into custody Tuesday.By Shaheem Reid, with additional reporting by Jayson Rodriguez

Arrests and raids due to the distribution of what authorities consider bootleg CDs is nothing new. A sprinkling of mom-and-pop stores throughout the country have been shut down in recent years, but this is the first time that the crackdown has hit a name as big as Drama, arguably the current top mixtape DJ. His *Gangsta Grillz* series has become a street staple and a promotional tool for emerging artists.

From Monterey Pop to Altamont
OPERATION CHAOS

The CIA's War Against the Sixties Counter-Culture
by Mae Brussell, November 1976 (unpublished)

http://www.newsmakingnews.com/vmmbchaos11,12,01.htm
DEATH, DRUGS, AND DEPRESSION

American and British pop/rock music during the 60's created an art form that has been described as one of the most important cultural revolutions in history. Within a few years, between 1968 and 1976, many of the most famous names associated with this early movement were dead. Mama Cass Elliott (earlier with the Mamas and Papas), Jimi Hendrix, Otis Redding, Brian Jones (helped form the Rolling Stones with Mick Jagger and Keith Richards), Janis Joplin were all at the Monterey Pop celebration, summer 1967.

Family and friends accepted the musicians' depressions or accidents as having to do with alcohol, drug usage, or both. Was anything added to their beverages or drugs to cause personality changes and eventual suicides? Almost every death was shrouded with unanswered questions and mystery. Persons around the musicians had strange backgrounds and were often suspect. All of these musicians were at the peak of a creative period and success at the time they were offered LSD. Their personalities altered drastically. Optimism and gratification were replaced with doubt and misery.

Why would young people with so much talent and influence as Phil Ochs, Janis Joplin, Gram Parsons, or Brian Jones wallow in suffering, self doubt, and despondency? They were all loved, making important contributions to their concerts and compositions, cutting new records, being recognized for their talent. It just doesn't make sense. By 1968, the FBI's Counterintelligence Program, and the CIA's Operation Chaos, had included among their long list of domestic enemies "Advocates of New Lifestyles," "New Left," "Apostles of Non-Violence and Racial Harmony" and "Restless Youth."

Justification for indexing 300,000 law abiding citizens into files, and wiretapping, bugging, or burglarizing offices was rationalized on the basis that violence was prevalent, the cities were burning. Now we find out that being "non-violent" and wanting "racial harmony," according to recent Congressional investigations, was also a crime.

The meeting place for this social, economic, and soon to become political, revolution was at the folk festival, rock concerts, free park love-ins, at the FM radio stations, or home with favorite records. In the music there were many messages. Everything was beautiful until the insanity began. The CIA got into the business of altering human behavior in 1947. "Project Paperclip," an arrangement made by CIA Director Allen Dulles and Richard Helms, brought one thousand Nazi specialists and their families to the United States. They were employed for military and civilian institutions. Some Nazi doctors were brought to our hospitals and colleges to continue further experimentations on the brain. American and German scientists, working with the CIA, then the military, started developing every possible method of controlling the mind. Lysergic Acid Diethylamide, LSD, was discovered at the Sandoz Laboratories, Basel, Switzerland, in 1939 by Albert Hoffman. This LSD was pure. No other ingredients were added.

ALLEN DULLES, RICHARD HELMS, Carmel Office and **FRANK WISNER** were the grand masters. If you were in a room with them you were in a room full of people that you had to believe would deservedly end up in **HELL**. I guess I will see them there soon." –James Angleton, CIA Chief of Counter Intelligence

Fela Kuti made mention that "With my music, I create change... I am using my music as a weapon." "After all, the military do not just dance to my music; they march to it, too." "To be spiritual is not by praying and going to church. Spiritualism is the understanding of the universe so that it can be a better place to live in." "...man is here against his will. Where do we come from? What was before us? When you think you die, you're not dead. It's a transition." "I want peace. Happiness. Not only for myself. For everybody." "A radical is he who has no sense... fights without reason... I have a reason. I am authentic. Yes, that's what I am." "A luta continua... a luta continua, no! It must not continue. The struggle must STOP!"

-- Fela Kuti

The U.S. Army got interested in LSD for interrogation purposes in 1950. After May, 1956, until 1975, the U.S. Army Intelligence and the U.S. Chemical Corps "experimented with hallucinogenic drugs." The CIA and Army spent $26,501,446 "testing" LSD, code name EA 1729, and other chemical agents. Contracts went out to forty-eight different institutions for testing. The CIA was part of these projects. They concealed their participation by contracting to various colleges, hospitals, prisons, mental hospitals, and private foundations. The LSD I will refer to is the same type of LSD that the CIA used because of the similarity of symptoms between their reports and what happened to musicians or hippies after 1967. We shall be speaking of CIA-LSD, not pure LSD.

Government agents and the ability to cause permanent insanity, identical to schizophrenia, without physician or family knowing what happened to the victim. "No physical examination of the subject is required prior to the administration of LSD. A physician need not be present. Physicians might be called for the hope they would make a diagnosis of mental breakdown

Government agents and the ability to cause permanent insanity, identical to schizophrenia, without physician or family knowing what happened to the victim

which would be useful in discrediting the individual who was the subject of CIA interest. Richard Helms, CIA Director, argued that administering drugs, including poisonous LSD, might be on individuals who are unwitting as this is the only realistic method of maintaining the capability considering the intended operational use to influence human behavior as the operational targets will certainly be unwitting."

-- "Senate Report to Study Governmental Operations with Respect to Intelligence Activities" Book I, page 401, April 1976

When the first reports came out that the CIA could administer a tasteless substance into the beverage of one of their most responsible co-workers, and drive that man into a mental institution, or cause him to jump out of a window to his death, all existing CIA records were destroyed.

Hippies and musicians, previously normal and creative, with families and loved ones identical to Dr. Frank Olson, responded in the same manner as Dr. Olson after their introduction to the same drugs. Valuable documentation of LSD experiments should not have been in the hands of CIA Director Richard Helms. January 31, 1973, one day before he retired from the CIA, he removed some possible answers as to the fate of persons' minds the past ten years. Helms had been behind all the types of experimentations since 1947. Mind altering projects went under the code names of Operation Chatter, Operation Bluebird/Artichoke, Operation Mknaomi, Mkultra, and Mkdelta.

By 1963, four years before Monterey Pop, the combined efforts of the CIA's Directorate of Science and Technology, Department of U.S. Army Intelligence, and U.S. Chemical Corps were ready for any covert operations that seemed necessary. U.S. agents were able to destroy any person's reputation by inducing hysteria or excessive emotional responses, temporary or permanent insanity, suggesting or encouraging suicide, erasing memory, inventing double or triple personalities inside one mind, causing prolonged lapses of memory, teaching and inducing racism and hatred against specific groups, causing subjects to obey instructions on the telephone or in person, hypnotically assuring that no memory remains of the assignments.

The CIA has poison dart guns to kill from far away, tranquilizers for pets so the household or neighborhood is not alerted by entry or exit. While pure LSD is usually 160 micrograms, the CIA was issuing 1600 micrograms. Some of their LSD was administered to patients at Tulane University who already had wired electrodes in their brain. Was being crazy an occupational disease of being a musician? Or does this LSD, tested and described in Army documents, explain how a cultural happening that was taking place in 1967-68 could be halted and altered radically?

Jimi Hendrix was given a tab of acid just before his show at Madison Square Garden where he was playing with Buddy Miles and Bill Cox. The audience, as well as Hendrix, was completely freaked out by his irrational behavior. The result was that Hendrix was discredited. The effect of one LSD dose could cause permanent brain injury. Anything Hendrix did after this experience, up to and including the time of his death, could be attributed to that earlier event.

He didn't die from a drug overdose. He was not an out-of-control dope fiend. Jimi Hendrix was not a junkie. And anyone who would use his death as a warning to stay away from drugs should warn people against the other things that killed Jimi—the stresses of dealing with the music industry, the craziness of being on the road, and especially, the dangers of involving oneself in radical, or even unpopular, political movements. COINTELPRO was out to do more than prevent a Communist menace from overtaking the United States, or keep the Black Power movement from burning down cities. COINTELPRO was out to obliterate its opposition and ruin the reputations of the people involved in the antiwar movement, the civil rights movement, and the rock revolution. Whenever Jimi Hendrix's death is blamed on drugs, it accomplishes the goals of the FBI's program. It not only slanders Jimi's personal and professional reputation, but the entire rock revolution in the 60's.

    -- John Holmstrom. "Who Killed Jimi?"

JIMI HENDRIX, 27 yrs., Sept. 18, 1970. Cause of death clouded. Suggestions of drug plants, mafia connections, murder. Kidnapped shortly before he died. Surrounded by groupie females, one of whom boasted giving him his first acid trip. Affected by acid, depression interfered with performances. One of top stars at Monterey Pop. Into rock-blues, jazz. Media assumption of "suicide" or "drug overdose" like Joplin. Earned millions. Freaked out and couldn't do his serious music

As the music of youth and resistance fell under the crosshairs of the CIA's CHAOS war, it was probable that Jimi Hendrix—the tripping, peacenik "Black Elvis" of the '60s—should find himself a target.

Government manufactured LSD included countless combinations of chemicals. New York State Psychiatric Institute was granted the first known contract for research into psychochemical drugs. The purpose was to determine the psychological effect of psychological chemical agents on human subjects. These subjects were given derivatives of LSD and mescaline. Other chemicals that were tested, which could be distributed at a later date included morphine, demerol, seconal, scopolamine, ditan, atropine, psilocybin, BZ (benzilate), glycolate, atropine substitutes, dimethyl, tryptamine, chlorpromazine, LSD with Dibenzyline (blocking agents), LSM (Lysergic acid morpholide), LSD like compounds, psilocybin, and various chemical glycolate agents.

It is no easy feat to alter society's consciousness. An arsenal of weapons was available. Included among the chemicals were also choking agents, nerve agents, blood agents, blister agents, vomiting agents, incapacitating agents and toxins. "The glycolates cause incapacitation by interfering with muscle, gland functions and the central nervous system; they depress or inhibit nervous activity. In addition to delirium, there is physical impaired coordination, blurred vision, inhibition of sweating and salivation, rapid heart rate, elevated blood pressure, increased body temperature and, at high doses, vomiting, prostration, and stupor or coma. The onset may be minutes, hours, or days."

> **-- U.S. Army "Use of Volunteers in Chemical Agent Research"**
> **Released from the Pentagon March 1976**

THE ENEMY

Why were Hippies such a threat, from the President on down to local levels, objects for surveillance and disruptions? Many of the musicians had the potential to become political. There were racial overtones to the black-white sounds, the harmony between people like Janis Joplin, Otis Redding, and Jimi Hendrix. Black music was the impetus that got the Rolling Stones into composing and performing. The war in Vietnam was escalating. What if they stopped protesting the war in Southeast Asia and turned to expose domestic policies at home with the same energy?

One of the Byrds stopped singing at Monterey Pop to question the official Warren Report conclusion that Lee Harvey Oswald was a "lone assassin." John and Yoko Lennon were protesting the Vietnam War. The State Department wrote documents describing them as "highly political and unfavorable to the administration." It was recommended their citizenship be denied, and they be put under surveillance. Mick Jagger, before he was offered Hollywood's choicest women and heavy drugs, was concerned about the youth protests in Paris, 1968, and the anti-war demonstrations at the London Embassy.

"War stems from power-mad politicians and patriots. Some new master plan would end all these mindless men from seats of power and replace them with real people, people of compassion."

-- Mick Jagger

http://www.icdc.com/~paulwolf/cointelpro/cointel.htm

http://www.sixtiescity.com/Events/Events67.shtm

THE BATTLEGROUND

July, 1968, the FBI's counterintelligence operations attacked law-abiding American individuals and groups. The stated purpose of these assaults was to disrupt large gatherings, expose and discredit the enemy, and neutralize their selected targets. Neutralization included killing the leaders, if necessary. Preferably, turn two opposing segments of society against each other to do the dirty work for them.

Remember that among these dangers to the security of the United States were persons with "different lifestyles" and also "apostles of non-violence and racial harmony." CIA Director Richard Helms warned National Security Advisor Henry Kissinger, Feb. 18, 1969, that their study on "Restless Youth" was "extremely sensitive" and "would prove most embarrassing for all concerned if word got out the CIA was involved in domestic matters." The FBI sent out a list of suggestions on how to achieve their goals. They can all be applied to what happened to musicians, youngsters at folk rock festivals, and hippies along the highway. Gather information on their immorality. Show them as scurrilous and depraved. Call attention to their habits and living conditions. Explore every possible embarrassment. Send in women and sex, break up marriages. Have members arrested on marijuana charges. Investigate personal conflicts or animosities between them. Send articles to the newspapers showing their depravity. Use narcotics and free sex to entrap. Use misinformation to confuse and disrupt. Get records of their bank accounts. Obtain specimens of handwriting. Provoke target groups into rivalries that may result in death.

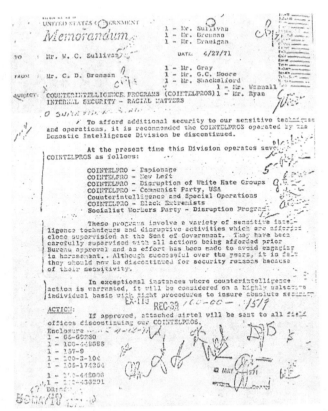

"Intelligence Activities and Rights of Americans"
Book II, April 26, 1976
Senate Committee Study with Respect to Intelligence

The IRS admitted that "people who attend rock concert festivals" were listed among targets for investigation by its special staff. Agent Leon Levine said that "ideological groups such as rock festival patrons were to be watched." Employees at the CIA's Langley, Virginia, headquarters don't have to stand in line to get tickets to these events. They have a top-secret Ticketron outlet for rock concert appearances. Korea has a list of 260 decadent rock-folk and protest songs. Among them is "I Shot the Sheriff" and "We Shall Overcome."

"Peace Pills" were distributed at the Santa Clara Fairgrounds for a folk-rock festival. Youngsters were hospitalized. A strange drug was handed out freely and poured into drinks. All of those who took the drug were treated, but sent home without any knowledge of the psychological damage. A man had jumped on the musician's platform and announced they had 4,000 pills to hand out. The pills caused "marked disorientation as to time and space, inability to sustain directed thought, presence of a trance-like state." This kind of scene was so common that large groups were discouraged from performing in the manner they had before these assaults took place.

The irreplaceable loss of lives and talent has been noticed by persons sensitive to the rock-folk music. We can't bring them back to life. We might take time to examine their deaths, if only to stop the attack still going on upon certain artists and musicians. Some of my information on the details of these deaths is incomplete. The circumstances surrounding them caused me to ask some hard questions.

ISRAELI MONEY LAUNDERING AND THE DIRTY TRUTH

Is it a coincidence record companies promote so many jewish rock acts?

http://www.intmensorg.info/zionism2.htm

WHO'S STOLEN THE WORLD'S MONEY?

IRS

Department of the Treasury
Internal Revenue Service

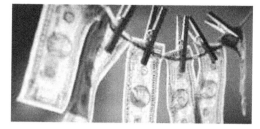

Jews being arrested on money laundering

58

AL JACKSON, 39yrs., October, 1975. Former drummer with Booker T. and the MG's. Back-up drummer for Otis Redding. Shot five times to his death in Memphis, TN. Cause of death "apparent robbery." Produced Stax Records.

OTIS REDDING, 26 yrs., December 1967. Airplane crash over Wisconsin. First star of Monterey Pop to die. Brought soul to every American city. Best known hit record "By the Dock of the Bay." A poll before his death claimed Redding the most popular musical star in Europe.

PAUL WILLIAMS, 34 yrs., Aug. 23, 1973, Detroit, Michigan. Found dead in the car, gun on his lap. One of the original Temptations. Did the choreography for Temptations. Had solved drinking problems, emotional crisis. Dead only a few blocks from Motown, where first records made.

VESTA WILLIAMS

My good friend **Vesta Williams** is gone and I simply can't **Rest In Peace | R&B singer Vesta Williams found dead at 53** ---Big-voiced R&B diva Vesta Williams, perhaps best-known for her 1980s hits "Don't Blow A Good Thing" and "Congratulations," has been found dead of a possible drug overdose in a Southern California hotel room, coroner's investigators said Friday. She was 53. Williams was found dead at 6:15 p.m. Thursday in an El Segundo hotel room.

MICHAEL JACKSON Did the Illuminati kill Michael Jackson?

Yes, the illuminati DID kill Michael Jackson. As you probably know, he was getting ready to begin a "come back" tour and was planning on performances all over the world.

There is not enough time or space in this posting to go into all the details, but the same group of people bent on world domination for decades are getting ready to "seal the deal" on the world. Michael was preparing to use his postion and influence to warn the entire world of what these people (the Rothschild, Rockafellers, the International Bank of Settlements, etc) are planning. In particular, their plans to drastically reduce the world's population by mass extermination through a program of forced "vaccinations" against the bogus swine flu. Investigative journalist Jane Burgermeister just filed a complaint with the FBI against the UN and the WHO (world health organization) for among other things, conspiracy to commit mass murder...here's the full story:

http://cotocrew.wordpress.com/2009/06/25/natnews-journalist-files-charges-against-who-and-un-for-bioterrorism-and-intent-to-commit-mass-murder/

There are some very sinister forces at work, and the people of the earth need to stand together to defeat them. These same monsters have manipulated nations into wars for centuries, in order that these same nations would be in a postion to need to borrow money thus plunging these nations (including ours) into deeper and deeper debt. This is a link to a video about the federal reserve and the international banking system and how it keeps the population enslaved:

http://video.google.com/videoplay?docid=5232639329002339531

KRS ONE

KRS ONE's Temple Of Hip-Hop has posted "The Hiphop Declaration of Peace." This was not posted in response to recent events, but to guide "Hiphop Kulture toward freedom from violence, to establish advice and protection for the existence and development of the international Hiphop community... and establish a foundation, of health, love, awareness, wealth, peace and prosperity for ourselves, our children and their children's children, forever." Peace starts in the heart so this is definitely something to read.

KRS ONE

Minister Server and KRS ONE

his Hiphop Declaration of Peace guides Hiphop Kulture toward freedom from violence, and establishes advice and protection for the existence and development of the international Hiphop community. Through the principles of this Hiphop Declaration of Peace we, Hiphop Kulture, establish a foundation of Health, Love, Awareness, Wealth, peace and prosperity for ourselves, our children and their children's children, forever. For the clarification of Hiphop's meaning and purpose, or when the intention of Hiphop is questioned, or when disputes between parties arise concerning Hiphop; Hiphoppas shall have access to the advice of this document, The Hiphop Declaration of Peace, as guidance, advice and protection.

"24.9 percent of American children live in poverty, while the proportions in Germany, France and Italy are 8.6, 7.4 and 10.5 percent. And once born on the wrong side of the tracks, Americans are more likely to stay there than their counterparts in Europe. Those born to better-off families are more likely to stay better off. America is developing an aristocracy of the rich and a serfdom of the poor - the inevitable result of a twenty-year erosion of its social contract."

-- Will Hutton, The American Prosperity Myth
Albert Einstein quotations

Hip-Hop's Letter to President Bush
Russell Simmons and the Hip-Hop Summit
Released a Letter to President Bush

HIP-HOP SUMMIT ACTION NETWORK
512 Seventh Avenue
43rd Fl
New York
New York 10018

OPEN LETTER TO
PRESIDENT GEORGE W. BUSH

March 10, 2003

Dear Mr. President:

As you approach your final decision on a war to disarm Iraq, we are writing urgently to recommend that you use your good office and stature as a world leader to win disarmament of Iraq without going to war. Thus far, without a full-scale war, you have been successful in marshalling the United Nations and the world community to affirm the importance of disarming Saddam Hussein of all weapons of mass destruction.

The United Nations' inspectors are making progress. The worldwide demand that Iraq complies completely with UN Resolution 1441 has produced results and important information that will enhance the effectiveness of the ongoing UN inspection process.

Rather than establishing a deadline for war, you could strengthen the lifeline for peace and disarmament in Iraq: continued UN inspections.

Peace is not the absence of war, but it is the presence of justice. There is no justification for the massive killing of innocent people in an avoidable war on Iraq. The wrongness of this war will prevent a lasting peace in the Middle East and circumvent the progress that the UN is finally making in getting Saddam Hussein to comply.

Domestically, Mr. President, rampant poverty is on the rise and the hopes and aspirations of millions of youth are being triaged on the altar of national neglect. We in the hip-hop community know and feel the pain, misery and wretchedness of the social condition of our communities. Now with the prospect of a multi-trillion dollar federal budget deficit, an unnecessary war on Iraq is only going to increase the cold damp hands of social dereliction that have a deadly choke hold on too many Americans across the nation.

Give peace a greater chance. War on Iraq now is not the solution. We can win peace and disarmament without war.

Sincerely,

Russell Simmons
Chairman

Benjamin F. Chavis
President
===========================

The FNV Newsletter c 2002
Send comments to
misterdaveyd@earthlink.net

CONGRESS TRYING TO BAN HIP HOP SHOWS

Prosecutors May Be Raving About Jailing Hip Hoppers Very Soon
by: Opio Lumumba Sokoni, J.D.

Would you believe that there are laws being proposed in Congress that would shut down venues and jail owners and promoters of Hip Hop concerts? If something is not done now, the government will have the legal right to jail and fine innocent venue owners and promoters for some other person's drug use.

One of these laws, which was introduced in the U.S. House of Representatives, is called the "RAVE Act of 2003" (H.R. 718) - sponsored by North Carolina Republican Howard Coble and co-sponsored by Texas Republican Lamar Smith. Let me not fail to mention that Congressman Coble (who is the chairman of the Judiciary Subcommittee on Crime, Terrorism and Homeland Security) said on a radio show last month that the internment of Japanese-Americans during World War II was appropriate. It's no wonder that he is sponsoring this law.

There is no hip way to break this bad bill down. But to make it simple, the "RAVE Act" expands the scope of the previously passed bill often referred to as the "crack house statute." This bill would make it easier for the federal government to prosecute owners and managers of businesses and real estate if customers, employees, tenants, or other persons on their property commit a drug-related offense. Persons convicted under this new law could be sentenced to up to 20 years in prison, fined $500,000 and have their business or property confiscated under current forfeiture laws.

Formerly introduced in 2002, the RAVE Act came close to passing the Senate last year and might have become law if it wasn't for a national campaign led by Drug Policy Alliance (DPA). Tens of thousands of voters urged Senators to reject it. Business interests collected nearly 20,000 signatures on a petition that warned that the RAVE Act "is a serious threat to civil liberties, freedom of speech and the right to dance." Protests were held in cities around the country, including a protest in the form of a "rave" (a dance party with electronic music) held on the lawn of Congress. Ultimately, two of the original Senate co-sponsors withdrew their support. Supporters of the bill are determined to pass it this year.

The second bill being proposed is the CLEAN-UP Act, sponsored by California Republican Doug Ose. This is a seemingly harmless bill that provides more money and training for the clean up of illegal methamphetamine laboratories. But look deeper into the bill and you will find provisions that would make it a federal crime - punishable by up to nine years in prison - to promote "any rave, dance, music or other entertainment event" that might attract some attendees that would use drugs.

Some may say, "So what - they should get popped if they let people use drugs at their spots." That's not the point. The real issue is that businessmen and women could be prosecuted even if they were not involved in drugs - and even if they took steps to stop drug use on their property.To take it further, if these bills become law, property owners may be too afraid to rent or lease their property to groups holding dance parties and other musical events - effectively stifling entrepreneurs who are doing the right thing. If that doesn't scare you, let's try this. These laws would also make it where anyone who threw an event at their own home (such as a party or barbecue) in which one or more of their guests used drugs, they could potentially face a $500,000 fine and 20 years in federal prison. All it takes is a snitch and a racist prosecutor - and we all know that there is no shortage of either.I am a lobbyist for DPA (www.drugpolicy.org), which is the leading organization fighting this law. This organization also fights against America's drug war which has lacked reason, compassion and justice. My work has been more on "treatment instead of incarceration" (www.dcmeasure62.com) for non-violent, low level drug offenders. I work on solutions to prevent the massive incarceration of Blacks (in particular) who need drug treatment, counseling, job training and jobs versus jail. My interest in the RAVE Act was peaked when one of my best friends, a DJ and promoter, talked extensively about how the RAVE Act would affect him. But, my research also lead me to understand how, if these laws were passed, hip hop would be further harassed by the government. So, I took a couple steps over to Bill Piper's office (he successfully fought to kill the RAVE act last year) and began asking questions about these bills. Mr. Piper, who is the Associate Director of National Affairs for DPA, said that these proposed laws make it easier to punish people for the actions of others and could bankrupt nightclubs, arenas and stadiums and put their owners in jail. He also added that it is clear that dancing, singing, and playing music may soon become the next casualty in the War on Drugs.

To take action on this matter just click on http://actioncenter.drugpolicy.org/action/ and participate in the fax campaign to kill this bill.

[Opio Lumumba Sokoni is a Howard University trained lawyer working as the Implementation Coordinator for DC's "Treatment Instead of Jail" initiative. He has previously worked for TransAfrica, Amnesty International and the Interfaith Action Communities. His writings have appeared in the Boston Globe, the Black Commentator and the Washington Times. He has been quoted in a number of publications including the Washington Post. Opio Sokoni is the author of an award winning children's book entitled, "I Want to Be a Lawyer When I Grow Up." He is also a Hip Hop enthusiast.]

We were as hypnotized by the enemy's propaganda as a rabbit is by a snake.
-- **General Eric Von Ludendorf, German General Staff, 1918**

3ʳᵈ DEGREE

The Illuminati's Takeover of Hip Hop

Strategic PSYOP proved to be the instrument through which the U.S. and Coalition Forces were successfully able to isolate the enemy and deny him acceptance by the world community. - -
General Carl Stiner, Former CINCSOC

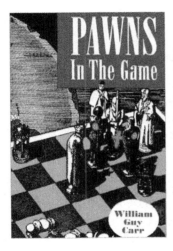

On August 15, 1871, Pike told Mazzini that after World War Three is ended, those who aspire to undisputed world domination will provoke the greatest social cataclysm the world has ever known. We quote his own written words (taken from the letter catalogued in the British Museum Library, London, Eng.) :

"We shall unleash the Nihilists and Atheists, and we shall provoke a formidable social cataclysm which in all its horror will show clearly to the nations the effect of absolute atheism, origin of savagery and of the most bloody turmoil. Then everywhere, the citizens, obliged to defend themselves against the world minority of revolutionaries, will exterminate those destroyers of civilization, and the multitude, disillusioned with Christianity, whose deistic spirits will be from that moment without compass (direction), anxious for an ideal, but without knowing where to render its adoration, will receive the true light through the universal manifestation of the pure doctrine of Lucifer, brought finally out in the public view, a manifestation which will result from the general reactionary movement which will follow the destruction of Christianity and atheism, both conquered and exterminated at the same time."

William Carr, Pawns in the Game
the synagogue of Satan, who controlled the Illuminati AT THE TOP, planned to use wars and
revolutions to bring about the establishment of one kind or another of a One World Government, the powers of which they intended to usurp as soon as it was established.

In 1785, the Bavarian Government outlawed the Illuminati and closed the lodges of the Grand Orient. In 1786, they published the details of the conspiracy. The English title is "The Original Writtings of the Order and Sect of The Illuminati". Copies of the conspiracy were sent to the heads of church and state. The power of the Illuminati was so great that this warning was ignored, as were the warnings Christ had given the world.
The Illuminati went underground. Weishaupt instructed his Illuminists to infiltrate into the lodges of Blue Masonry and form a secret society within secret societies.
Only masons who proved themselves Internationalists, and those whose conduct proved they had defected from God, are initiated into the Illuminati.

It was Myron Fagan, I believe, back in the 60's.   And he said, now just why did the conspirators choose the word Illuminati for their satanic organization. Adam Weishoff himself said that the word is derived from Lucifer and it means "holder of the light."

Illuminati. Cinema Educational Guild, 1967.

Myron Fagan came to prominence in the late 1940s and early 1950s as one of the leaders of the movement to expose supposed communist influence in Hollywood. Operating chiefly under the guise of the Cinema Educational Guild--an organization he founded to distribute anti-communist publications--Fagan sought to demonstrate that Hollywood was "as Red controlled as Moscow" and to counteract that influence. He was reportedly the major force behind the creation of *Red Channels,* a 1950 booklet that listed alleged communist sympathizers in the movie industry, many of whom film executives subsequently blacklisted.

By the 1960s, Fagan had broadened his efforts to root out anti-American infiltration, and he picked up on the popular conservative theme of a plot to subvert US sovereignty by accession to a "one-world government." Like other commentators, Fagan pointed to the activities of the United Nations as evidence of this plot. (For other examples of this theme, see: "The Tower of Babble," "United Nations: The Modern Trojan Horse," and "The Strange Origin of the U.N. Flag," all below.) But in this 1967 record series, *Illuminati: The Council on Foreign Relations,* he spent most of the two-and-a-half hours covering six LP album sides decrying the eponymous think tank as the home base for US members of the "Illuminati," a cult which Fagan claimed had been working to forge a "satanic" world-wide government since the eighteenth century.

Weishaupt and the Illuminati

In 1784 an "Act of God" placed the Bavarian government in possession of evidence which proved the existence of the continuing Luciferian Conspiracy. Adam Weishaupt, a jesuit-trained professor of canon law, defected from Christianity, and embraced the Luciferian ideology while teaching in Ingoldstadt University. In 1770 the money lenders (who had recently organized the House of Rothschild), retained him to revise and modernize the age-old 'protocols' designed to give the Synagogue of Satan ultimate world domination so they can impose the Luciferian ideology upon what remains of the Human Race, after the final social cataclysm, by use of satanic despotism. Weishaupt completed his task May 1st, 1776.

The plan required the destruction of ALL existing governments and religions. This objective was to be reached by dividing the masses into opposing camps in ever increasing numbers on political, racial, social, economic and other issues. The opposing sides were then to be armed and an 'incident' provided which would cause them to fight and weaken themselves as they destroyed national governments and religious institutions.

In 1776 Weishaupt organized the Illuminati to put the plot into execution. The word Illuminati is derived from Lucifer, and means 'holders of the light'. Using the lie that his objective was to bring about a one world government to enable men with proven mental ability to govern the world he recruited about two thousand followers. These included the most intelligent men in the field of arts and letters, education, the sciences, finance and industry. He then established the Lodges of the Grand Orient to be their secret headquarters.

In 1776 Adam Weishaupt officially completes his organization of the Illuminati on May 1 of this year. The purpose of the Illuminati is to divide the goyim (all non-Jews) through political, economic, social, and religious means. The opposing sides were to be armed and incidents were to be provided in order for them to: fight amongst themselves; destroy national governments; destroy religious institutions; and eventually destroy each other.

If you type in illuminati backwards in googles search engine you get...........

http://www.nsa.gov/

Pike's plan was as simple as it has proved effective. He required that Communism, Naziism, Political Zionism, and other International movements be organized and used to foment the three global wars and three major revolutions. The first world war was to be fought so as to enable the Illuminati to overthrow the powers of the Tzars in Russia and turn that country into the stronghold of Atheistic-Communism. The differences stirred up by agentur of the Illuminati between the British and German Empires were to be used to foment this war. After the war ended, Communism was to be built up and used to destroy other governments and weaken religions.

World War Two was to be fomented by using the differences between Fascists and Political Zionists. This war was to be fought so that Naziism would be destroyed and the power of Political Zionism increased so that the sovereign state of Israel could be established in Palestine. During world war two International Communism was to be built up until it equalled in strength that of united Christendom. At this point it was to be contained and kept in check until required for the final social cataclysm. Can any informed person deny Roosevelt and Churchill did not put this policy into effect ?

World War Three is to be fomented by using the differences the agentur of the Illuminati stir up between Political Zionists and the leaders of the Moslem world. The war is to be directed in such a manner that Islam (the Arab World including Mohammedanism) and Political Zionism (including the State of Israel) will destroy themselves while at the same time the remaining nations, once more divided against each other on this issue, will be forced to fight themselves into a state of complete exhaustion physically, mentally, spiritually and economically. Can any unbiased and reasoning person deny that the intrigue now going on in the Near, Middle, and Far East isn't designed to accomplish this devilish purpose?

"That which we must say to the **CROWD** is: we worship a god, but it is the god that one adores without superstition. To **YOU** Sovereign Grand Inspectors General, we say this, that you may repeat it to the brethren of the 32nd, 31st and 30th degrees – the **MASONIC RELIGION** should be, by all of us initiates of the *high* degrees, maintained in the purity of the **LUCIFERIAN** doctrine. If Lucifer were not god, would Adonay (Jesus)... calumniate (spread false and harmful statements about) him?... **YES, LUCIFER IS GOD...**"*

*A.C. De La Rive, *La Femme et l'Enfant dans la Franc-Maçonnérie Universelle* (page 588).

Baphomet

General Albert Pike, 33˚

In hip hop the **Hegelian Dialectic** principle was played out, and it worked just as they planned it would

KANYE WEST **Vs**. **50 CENT**: A Quarter A Million Copies Sold

William Carr, Pawns in the Game

http://littlemary.excerptsofinri.com/prayers/prayers.html

The Old Testament is simply the history of how Satan became prince of the world, and caused our first parents to defect from God. It relates how the synagogue of Satan was established on this earth, it tells how it has worked since to prevent God's Plan for the rule of the universe being established on this earth. Christ came to earth when the conspiracy reached the stage that, to use his own words, Satan controlled all those in high places. He exposed the synagogue of Satan (Rev. 2:9; 3:9;) he denounced those who belonged to it as sons of the devil (Lucifer), whom he castigated as the father of lies (John 8:44) and the prince of deceit (2 Cor. 11:14). He was specific in his statement that those who comprised the synagogue of Satan were those who called themselves Jews, but were not, and did lie (Rev. 2:9; 3:9). He identified the Money-Changers (Bankers) the Scribes, and the Pharisees as the Illuminati of his day. What so many people seem to forget, is the fact that Christ came on earth to release us from the bonds of Satan with which we were being bound tighter and tighter as the years rolled by. Christ gave us the solution to our problem when he told us we must go forth and teach the truth, regarding this conspiracy (John 8. 31:59;), to all people of all nations. He promised that if we did this, knowledge of the truth would set us free (Matt. 28:19;). The Luciferian Conspiracy has developed until it is in its semi-final stage (Matt. 24: 15:34;), simply because we have failed to put the mandate Christ gave us into effect.

Satan's goal: the ruin of souls

Learned theologians have stated that Lucifer, Satan, or call the head of the Forces of Evil simply "The Devil", knows he did wrong and knows that he was wrong. He is a pure spirit and therefore indestructible. Knowing he is wrong he still is determined to drag as many souls as possible into hell with him to share his misery. This being a fact our duty is clear: We have to make known the TRUTH in this regard to as many others as quickly as possible so they can avoid the snares and pit-falls set by those who serve the devil's purpose and penetrate the lies and deceits of those who wander about the world seeking the ruin of souls. Weishaupt's plot requires :

1. Abolition of ALL ordered national governments.

2. Abolition of inheritance.

3. Abolition of private property.

4. Abolition of patriotism.

5. Abolition of the individual home and family life as the cell from which all civilizations have stemmed.

6. Abolition of ALL religions established and existing so that the Luciferian ideology of totalitarianism may be imposed on mankind.

The term "Illuminati" was coined by Adam Weishaupt, a man of Jewish descent who converted to Catholicism and studied and taught Canaanite law as a Jesuit priest in Ingolstadt, Germany before defecting from Catholicism to embrace the Luciferian Doctrine. Weishaupt, funded by the Rothschild family, was instructed to go seek out and recruit like minded "Illuminist" from among the smartest and most accomplished men of the time within the arts, sciences, government and other fields to officially form The Illuminati on May 1, 1776. Weishaupt would recruit up to 2,000 members of this new movement and establish lodges of the Grand Orient, a secret society, as well as infiltrate and establish Freemasonic lodges as their headquarters for operation. The word "Illuminati" means "holders of the light" as derived from Lucifer, the Light Bearer. http://itzallahustle.ning.com/profiles/blogs/the-illuminati-1

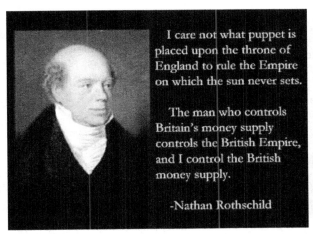

I care not what puppet is placed upon the throne of England to rule the Empire on which the sun never sets.

The man who controls Britain's money supply controls the British Empire, and I control the British money supply.

-Nathan Rothschild

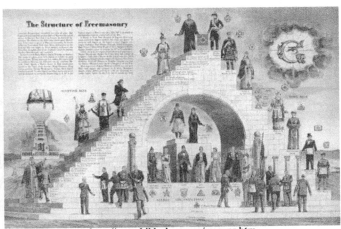

http://www.bilderberg.org/masons.htm

What is the Hegelian Dialectic?

By **Niki Raapana** and **Nordica Friedrich**

In order to discover the causes which have produced the effects we experience to-day all available evidence must be studied carefully. Truths must be separated from falsehoods, and fiction from fact. Past events must be studied to see how they have affected and influenced conditions existing to-day. William guy Carr "pawns in the game"

Introduction: Why study Hegel?

"...the State 'has the supreme right against the individual, whose supreme duty is to be a member of the State... for the right of the world spirit is above all special privileges.'" Author/ historian William Shirer, quoting Georg Hegel in his *The Rise and Fall of the Third Reich* (1959, page 144)

In 1847 the London Communist League (Karl Marx and Frederick Engels) used Hegel's theory of the dialectic to back up their economic theory of communism. Now, in the 21st century, Hegelian-Marxist thinking affects our entire social and political structure. The Hegelian dialectic is the framework for guiding our thoughts and actions into conflicts that lead us to a predetermined solution. If we do not understand how the Hegelian dialectic shapes our perceptions of the world, then we do not know how we are helping to implement the vision. **When we remain locked into dialectical thinking, we cannot see out of the box.**

Hegel's dialectic is the tool which manipulates us into a frenzied circular pattern of thought and action. Every time we fight for or defend against an ideology we are playing a necessary role in Marx and Engels' grand design to advance humanity into a dictatorship of the proletariat. The synthetic Hegelian solution to all these conflicts can't be introduced unless we all take a side that will advance the agenda. The Marxist's global agenda is moving along at breakneck speed. The only way to completely stop the privacy invasions, expanding domestic police powers, land grabs, insane wars against inanimate objects (and transient verbs), covert actions, and outright assaults on individual liberty, is to **step outside the dialectic. This releases us from the limitations of controlled and guided thought.**

So the Illuminati, and now they've set forth some goals way back in, I believe, 1876, with Adam Weishaupt, so all they did was carry those goals and re-fashion those goals to fit into a modern-day paradigm, a modern day matrix. That's it. But the goals are still the same.

1. Monetary and sex bribery was to be used to obtain control of men already in high places in the various levels of all governments and other fields of endeavor. Once influential persons had fallen for the lies, deceits, and temptations of the Illuminati, they were to be held in bondage by application of political and other forms of blackmail, threats of financial ruin, public exposure, and physical harm, even death to themselves and family members.

2. The Illuminati who were on the faculty of colleges and universities were to cultivate students possessing exceptional mental ability and who belonged to well-bred families with international leanings, and recommend them for special training in Internationalism. Such training was to be provided by granting scholarships, like the Rhodes Scholarship, to those selected by the Illuminati. All such scholars were to be first persuaded and then convinced that men of special talent and brains had the right to rule those less gifted on the grounds that the masses do not know what is best for them physically, mentally, and spiritually.

3. All influential people who were trapped to come under the control of the Illuminati, plus the students who had been specially educated and trained, were to be used as agents and placed behind the scenes of all governments as experts and specialists. They would advise the top executives to adopt policies which would, in the long run, serve the secret plans of the Illuminati's New world Order, bringing about the destruction of governments and religions they were elected or appointed to serve.

4. They were to obtain absolute control of the press so that all news and information could be slanted to convince the masses that a one world government is the only solution to our many and varied problems. They were also to own and control all the national radio and TV channels. Also, remember those studies that stated that "TV violence doesn't affect children's behavior" years ago? Guess who funded them? They are a bunch of bull crud. What a person watches DOES influence them, and this is well known by the behaviorists in the group. In fact, they know that TV is a tool that they purposely use to influence "the masses." It cannot create a total personality change in the average citizen, but it can desensitize us increasingly to violence, pornography and the occult, and influence the perceptions of young children. Many of the top pop singers come from an internship with the "Mickey Mouse club" (yep, good old Walt the Illuminist's Empire). How many lyrics advocate suicide, violence, despair, or New Age spirituality in pop/rock today? Or just get a copy of the words and read (but be aware that many are possibly triggering to survivors of mind control).

Weishaupt and others would then help to start both the French and American revolutions while the banking families would finance both sides of each conflict. Eight years after their official formation, the Illuminati were forced underground when their plot was discovered by the Bavarian government. In 1786 the Original Writings of the Order and Sect of the Illuminati was published by the British and sent to all European governments. Weishaupt and other Illuminati members would then infiltrate Freemasonic orders and form inner secret societies. In 1798, after rejecting an invitation to join the Illuminati, John Robison would publish the book, "Proofs of a Conspiracy," that would expose the plot to form a One World Government. From that point forward, members of the Illuminati would hide their true agenda in different organizations under the guise of humanitarianism and philanthropy. The wealth attained through these front companies would then be funneled through their Tax Exempt Foundations and Non Profit Organizations. Some of these organizations are as follows:

- **The United Nations**
- **Council on Foreign Relations**
- **Trilateral Commission**
- **Bilderberg Group**
- **The Central Intelligence Agency (C.I.A. created by Skull and Bones members)**
- **International Monetary Fund (IMF)**
- **World Bank**
- **World Trade Organization**
- **World Council of Churches**
- **Tavistock Institute**
- **The Rand Corporation**
- **The Rockefeller Foundation**

These foundations, organizations and think tanks, funded by the Illuminati, would consist of recruited globalist, politicians, academics and scientist who would create and advise policies to the nations of the world to advance the New World Order agenda for One World Government and a One World banking system. http://itzallahustle.ning.com/profiles/blogs/the-illuminati-1

There are 33 sections to the United Nations on the inner emblem logo.
21 14 = 2+1=3 1-4=3 3 and 3 make 33
U. N. United Nations

"No one will enter the New World Order unless he or she will make a pledge to worship Lucifer. No one will enter the New Age unless he will take a LUCIFERIAN Initiation." (David Spangler, Director of Planetary Initiative, United Nations)

www.theforbiddenknowledge.com/hardtruth/
destruction_of_the_trade_centers.htm

Here is my conversation with Brother Corey from XXL Magazine

Excerpts of the interview i gave to xxl magazine.

Qoutes were given clarity and detailed references

This information is an over view as to what was actually stated in the magazine.

Please visit http://panachereport.com/, http://vigilantcitizen.com/?cat=46 , and http://www.truthcontrol.com/node/illuminati

Also fanning the flames of conspiracy in the direction of the Jigga man, was rapper Prodigy's handwritten note to URB magazine.

Peep ithttp://tckonbroadway.wordpress.com/2008/12/11/investigative-reports-hip-hop-illuminati/

Rapper Prodigy from the mythical group Mobb Deep has occasionally denounced Jay-Z's affiliation with the Illuminati in the last years. **Here's [see Jay-Z's Inspiration DVD] a URB article on the subject.**

Bro. Corey: Okay. And in modern time the connection between Illuminati and hip hop - how do those two things work?

Prof. Griff: Well, they don't work together. The information that I was putting out over the past 5 to 6 years started out as the "The Pacifi Antidote" and ended up becoming a book the "Psychological covert war on Hip Hop." The research team of people that I study with, we exchange information and support one another's work. One of those people is a brother by the name of Black Dot who wrote the book Hip Hop Decoded: From Its Ancient Origins To Its Modern-Day Matrix. We started seeing patterns not only inside of hip hop but in the entertainment industry as a whole; we started seeing behavior patterns and signs and symbols that spoke volumes. Hip-Hop had an organic vibe in its inception; as the multi-national corporations began to target hip hop to sell their agenda through their products, we started to notice the music began to change. If I could just mention two or three of these obvious and noticeable changes, that will give you an idea of what we began seeing so you can see it from our point of view.

Mobb Deep's Prodigy Speaks On The Illuminati, President Obama & Jay-Z

by Andres Vasquez

P chops it up with radio show host Alex Jones about the Illuminati, saying, "It's definitely not a joke." He also says Jay-Z "knows what time it is" and more.

New York's Prodigy of Mobb Deep recently visited The Alex Jones Show to speak about the Illuminati and more. After famously saying, "Illuminati want my mind, soul and my body," Prodigy took his lyrics further in the recent interview with the controversial Jones. Speaking on how society has been brainwashed, talking about President Obama and more, Prodigy shared his feelings about the world's "conspiracies."

Analyzing his role in Hip Hop and how other elements play a part in the formation of the culture, Prodigy said he is unhappy with how his friends and others are "brainwashed." Like he does in his monthly blog on Vibe.com, the incarcerated Prodigy recently spewed more of his conspiracy theories via a handwritten letter to URB. This time, he reveals the moment his eyes were opened to the sham he calls "the government, religions, politics, the Federal Reserve, and I.R.S." According to P, in 1996, after reading a book by Dr. Malichi Z. York titled **Leviathan 666**, he was moved so much, he cried, and that was his "moment of clarity."

Okay. So if the Illuminati worship Satan/Lucifer and they have to galvanize certain energies at certain times of the year with large masses of people, there is a blood ritual and a blood sacrifice that initiates have to make when they go through their rituals. So we're gonna set that aside for a second because we started to see the blood sacrifice and the blood rituals inside of hip hop! People were being sacrificed so that the agenda can push forward. Other people were being used. One right now, Niki Minaj, says there's a male entity, a violent rough and tough male entity that exists inside of her, and she gives him the name Roman. That's demonic possession! Beyonce' says that there's a dark, demonic character in her that takes over her when she is on stage and she calls her Sasha Fierce. This is what you call demonic possession.

Deeper than that, I ask the question why are all the albums that are released, why are they always released on a Tuesday. So we started studying the teachings of the Illuminati, and we found out that Tuesday is the name for the Norse war god, because these people are constantly at war for the souls and hearts and minds of the people.

Tuesday is the name for the Norse war god replacing the Roman god Mars. The day Tuesday had already been named for the Roman God. There are a lot of things that went down on a Tuesday, like this so-called attack on America went down on September 11th, 2001 which was on a Tuesday.

All of this is a part of keeping that demonic energy and that frequency alive. But now, how did it marry itself onto hip hop? That's interesting. Because now we're starting to see the signs and symbols inside of hip hop, and no one can deny that. When we start to dig up information like Fritz Springmeyer's **Bloodlines of the Illuminati**, we start to see who the blue bloods are. And then keeping that in mind, when you hear Jay-Z saying he was sipping Krystal with the blue bloods, I'm like wait a minute! This cannot be true! So when you do the research and you start the language that Jay-Z and some other people are using, we're just like wow – this is critical! We couldn't believe it at first, and then we did more research and we dug up **Codex Magica** by Tex Mars and we started to see the signs and the symbols being thrown up by T Pain, Kanye West and some other people. I was like wow - this is actually really going on? And I said to myself, if I reveal this, I know that people are going to come at me. And they're going to say – ah, you're kinda making this up, so I'm gonna have to have my proof. And I dug up the proof, and I have been showing people for 5, 6, 7 years now. But every time I see it on the front page of a magazine or something talking about the illuminati it's always someone other than me that gets the credit. I'm not in this to get the credit, brother; I'm in this to tell the truth and to make the people aware, like I've always been doing, ever since you've heard of a Public Enemy and Professor Griff.

Bro. Corey: Yes, definitely. That's why I wanted to ask, because you say you've definitely been talking about this for a long time; why do you think, because at the turn of the millennium it was talked about, the new world order and such, and then it kind of died down, the Illuminati and hip hop, and then I'd say for the last two years or so, at least for the last year, it's been highly talked about where rappers are making songs about it. Why do you think it went through that phase of not much attention being paid to it and now it's become the thing to talk about among rappers?

Prof. Griff: To be honest with you, I did not – and I'm not taking all the credit for that, because there's other brothers, Steve Cokely, Red Pill, Blue Pill, of course Black Dot, Phil Valentine and Bobby Hemmitt and some other brothers… I think because I'm Prof. Griff from Public Enemy, and when it went viral thanks to the brothers over there at worldstarhiphop.com and occult science and these kind of blog talk radio and internet websites that millions of people were exposed to the information.

The Innermost Secrets of the Illuminati Beckon You

They vowed you would never know. They thought there was no way you could possibly unmask the sick things they have been hiding. They were wrong. Now, thanks to the incredible revelations in this amazing book, you can discover their innermost secrets. You can identify the members of the Illuminati and unravel their astonishing plan to control and manipulate. You can crack the Illuminati code. Codex Magica is awesome in its scope and revelations. It contains over 1,000 actual photographs and illustrations. You'll see with your own eyes the world's leading politicians and celebrities - including America's richest and most powerful - caught in the act as they perform occult magic.

http://www.sacred-texts.com/sro/
mhj/index.htm

Once you understand their covert signals and coded picture messages, your world will never be the same. Destiny will be made manifest. You will know the truth and everything will become clear.

-- Texe Marrs. The Innermost Secrets of the Illuminati Beckon You

They vowed you would never know. They thought there was no way you could possibly unmask the sick things they have been hiding. They were wrong. Now, thanks to the incredible revelations in this amazing book, you can discover their innermost secrets.

You can identify the members of the Illuminati and unravel their astonishing plan to control and manipulate. You can crack the Illuminati code.

Check out these pictures of Obama's graduation. The emphasis seems to be on the handshake, not the diploma. The tell tale sign of a masonic handshake is when one person places his thumb on the other person's knuckle. This is a very peculiar way to shake hands. Try it the next time that you shake someone's hand and decide for yourself whether or not it seems odd. The other strange thing about this picture is the very fact that it even exists. Do you have a picture of your own graduation handshake receiving your diploma?

75

They Have Their Own Hidden Language

Codex Magica is awesome in its scope and revelations. It contains over 1,000 actual photographs and illustrations. You'll see with your own eyes the world's leading politicians and celebrities - including America's richest and most powerful - caught in the act as they perform occult magic.

Once you understand their covert signals and coded picture messages, your world will never be the same. Destiny will be made manifest. You will know the truth and everything will become clear.

Texe Marrs is author of over 37 books, including the #1 bestseller Dark Secrets of the New Age and

Circle of Intrigue: The Hidden Inner Circle of the Global Illuminati Conspiracy.

A retired career U.S. Air Force officer, he has taught at the University of Texas at Austin and has appeared on radio and TV talk shows across America.
Last night I saw upon the stair a little man who wasn't there. He wasn't there again today. Oh gee, I wish he'd go away!

I did an interview with Curtis Davis and this particular interview is in my book, **Analytixz**. I did an interview and 40 people, brother, were on that blog talk that night. 40 people! I went on vacation and my phone started blowing up because I made the mistake of putting my phone number in the interview. And young people like 13, 14, and 15 year olds were calling me talking about "what is this thing called the Illuminati?" and "are people

really sacrificing their family members for fame and money?" And at that point, I knew something needed to be said about the subject in a major way. I later learned that someone at worldstarhiphop.com took my interview and added images to it and put it up on their site. And I was thinking about getting a new phone number because my phone, it was ridiculous. I think I've logged in over 700,000, not phone calls but 700,000 hits on Worldstar, which is ridiculous. You understand what I'm saying? So that many people were calling me, asking me about the Illuminati. So I said at that time, I better go and put it out on YouTube to let people know exactly what it is so they can stop calling me. Well it didn't work. More people started calling me because as we put the information out, they started seeing the signs and symbols because they became awake and aware of what was going on in the music industry.

Bro. Corey: Now, why do you believe these particular artists, the people that you mentioned, the Jay-Z's, Beyonce's, the Diddy's, are the key players or key cards, whatever you want to call them, in this union between the Illuminati, what particular role would they serve in that union?

Prof. Griff: I think the Illuminati have goals. In order to carry out goals and capture the souls, hearts and the minds of the people, they don't have to control millions if not billions of people. All they have to do is control that handful of people that have influence over the millions and billions of people. This is where we pull the curtain back and we start to see the P Diddy's and the Jay-Z's and Beyonce's and the Lady Gaga's and these kinds of people, for whom and what they really are. I need to add they are not the Illuminati, they are the workers of iniquity. Foster children of the bloodlines of the Illuminati.

Apparently Jay-Z is an Aleister Crowley fan.

Many artists are themselves involved in the Occult and members of secret societies like the ones mentioned above, and the Church of Satan [1]. They are practicing Occultism and Black Magic (like Marilyn Manson, Ozzy Osbourne, Led Zeppelin to name a few), and this web site has the ambition to reveal what is behind the "glamour." Their task is to demoralize our youth, to create a society where no one is able to think for themselves (contrary to what the pop culture is trying to teach us about the "rebellious" rock music).

The Art Industry creates "Icons" with degrading and satanic messages, which are supposed to be a replacement for the 'invisible' God. The musicians are also often acting degraded and high or low on drugs, so their fans start acting the same. The purpose is to create apathy and decay. Quite a few recordings have subliminal backward messages in their music, like Led Zeppelin, Michael Jackson, The Eagles, and more. Here is a website that tells you more about Back masking: http://www.nauglefest.net/backmask.htm. There is no doubt these backward messages exist, but the question is, who put them there? The record companies? The musicians? Demons? In the long run, it doesn't matter that much. It's there, and it DOES affect our subconscious minds, and it's not positive...

Thank you,

Wes Penre

http://benryandkit.wordpress.com/
2011/02/07/moral-panic-fear-the-music/

Back-masking is a deliberate process in which audio is recorded backwards on a recording which is meant to be played forward. This basically means that when you play the record in reverse you can hear the audio that was recorded backwards. The process was popularised by The Beatles who used backward recordings of vocals and instrumentation and has been used by countless other bands since then, including The Stone Roses who even had backward recordings of complete songs their releases. Back-masking is commonly used in songs which may contain profanities, so that a 'radio-friendly' version of the song can be produced with the offending words being played backwards.

Kanye West Says: "I Sold My Soul to the Devil" & Brags About Having a "Bad White B*tch Like Ice-T"

Kanye West freestyles "He sold his soul to the devil" in LA at a Kid Cudi concert on 22nd December 2009

"I sold my soul to the Devil/I know its a crappy deal/least it came with a few toys and a happy meal/I'm spaced out God/ I be on that moon talk/ I wonder if God ask Mike how to moon walk..."

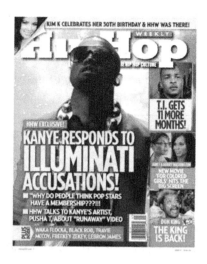

Lupe Fiasco

Wow, Lupe Fiasco Goes In On MTV "Illuminati's Favorite Network, Corporate Garbage Pushing Plastic Lifestyles & Wasteful, Destructive Behavior Into The Brains Of The Youth Of The World"

"For rebellion as is the sin of witchcraft." 1 Samuel, 15:23

You could call them; they are styled in the scriptures as workers of iniquity. They are styled in certain places as demons that do the work of Satan. They're styled in the scripture and they're styled in different writings as different things. But it's important that we understand it because their light has to constantly shine. See brother, we use that language in our daily conversations. You know when you have a little nephew or niece or something that's very smart, we say they're very bright, right?

Jay-Z's clothing line, "Rocawear," has incorporated obvious occult symbols in its designs. Some are so blatantly Masonic that he probably couldn't get away with it if he wasn't effectively implicated with them. In interviews, Jay-Z has said to be actively involved in the choices of designs of his clothing line.

"Masters of the Craft" is a 100% Masonic saying and the All-Seeing Eye of the Great Architect depicted here is directly taken from Masonic works. Notice also the secret handshake depicted in a circle. Here are some examples:

Israeli Prime Minister Ariel Sharon and President George W. Bush. (Notice the Hand Posturing and sign)

This scene is set at the White House in March, 2001, with Israeli Prime Minister Ariel Sharon and President George W. Bush both presenting mirror-image descending (female, delta, or vulva) triangles. Two triangles joined together constitute a Jewish Star of David. For added subliminal power, the room was arranged so that the bush of Lincoln was directly behind Sharon. The message:

In bludgeoning hapless Palestinians and denying them their own state, Sharon is simply being Lincolnesque. After all, Lincoln put down the Southern insurrection right?The scene is set at the White House in March, 2001, with Israeli Prime Minister Ariel Sharon and President George W. Bush both presenting mirror-image descending (female, delta, or vulva) triangles. Two triangles joined together constitute a Jewish Star of David. For added subliminal power, the room was arranged so that the bush of Lincoln was directly behind Sharon. The message: In bludgeoning hapless Palestinians and denying them their own state, Sharon is simply being Lincolnesque. After all, Lincoln put down the Southern insurrection right?

Aleister Crowley was born October 12th, 1875 at 36 Clarendon Square, Leamington, Warwickshire, England as Edward Alexander Crowley into a wealthy and religious family at the height of the Victorian era. Crowley despised and rebelled against his family at every turn, even renaming himself 'Aleister' to avoid sharing the same first name as his father, who passed away when Crowley was 11.

Like many naughty young boys, Aleister entertained himself through several activities, notably creating a "homemade firework" with which he nearly killed himself, as well as torturing a cat in several horrible ways to test the "nine lives" theory.

"Do what thou wilt" shall be the whole of the law.

79

He dispensed of his virginity at age 14 with the help of a maid. At 17, he contracted gonorrhea with the help of a street walker. According to Crowley's own account, while (unsuccessfully) trying to summon sylphs for his wife's amusement, she began to receive a very powerful psychic message from the Ancient Egyptian god Horus.

Crowley adopted 666 as his personal moniker in rebellion to his religious upbringing many years before. After invoking Horus, Crowley made his fateful breakthrough. For three days Crowley took dictation from the entity identifying itself as Aiwass. The resulting text, Liber AL vel Legis, became what is now known as The Book of the Law.

Interpretation of what "Do What Thou Wilt..." in contemporary times seems to have deteriorated into "do whatever you want...;" however, it seems clear that the meaning was more along the lines of 'doing that which your higher self dictates.' The higher self or "Will" is present in all of enlightened people. In order to follow your "Will," one must know oneself. And self-knowledge is the central basis of most successful philosophies.

According to Crowley, Mathers reportedly sent one of his followers, a vampire, to him. She appeared to him in the guise of a "young woman of bewitching beauty," but he was able to defeat her, and she was "transformed into a hag of sixty, bent and decrepit." Mathers then sent a "current of evil" which struck Crowley's bloodhounds dead and caused his servants to fall ill. Crowley retaliated by summoning up the forces of the demon Beelzebub and his 49 attendant fiends. Following this effort, Mathers' magical assaults on Crowley ceased. Years later, when Mathers passed away of influenza, many felt that Crowley had murdered him with magic.

In 1910, Crowley was contacted by the head of a German magical order known as the Ordo Templi Orientis, often referred to as the OTO (alternately translated as either "the Order of the Templars of the East" and "the Order of the Temple of the Orient" in a variety of sources). The OTO accused Crowley of having published the secret of their IXth degree. Crowley was mystified until a conversation revealed that a passage he published led the OTO to assume that Crowley was involved in sex magic which they used in their rituals. He joins the order shortly thereafter, and in 1912, became the head of the English speaking branch of the Order.

http://famouspoetsandpoems.com/poets/aleister_crowley/biography

Aleister Crowley 1875-1947--Aleister Crowley is the occultist and Satanist that is maybe the most well known. His works "The Book of the Law", "Magick in Theory and Practice" and "The Book of Thoth" are broadly used in occult circuits. Crowley himself didn't take much credit for having written them, as he stated they were written by automatic handwriting, being channeled from a higher being called Aiwaz (or Aiwass)

- **My number is 11, as all their numbers who are of us** *Aleister Crowley's Book Of The Law line 60, of Chapter One as channeled from Aiwass*

- *http://www.theforbiddenknowledge.com/hardtruth/destruction_of_the_trade_centers.htm*

(Musician, Special Collector's Edition, – Beatles and Rolling Stones, 1988, p.12). One of the Beatles' heroes included on the cover of Sgt. Pepper's was — the infamous Satanist, Aleister Crowley! Most people, especially in 1967, did not even know who Crowley was — but the Beatles certainly did. Crowley's photo appeared on the Beatles' Sgt. Pepper album cover (click to enlarge: upper left hand corner). The Beatles testified that the characters who appeared on the album were their "heroes." Adolph Hitler was to be on the album but Lennon took it off at the last minute.

John Lennon explained to Playboy magazine that "the whole Beatle idea was to do what you want … do what thou whilst, as long as it doesn't hurt somebody" (Lennon, cited by David Sheff,

The Playboy Interviews with John Lennon and Yoko Ono, p. 61). This was precisely what Crowley taught. Here is another picture drawn by Crowley himself with the phrase "Do What Thou Wilt" across the top that the rock group KISS clearly imitated. (BELOW LEFT and RIGHT).

http://theconspiracyzone.podcastpeople.com/posts/32765

"Popular culture" (music, TV, movies, books, fashion etc.) is NOT spontaneous but corporate controlled and manufactured. EIR compares it with the drug trade in general: "Today's mass culture operates like the opium trade: The supply determines the demand." (545) For example, the bankers' social engineering branch, the Tavistock Institute, manufactured the Beatles phenomenon. The screaming teenagers were bused in.

-The Beatles were created and put together by Tavistock a mind control center in America.

An outstanding example of social conditioning to accept change, even when it is recognized as unwelcome change by the large population group in the sights of Stanford Research Institute, was the "advent" of the BEATLES. The Beatles were brought to the United States as part of a social experiment which would subject large population groups to brainwashing of which they were not even aware.

Tavistock and its Stanford Research Center created trigger words which then came into general usage around "rock music" and its fans. Trigger words created a distinct new break-away largely young population group which was persuaded by social engineering and conditioning to believe that the Beatles really were their favorite group. All trigger words devised in the context of "rock music" were designed for mass control of the new targeted group, the youth of America.
http://www.illuminati-news.com/rock_and_mc.htm

"In 1963 the Beatles appeared on the Ed Sullivan show. They combined rock and mystical music, long hair, and Hindu worship. Drugs were suggested in many of their songs: "Yellow Submarine" (a "submarine" is a "downer"), "Lucy in the Sky With Diamonds" (the initials of the main words are LSD), "Hey Jude" (a song about methadrine), "Strawberry Fields" (where opium is grown to avoid detection) and "Norwegian Wood" (a British term for marijuana). John Lennon's song "Imagine" attacked religion ("Imagine there's no heaven, It's easy if you try, No hell below us, Above us only sky"), espoused a do-your-own-thing philosophy ("Imagine all the people, Living for today"), attacked nationalism ("Imagine there's no countries"), attacked religion ("It is isn't hard to do, Nothing to kill or die for and no religion too"), called for the abolition of private property ("Imagine no possessions"). It supported a new international order ("I wonder if you can, No need for greed or hunger, A brotherhood of man, Imagine all the people, Sharing all the world") and advocated a one-world government ("You may say I'm a dreamer, But I'm not the only one, I hope someday you'll join us, and the world will be as one.") Lennon called for abolition of private property and then left his Japanese-born widow a $250 million estate."

-- Dr. Henry Makow

Aleister Crowley (Barbara Bush's father and the grandfather of George W Bush), Book of Law & Pop Culture

Lest you think that Aleister Crowley (born Edward Alexander Crowley, 1875-1947) was just some crazy fool that no one took seriously, think again. Crowley has had a large influence upon modern rock music.

Guitarist Jimmy Page of Zeppelin is a devout follower of Satanist, Aleister Crowley, who proclaimed himself as "The Beast 666." Aleister Crowley was also a 33rd Degree Scottish Rite Freemason and 97th Degree Memphis Rite Freemason and is recognized as the master Satanist of the 20th century. In 1971, guitarist Jimmy Page bought Crowley's Boleskine House on the shore of Loch Ness where Crowley practiced his hellish, satanic sex-magic rituals, including human sacrifices. Guitarist Jimmy Page actually performed Crowley magical rituals during their concerts. Their song "Stairway to Heaven" carries the reference "May Queen," which is purportedly the name of a hideous poem written by Crowley. Page had inscribed in the vinyl of their album Led Zeppelin III, Crowley's famous "Do what thou wilt. So mete it be." Page and Robert Plant claim some of Zeppelins' songs came via occultic "automatic handwriting," including their popular "Stairway to Heaven."

The cover of the Sergeant Pepper's album by the Beatles showed a background of, according to Ringo Starr, people "we like and admire" (Hit Parade, Oct. 1976, p.14). Paul McCartney said of Sgt. Pepper's cover, ". . . we were going to have photos on the wall of all our HEROES . . ." (Musician, Special Collector's Edition, - Beatles and Rolling Stones, 1988, p.12). One of the Beatle's heroes included on the cover of Sgt. Pepper's was — the infamous Satanist, Aleister Crowley! Most people, especially in 1967, did not even know who Crowley was — but the Beatles certainly did.

The Beatles apparently took Crowley's teaching very serious — Beatle John Lennon, in an interview, says the "whole idea of the Beatles" was — Crowley's infamous "do what thou wilt": "The whole Beatle idea was to do what you want, right? To take your own responsibility, do what you want and try not to harm other people, right? DO WHAT THOU WILT, as long as it doesn't hurt somebody. . ." ("The Playboy Interviews with John Lennon and Yoko Ono", by David Sheff and G. Barry Golson, p. 61)

Crowley has had a great influence on rock & roll. The International Times voted Crowley the unsung hero of the hippies. One man who helped popularized Crowley's work among rockers is avant-garde film artist Kenneth Anger. He claimed that his films were inspired by Crowley's philosophy and called them visual incantations and moving spells. Anger considered Crowley a unique genius. Mick Jagger of the Rolling Stones and Jimmy Page of Led Zeppelin both scored soundtracks for Anger's films about Crowley. See Led Zeppelin for more about Pages enthusiasm for Crowley.

Ozzy Osbourne called Crowley a phenomenon of his time (Circus, Aug. 26, 1980, p. 26). Ozzy even had a song called Mr. Crowley. You fooled all the people with magic / You waited on Satan's call / Mr. Crowley, won't you ride my white horse.On the back cover of the Doors 13 album, Jim Morrison and the other members of the Doors are shown posing with a bust of Aleister Crowley.

Jimmy Page of Led Zeppelin

Mick Jagger of the rolling stones band

The spiritual significance here is brought out in this Old Testament passage, "For rebellion is as the sin of witchcraft." (1 Samuel 15: 23) Biblically, witchcraft is synonymous with satanism and rebellion is its root.

- **"For I stand forth to challenge the wisdom of the world; to interrogate the "laws" of man and of "God". He who saith 'thou shalt' to me is my mortal foe." (The Book of Satan, 1: 3&5)**

Madame Blavatsky

"[Modern] Theosophy is no new candidate for the world's attention, but only *the restatement* of principles which have been recognised from the very infancy of mankind."
Master K.H., *The Mahatma Letters*, Letter 8. Italics added.
". . . We have broken *the silence of centuries* . . . ."
Master K.H., *Letters from the Masters of the Wisdom*, Series One, Letter 4. Italics added.

". . . Our [esoteric] doctrine . . . is now being partially taught to Europeans for the first time."
Master K.H., *The Mahatma Letters*, Letter 18.

"Our [modern] knowledge of this Wisdom called Theosophy sprang from two sources, . . . [*The Mahatma Letters*] and the writings of H.P. Blavatsky. From these Letters A.P. Sinnett wrote *The Occult World* and *Esoteric Buddhism*; from the knowledge gained from these Masters, H.P. Blavatsky gave the world *Isis Unveiled*, *The Secret Doctrine*, *The Key to Theosophy*, *The Voice of the Silence*, and much besides. . . . 'H.P.B.' ... was the Founder of the Theosophical Movement, and the Masters' chosen and beloved pupil, agent and scribe. . . . "
Christmas Humphreys and Elsie Benjamin, *The Mahatma Letters* (Preface to 3rd Ed.)

Blavatsky Brooch and Symbol

After its establishment the Theosophical Society expounded the esoteric tradition of Buddhism aiming to form an universal brotherhood of man, studying and making known the ancient religions, philosophies and sciences, and investigating the laws of nature and divine powers latent in man. The direction of the society was claimed to be directed by the secret Mahatmas or Masters of Wisdom.

http://www.bofads.com/stories/jacksonsecrets.htm

Madame Blavatsky also wrote:

" . . . I was the first in the United States to bring the existence of our Masters into publicity; and . . . exposed the holy names of two members of a Brotherhood hitherto unknown to Europe and America (save to a few mystics and Initiates of every age), yet sacred and revered throughout the East, and especially India . . . . " "The Theosophical Mahatmas." *The Path*, December, 1886.

"I was crying for all of humanity, but mostly for my Black people 'cause I then realized it was all a sham," Prodigy writes in his letter to URB. "The government, religions, politics, the Federal Reserve, the I.R.S., and everything that we believe and live by are a joke." Even worse, the rapper says that many popular rappers are aware of these society secrets, but choose not to speak on it for fear of not being accepted by corporate America. One, in particular, is Jay-Z.

Aleister Crowley was an occultist who practiced sex magick, studied mysticism, the same esoteric symbols Jay Z displays on his clothing line, and promoted anarchy (rebellion against God). Notice Aleister Crowley has the same symbol on his head hundreds of years ago that Jay Z has on his shirt above.

Occult Secrets of Jay-Z, Kanye & Nas

"Jay-Z knows the truth, but he chose sides with evil in order to be accepted in the corporate world. Jay-Z conceals the truth from the Black community and the world, and promotes the lifestyle of the beast instead," he wrote. Prodigy says that Jay grew up grew up in Dr. York's "Nuwabian" community in Brooklyn as a kid, and is "aware" of these evils — rogue government, elitists running the country, etc. Because of Jay-Z's refusal to speak on the topics Prodigy has been speaking on since his incarceration, he will make it a point to wage war against him.

"Jay-Z is a God damn lie. I have so much fire in my heart that I will relentlessly attack Jay-Z, Illuminati, and any/every other evil that exists until my lights are put out," P writes. "This negativity I speak of is an actual living entity that uses us as food. We must sever ties with it in order to see things for what they really are. This negative energy is created and harnessed by the Illuminati secret government and they will make you spread this energy without you even knowing it. But people like Jay-Z are very well aware. He was schooled by Dr. York," he continued

Nas and Jay Z

Religious deception is painless inoculation against truth. It cannot be removed from the conscience with surgery, yet it is the motivator of our actions and directly controls our lives. Once man gives over to false religion, he is no longer rational because he originated no thought. His life is controlled by whoever controls his religion. The veil of false religions the sword of Damocles and its power to control humanity defies even the imagination of tyrants who used it.

This is not to say that George Washington was a traitor willingly, or knowingly. He was beguiled into a satanic religious order that insidiously controls men's minds.

Prof. Griff: See, that's the language that the Illuminati use because they are the holders of the light. They see themselves as not the guardians, but the ones that are going to lead people into everlasting life and light and intellect and power …

… but we don't know who these people are, so I began to try to demystify them. So when you see someone like Jay-Z throwing up the hand signs and showing us in his clothing line Masters of the Craft the signs and symbols of the Freemasons, the Freemasons basically, or the Masonic order was infiltrated by the Illuminati. So by bringing Jay-Z in as a Mason then a Freemason, and elevating him and keeping him in the public's eye and galvanizing the mind of the masses of the people, they're able to control the masses of the people just by controlling someone like Jay-Z, someone like P Diddy, and then they bring people in and manufacture Illuminati tools like Lady Gaga. This chick came from absolutely nowhere! Are you following me? Black people weren't into white European and all this like Lady Gaga and this kind of thing. We didn't resonate with that kind of madness. But it was presented in such a way and packaged in such a way and aimed and geared toward young Black children to capture their minds. All brought to you by Akon.

"...this is God engineering...I'm on my 3rd six [666]..." - *Jay-Z*, *"Freemason"* **featuring Rick Ross.**

Bro. Corey: Yeah. Now, what do you say to the people, cause I've spoken to a lot of people on this topic and I guess a minority of people believe that race is a factor and people like Jay-Z or a Diddy could not be a part of the Illuminati because of their race, because the people, those controllers, do not associate with minorities, Black folk, African Americans in general.

Lady gaga and akon

Jay-Z and the occult...one too many coincidences..

Let me briefly show you how Jay Z is no longer dealing crack to the urban community, but something much worse...

Prof. Griff: No, and they are absolutely correct, but the average person doesn't know that, are you following me? So when you point to Illuminati, since we don't know who they are and we can't demystify who they are, we point at their representatives. And their representatives are the people that we know that are in front of us, that are carrying out their agenda. So we point to the P Diddy's and we point to the Kanye West's. We can see it in the videos and we hear it in the lyrics, and we point to them as they become the representatives of the Illuminati. You see how slick the Illuminati is? This is how they work, brother! They'll put a Jay-Z out there and make Jay-Z think that he's part of the program – he is part of the program, but the ultimate program, Jay-Z's not a part of that! They'll dismiss Jay-Z in a heartbeat. Are you following me? They'll dismiss Barack Obama, Barry Davis, in a heartbeat! They'll get rid of; they'll trump up some charges on P Diddy and have him locked down tomorrow.

hat's how they work. There is a movie out entitled "**Brotherhood of the Bell**." I ιggest that you watch that movie because it spells out exactly how the Illuminati ork. It's called "**Brotherhood of the Bell**." So they use Jay-Z. They use P Diddy to ιrry out their particular goal. Now, they feed into the desire, the wants and needs, of ϵople like Jay-Z. Of course, they'll make you rich. They'll give you a Billion dollars. hat's nothing to them. They own the Fed (The Federal Reserve Bank). The Fed is no ιore federal than Federal Express.

Federal Reserve Directors: A Study of Corporate and Banking Influence

Staff Report, Committee on Banking, Currency and Housing, House of Representatives, 94th Congress, 2nd Session August 1976

The Rockefellers invented a scheme, used by the super rich today, whereby the more money you appear to give away, the richer and more powerful you become. Through the help of captive politicians, guided by some bright boys in the family law offices, legislation was written and passed which would protect the Rockefellers and other elite super-rich from the repressive taxation they have foisted on everyone else. The key to this system is giving up ownership but retaining control. For example, most people don't believe they really own something unless they retain title to it in their own name. The Rockefellers know this is a big mistake. Often it is better to have your assets owned by a trust or a foundation – which you control – than to have them in your own name.

http://educate-yourself.org/ga/RFcontents.shtml

Bro. Corey: Jay-z talked about a car. Someone mentioned that in another conversation I was having with him, I think it was a Chevrolet or one of the cars a blue…car what is that?

Prof. Griff: Right, but Jay-Z owns a color blue, and there's a reason for that. There's an esoteric reason for that, an esoteric meaning behind that, are you following me? He's lining himself up with the blue bloods.
Jay-Z unveiled the new gas guzzler he helped design for GM, a bright blue GMC Yukon Denali. Maybe the blue helps signify his "Water for Life" campaign, since designing SUVs and bringing water to the third world is so consistent:

Sure he owns part of the Nets, a piece of the Roc and may or may not be the best rapper alive, but when you collaborate with GM and they give you your own color, that's impressive. Painted "Jay-Z Blue," the SUV was developed through a partnership with the rapper during the past two years. Jay-Z, whose real name is Shawn Carter, worked with the company's global color studio to create the reflective blue color for the SUV.

The same with Barack Obama belonging to CFR council on foreign relations. The same with Oprah. I could mention a few more people. But a lot of times when you mention these people, people kind of come down on you because they want to see the proof that their I-Cons, the people they worship, are actually in on the plot. And it's not that I don't have the proof - I do. It's just that I don't have the platform to explain this. You and I are having this conversation today in 2011. I've been talking about this for the last 6 or 7 years and you're just now getting around talking to me. I was the lone voice for a while, right or wrong? There weren't too many voices out there talking about this. So Jamie Foxx's people Zoe Williams called me, and the Warren Ballentine's people, and somebody tried to connect me with Monique. She didn't have me, but she had Paul Mooney on, if you remember that recently.

Obama before he was elected
A close friend of Barack Obama is a big fan of my music and reached out to someone in my camp to set up a meeting. I was sick about what had happened with the country since 9/11, the wars and torture, the response to Hurricane Katrina, the arrogance and dishonesty of the Bush administration. I sat down with Barack at a one-on-one meeting set up by that mutual friend and we talked for hours.
More than anything specific that he said, I was impressed by who he was. He was my peer, or close to it, like a young uncle or an older brother. His defining experiences were in the 90s in the projects of Chicago, where he lived and worked as a community organiser before going to Harvard Law School. He'd seen me – or some version of me – in those Chicago streets. He even had the guts to tell the press that he had my music on his iPod. And he was black. This was big. – Decoded by Jay-Z

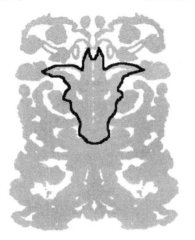

From saying "I don't pray to God, I pray to gotti" to calling himself Jahova, a name people have taken to mean Jehovah (one of the Hebrew names for God) Even Beyonce is not left out of all of this, her alter ego; Sasha Fierce has been said to be Beyonce possessed by a demon. Not to mention the Goat head ring she's been sporting recently which conspiracy theorists are calling the head of Baphomet which is notably the symbol of the church of satan.

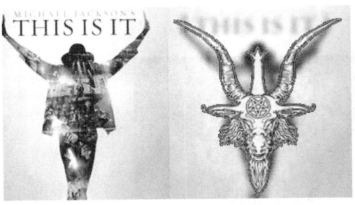

Baphomet is an imagined pagan deity (i.e., a product of Christian folklore concerning pagans), revived in the 19th century as a figure of occultism and Satanism. ..*Baphomet* is an imagined pagan deity (i.e., a product of Christian folklore concerning pagans), revived in the 19th century as a figure of occultism and Satanism. .

Ritual sacrifice to Moloch - THERE IS NO CHRISTINE. THERE IS ONLY MOLOCH.

An 18th century German illustration of Moloch ("Der Götze Moloch" i.e Moloch, the false god). In many depictions, the fiery alter of Molech was located within the 'Belly of the Beast'.

In a midrash (Genesis Rabbah 19) Samael, the lord of the satans, was a mighty prince of angels in heaven. Satan came into the world with woman, that is, with Eve (Midrash Yalkut, Genesis 1:23), so that he was created and is not eternal. Like all celestial beings, he flies through the air (Genesis Rabbah 19), and can assume any form, as of a bird (Talmud, Sanhedrin 107a), a stag (ibid, 95a), a woman (ibid, 81a), a beggar, or a young man (Midrash Tanchuma, Wayera, end); he is said to skip (Talmud Pesachim 112b and Megilla. 11b), in allusion to his appearance in the form of a goat.

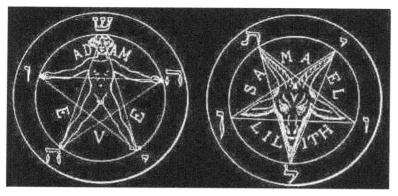

So Mote It Be..

Plaque illustrating ritual-murder of Simon of Trent.

HIGHEST PRICES PAID FOR BLOOD
MALE CHRISTIAN CHILDREN ONLY
MAXIMUM AGE SEVEN YEARS

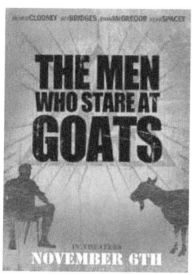

The last news about Men Who Stare At Goats.
George Clooney is a soldier with paranormal
powers! Watch the movie trailer soon.

Prof. Griff: I think because people's eyes are opening up to how it's really going down in the entertainment industry. Talent-less people are moving to the top of the charts and getting movie deals, while the people with true talent are getting kicked to the side unless you join onto this particular agenda. And I think now because people like you are asking the questions. And people like me already had the answer, but no one comes to me. Unless Jay Prince blasts me in the magazine, and then I gotta offer my apology to him and to Pimp C's family. And then young people read it and call me and say well, what is this Illuminati stuff? And then you have to explain the Boule, and the Boule is the Black Secret Society. And Boule means advisors to the King. And people are scratching their head and saying, wait a minute! There are private organizations and secret societies that are controlling things? Oh, no wonder I can't get a job. Or no wonder they gave that person the promotion instead of me. Or no wonder I couldn't get the loan at the bank. Or no wonder I couldn't get a loan to go to school. And it's starting to make sense now.

Prof. Griff: So we're connecting the dots. We're connecting the dots, as Steve Cokely said. But go on, I'm sorry...

Bro. Corey: No, when you hear someone like Kanye West talk about the Black Elite, what do you think when you hear that?

Prof. Griff: Oh, soon as he said it, I said okay – that Talented Tenth that WEB Dubois talked about, **the Boule,** I thought about Frederick Douglass, I thought about all the other secret societies that I've studied in the past, some known and some unknown, some spoken about, some only whispered about, that we know of. And that's the first thing that came to my mind. Freemasons came to my mind. Prince Hall Freemasons came to my mind, and those that are selected to carry out the Luciferian agenda. That's what came to my mind. And I said oh, if Kanye West is talking about this, he must have knowledge of it. Because the average person doesn't have that conversation, are you following me? So I start to watch Kanye West, Jay-Z, and the rest of them, and I notice the body language, the clothing lines, the handshakes, and the language that they use. Now brother, you have to admit that Kanye West has really changed right before our eyes. There is no more Jesus Walk, no more talk about the diamond mines and diamond trade. Are you following me? Videos have changed. Subliminal messages have been put in the videos and in the lyrics. So something is going on. This is just not conspiracy theory and Professor Prof. Griff reaching. Because if that was the case, you don't think I'd have been brought up on a lawsuit already? For slander? No one has come to me that way. Because they know that if they come, they better bring the information, 'cause I have it. I have a research team that's dynamite. And we bring up information that you would not believe, brother. This is just scratching the surface.

WHO IS PRINCE HALL?
September 12th, 1748 – December 4th, 1807

Prince Hall is recognized as the Father of Black Masonry in the United States. Historically, he made it possible for Negroes to be recognized and enjoy all privileges of free and accepted masonry.

Prince Hall clip art of Prince Hall passing on the Masonic apron to future generations of P.H.A. (Prince Hall Affiliated) Freemasons.

Bro. Corey: So someone – we talked about people who wanted proof – someone that actually wanted that proof a long time ago was Tupac Shakur. In interviews, he talked about the Illuminati and the reasons that his album, Kaluminati, was to dispel the rumors of the Illuminati. Do you agree with his take on it that it was something that was there to I guess take the credit away from young Black men for being successful, and give it to the white establishment. Do you agree with that, or have you heard that opinion that he shared like 15 years ago?

Prof. Griff: Well, like myself, I don't think Tupac was basing it on an opinion. It's not an opinion, its actual fact. He learned about the Illuminati in prison. He came out calling them Kaluminati because he had to put it in that way, in that language, in that vibratory frequency that young people would understand, so he said it in interviews and he put it in songs. Black people resonated with it, but we failed to do the research as to what Tupac was even talking about. And just to tag onto what Tupac was saying, it is true, they give the credit to the white establishment. All the signs and symbols that you see there in the Illuminati are ours. Study Ashra Kwesi's work, **The African Origin of Freemasonry**. All of these Masonic symbols are Black people's man, out of ancient Kemet and out of classical African civilization. They're ours. But they use them and put a demonic frequency and energy to them and they turn around and use them against us. Tupac was absolutely correct – they're ours. Are you following me?

To answer that question, we need to know who Walt Disney really was, what his corporation stands for, and what purpose it has. I strongly advise you to read Fritz Springmeier's excellent research on the Disney bloodline. You can read about it online: http://www.theforbiddenknowledge.com/hardtruth/the_disney_bloodlinept1.htm

Walt Disney was a 33° Freemason and an illuminist. Behind all those cartoons, magazines, movies etc., is a hidden agenda to mess up our children's minds. Disney's production over the years is filled with Masonic symbolism, occult over- and undertones, mind control and indoctrination. He is preparing our younger generations for the New World Order, and introduce them to sorcery (black magic) as being a "cool thing" . Read more about it in the above Springmeier article, it is amazing reading. Children who have disappeared at Disneyland and never been found again were kidnapped by the Disney Organization and sacrificed, or used as mind controlled slaves, although their disappearances have been blamed on crazy visitors who supposedly have used the children for sexual perversions.

Let's take a look at Walt Disney and Dizzyworld I call it, not Disneyworld. He was part of the Illuminati. His family was one of the 13 bloodlines of the Illuminati. What happened as a result of that? He started producing people that came out of that mind control experiment, and that mind control experiment was the Mouseketeers! So what happened in the Mouseketeers? The Mouseketeers started producing people that carried out the Luciferian agenda. Who are these people? Was Christina Aguilera a Musketeer?

"Because so much of the Illuminati programming involves the creation and programming of 3 alters linked into trinities, it is not surprising that Disney has helped such triad programming with a series of movies about threesomes, including: 3 Blind Mouseketeers, Three Caballeros, Three Little Pigs, Three Little Wolves, Three Lives of Thomasina, The Three Musketeers, Three Ninjas, Three Orphan Kittens."
-- **Fritz Springmeier**

92

Bro. Corey: Yes she was …

Prof. Griff: Was Britney Spears and Justin Timberlake and all of these people? Right?

Bro. Corey: Yeah.

Prof. Griff: Okay, we have to admit this. It was a mind control experiment. And it worked. Because all of the white artists ended up making music with Black people and they ended up at the top of the Black charts that we have in music. They ended up in Black programs. They were introduced to Black people. Tupac was absolutely correct.

The Satanic Ritual Abuse and Illuminati Mind-Control Sex Slave of JonBenet Ramsey

Many children are programmed to serve as sex slaves for pedophile politicians and heads of state; as the JonBenet Ramsey investigative team is well aware, the case includes aspects of possible mind-control and cult activity. The name "JonBenet" is very similar to an Illuminati term for the Devil - "Jonbet".

Britney Spears is a classic case of a Mouseketeer gone wild. After releasing a hit record, "…Baby One More Time," she had established herself as a sex symbol. Spears broke the record for highest album sales in its debut week by a solo artist after releasing Oops!… I Did It Again. The album ended by selling 10 million copies in the U.S. Spears married her childhood friend, Jason Alexander for 55 hours and then married Keven Federline a couple of years later.

Britney Spears is on Tour and is Still Under Mind Control

By VC | October 31st, 2011 | Category: Latest News | 108 comments

Britney Spears was mentioned a few times on this site, notably in the article entitled Britney Spears, Mind Control and "Hold it Against Me, which her links to Monarch Mind Control. Since then, a few articles were published describing Britney's complete lack of control over her life and career. Many have referred to the "empty look" in her eyes and her zombie-like demeanour. Her "boyfriend" is also her manager, which is often a sign that he is, in actuality, her handler. Here's a recent article describing the control her handlers have on her.

Disney-The Rescuers)

Walt and Roy Disney with Mickey Mouse and a special Academy Award

The Lion kng   Jessica in Roger Rabbit

I think we are destroying the minds of America and that has been one of my lifelong ambitions –

John Kricfalusi (creator of the *Ren and Stimpy Show*)

When Christina Aguilera was young, she sang The Star Spangled Banner at Pittsburgh Penguins, Pittsburgh Steelers, and Pittsburgh Pirates games. Shortly after that, she joined The New Mickey Mouse Club. Her co-Mouseketeers called her "the Diva." In 1999 and 2000, Aguilera released 3 singles, "Genie in a Bottle," "What a Girl Wants," and "Come on Over Baby." Later Aguilera created a sexually energetic album called "Stripped" and also went on tour with Justin Timberlake.

Other stars in this picture: **Christina Aguilera**, Justin Timberlake

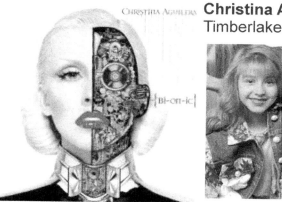

Justin Timberlake (Full name
Justin Randall Timberlake)

Justin Timberlake (Full name Justin
Randall Timberlake) was born on
January 31, 1981 in Memphis,
Tennessee, United States. He is a
famous American pop and R&B
singer, songwriter, record producer
and actor. He have won four
Grammy Awards and Emmy Award.

http://www.nydailynews.com/entertainment/tv/galleries/
disney_channel_stars_where_are_they_now/
disney_channel_stars_where_are_they_now.html

The Jesuits obviously wrote the Protocols because they have carried out every protocol in that little handbook. Alberto Rivera says that it was Jews aligned with the Pope who published the Protocols. Well, I tend to feel that it was just the Jesuits themselves because they and they alone, were the ones who were able to bring this to pass. They're the ones in the government. They're the ones behind professional sports. The owner of the Pittsburgh Steelers is a Knight of Malta. The owner of the Detroit Lions is a Knight of Malta. All your top owners of these ball clubs, for the most part, are Knights of Malta, getting the people whooped up in this hoopla over games and sports, while they're busy creating a tyranny. So, that was one of the things in the Protocols-that they would create 'amusements'.

95

Peter Hans Kolvenbach (front, center):
twenty-ninth Superior General, with his cosmopolitan general staff.
From the book Jesuits: A Multibiography by Jean Lacouture

Peter-Hans Kolvenbach, the General of the International Military Order of the Society of Jesus, commonly known as "the Black Pope", ordered the attack on the World Trade Center and the Pentagon on Tuesday, September 11, 2001, with the advice and consent of his General Staff, composed of five assistants (each representing a hemisphere and under whom are many advisory Provincials), an advisor (resembling the likes of a military commander to warn him of any faults or mistakes), and his confessor (to ease his conscience and absolve him of his many sins).

Another one they used was Walt Disney, 33rd-degree Freemason-Disneyworld, Disneyland. Another one was Milton Hershey, with Hershey Park. They create all of these amusements and games and pastimes to get the people drunk with pleasure, while they're busy overthrowing the Protestant form of government........ The High Knights are good, dear brothers with the High Mafia Dons-the Gambinos, the Luccheses, the Columbos, all of them. And they control Hollywood, not the Jews. It's only Jews who are front-men who are involved in Hollywood and working for the Mafia and for the Cardinal, just like in politics it would be Arlen Specter. Arlen Specter was Spelly's [Cardinal Spellman's] Jew in the assassination [of President Kennedy], and he would never say a word about it.

 -- Eric Jon Phelps

Nicolas 30th Superior General, Society of Jesus "**The Black Pope**"
Pope and Barry Davis (barrack Obama

For everyone who has seen the Stanley Kubrick flick **"Eyes Wide Shut"** with Tom Cruise... it is based around Illuminati sex rituals. It was also full of Illuminati symbolism, as well as symbolism about brainwashing. There is a conspiracy surrounding it and Kubrick mysteriously dying in his sleep. One theory says it's because he revealed to much about elitist Illuminati sex rituals.

"Only four days after Kubrick turned in the final cut of EWS to Warner Brothers, he was 'found' dead by his wife. He had no heart trouble, and wasn't ill before his sudden and shockingly unexpected death. Perhaps a clue into the nature of his death is the fact that it occurred precisely 666 days prior to the first day of the year in which his most famous film occurs – 2001: A Space Odyssey. Everyone was shocked by his death, and this group includes all who were working on EWS, and his family as well. Even though the official report was that he died of a heart attack, his wife did not accept the explanation. Stanley had not been ill, or even in seemingly bad health." [whose quote is this?]

 Here is the whole article which explains all the symbolism in the movie, what it has to do with brainwashing, the Illuminati, and how Kubrick died.

http://kentroversypapers.blogspot.com/2006/03/eyes-wide-shut-occult-symbolism.html

DEEPER INSIGHTS INTO THE ILLUMINATI FORMUL

Fritz Springmeier & Cisco Wheeler http://www.whale.to/b/disney.html

Bro. Corey: He was also of the belief that Black people could not exist among the Illuminati, so it was just a false thing. He wanted Black brothers and Black society to keep on moving forward rather than believing that this stuff was given to you because of your alignment with this society. What he's saying is partially stop giving the credit to someone else for the hard work that you put in, and focus most on the hard work. Now did he take this as not believing that the Illuminati exists or is that just to I guess encourage young Black males to keep striving on?

Prof. Griff: Well I'm gonna be honest with you, I don't care what people's beliefs are. If you look at **The 21 Goals of the Illuminati**, which you can put in a search engine and you can go along with me on this, The 21 Goals of the Illuminati written by John Coleman. John Coleman is the same gentleman whose book I introduced to Black people at the Tavistock Institute on Human Relations, and John Coleman laid out the 21 goals of the Illuminati in his other book called **Conspirators' Hierarchy on the Story of the Committee of 300** – it lays out the 21 goals of the Illuminati. So I don't give a damn what people believe. You can believe what you want to believe, but the actual facts stand to be true. And just to go over two or three of them, Number One says, and now this is at Educate-Yourself.org, The 21 Goals …

Bro. Corey: Yeah, we're looking at the same thing…

Prof. Griff: Okay, the 21 Goals of the Illuminati and The Committee of 300. "To establish a one world government, new world order, with a unified church and monetary system." Let's stop right there, we ain't gotta read the rest of it. Is it happening?

Bro. Corey: Yeah, the monetary system's definitely happening.

Prof. Griff: And the actual church is happening! There's gonna be one unified church, one religion. Fostered and maintained and controlled and financed by the Illuminati, the Committee of 300. Are you following me? Number Two, to bring about the utter destruction of all national identity and national pride, which was a primary consideration if the concept of a one-world government was to work. The whole idea of, "I'm an American." Are you following me?

Bro. Corey: Mmm-hmm.

Prof. Griff: So we have to all become Americans. The last one, which is probably the very most important one that I catch flack about: to engineer and bring about the destruction of religion, and especially the Christian religion. Now be careful when you print that one, brother, 'cause you're gonna catch some flack like I caught some flack. "You mean to tell me they're gonna destroy Christianity?"   Yeah, that's why Jay-Z goes hard in on Christianity. When you flip the words backward, its murder Jesus. Are you following me?

Bro. Corey: Mmm-hmm.

Prof. Griff: So this is where we are. This is where we are.

Bro. Corey: Yeah, those are the big picture goals. Where does hip hop fit in, as far as the ultimate goals of the Illuminati?

Prof. Griff: Hip hop fits in because hip hop became a voice of the voiceless. Everyone – White, Black, Asian - everyone resonated with hip hop. And since everyone resonated with hip hop, the Illuminati sought out hip hop to use hip hop as an Illuminati tool and a medium to get their agenda across, and they selected key players. And you cannot tell me on this phone right now that it didn't work – it worked! Are you following me?

Bro. Corey: Yeah, can you talk about the flack, and you mentioned that there have been threats to your life and your home – talk about why you think that stuff has come about because of what you're talking about.

Prof. Griff: I think because I mainly carried on the work that Public Enemy was doing and we spoke truth to power, and we spoke to the masses in an uncompromising kind of way. And when I reveal certain things to the masses of the people, if the masses of the people became awake and aware, this slows the Illuminati agenda down. So as you can see, the Rick Ross's and the Jay-Z's have to get together and make a song called Freemason to dispel what Prof. Griff is saying. We have to play around now and promote the Illuminati now, and to play it down. Are you following me? But if you study the monster drink that just came out, the three lines on the monster drink is actual Hebrew numerology for 666. You can't deny that. The Dr. Dre commercial actually spells out 666 if you watch it closely. Everything from the fish on the back of people's cars that's supposed to represent Jesus, to the Gucci symbol, to MasterCard, to Days Inn, to the Shell gas station, to McDonald's logo, to the General Motors logo, to the Fed Ex logo. It's all there, brother. And Prof. Griff didn't design all of this stuff. It's all there. Once you become symbol-literate, as Michael Tsarion teaches us, then we'll know what the signs and symbols are, and once you read into the signs and symbols, it actually spells out the Illuminati.

Theosophist, Helen Keller, and Her Satanic Hand Sign

I get e-mails from people from time-to-time, upset that I would dare say that Helen Keller's "I love you" hand sign is Satanic. Yet, Helen Keller was an occult Theosophist herself...

Light in My Darkness is a book, originally published in 1927 as *My Religion*, written by Helen Keller when she was 47 years old. The book was written as a tribute to Emanuel Swedenborg whom Helen regarded as "one of the noblest champions true Christianity has ever known." This book is regarded as Helen's Keller's spiritual autobiography in which she openly declares that "the teachings of Emanuel Swedenborg have been my light, and a staff in my hand and by his vision splendid I am attended on my way."
SOURCE: http://en.wikipedia.org/wiki/Light_in_my_Darkness

Bro. Corey: Why do you think a lot of the rappers that are mentioned don't speak up against the accusations that are thrown against them or the things that are being said about them? Like Jay-Z, he's mentioned it in song, but he's never in an interview acknowledged the things that have been said about him. Why do they avoid the topic?

Prof. Griff: I think they avoid the topic because they've been brought in and they've taken the oath. Now I don't know if you know anyone that's in the Masons, or the Freemasons, but once you take the oath, your life is on the line and if you reveal the secrets, they will slit your throat from ear to ear. This is very real, brother. I've known people in my family and other families - people have died in this kind of way because once you take the oath and reveal who these people are, then they have to deal with you in such a way. Because you've taken the oath. George "GM" James, who wrote Stolen Legacy, died in the same kind of way. But if you just study Myron Fagan's work, he laid out the entire story of the Illuminati. You can go on YouTube and put in Myron Fagan and the whole story of the Illuminati will come up. **The Illuminati and the Council on Foreign Relations** by Myron Fagan. M-y-r-o-n F-a-g-a-n. It spells out the entire plot and plan of the Illuminati.

I was privy to this information years and years and years ago. So when I put together my first album **Pawns in the Game**, I read the book by William Guy Carr, who wrote the book **Pawns in the Game**, and in the introduction of the book, it spelled out the plan of the Illuminati. I put it on my first album! I spelled it out for people! I spelled out how they were going to take the oath and how they were going to get people to support the Luciferian agenda. And when I started to spell things out, that's when I was poisoned, shot at, ended up getting a divorce, and as you know recently (2008) they burned my house down. Recently over the last couple of months, I was driving in a car from L.A. to Vegas and they shot the back window out. So they're letting me know that they're there. That's cool, though. You understand what I'm saying?

Bro. Corey: Mmm-hmm. So last question, why is it important – 'cause you're putting your life on the line, obviously, by putting this information out there – why is it important for you to get this message out there to the masses?

Prof. Griff: Because, you know, I said early on with Public Enemy, me and Chuck having private conversations, and I asked him and he asked me are we willing to go all the way with this? And I said I am. And we kind of figured we'd either be dead or in jail by now, or both. So I just basically said to myself, I'm gonna carry this and see this thing through. Once your name is on the list, you cannot pull it back, brother, are you following me? And I have to see it through until the day that they lower me into the ground, simply because I gave my work not only to Chuck, to members of my family, to members in my circle of people, and to the ancestors and to the Creator, that I would speak the truth and speak truth to Power and raise the conscious level of our people. And my work is beyond that now.

My work is to raise the consciousness of the human family, including those white people and Asian people that care to listen. So it's not something that I'm getting paid for, because I'm barely existing here, are you following me?

I'm not trying to sell a DVD or a book. I'm not on the popular talk shows and the late night infomercials. You don't see Griff there. I just now decided to do a blog talk radio show. I just now got a website, bro', so I'm not in this for the money. There is no money in this! I just set up www.ProfessorGriff.wordpress.com in order to give people information. That's a place they can go get it. I just created Great Oracle Dialects, the blog talk radio thing every Wednesday night at 9 o'clock, and I've yet to put anything on my website or establish the first show that's supposed to be January 12th, so I'm kind of behind the game. I'm not doing this for money. Are you following me? I'm doing this so we can teach our people, man.

Bro. Corey: You're definitely risking a lot by putting this information out there, so...

Prof. Griff: Can I just say something as a result of that? I would like to live the kind of life you live – comfortable, in a nice penthouse apartment in Upper Manhattan – I don't know if you live like that, I'm just saying...

Bro. Corey: I wish!

Prof. Griff: I'd like to live comfortable like everyone else lives. I don't need to be rich, I just want to be comfortable so I can raise my children and live my life, you understand? But there's something that happens to me at 3 or 4 in the morning that wakes me up, that sends me to the computer and sends me to my library studying so I can reveal this truth, are you following me? Greater men than me have lost their lives trying to establish the truth. It's those shoulders of those brothers and sisters that I stand on, that I have to continue this work. And guess what, brother, now you're a part of my work, believe it or not.

The remains of Griff's library

Griff still managing to work in behalf of black people and the human family

Professor Griff's house is burned down

Bro. Corey: Well I've been following it and it's interesting, very interesting.

Prof. Griff: Oh, Give Thanks.

Bro. Corey: And ultimately, where is hip hop going to go with this, this involvement with the Illuminati?

Prof. Griff: To be honest with you, if you would take this next statement with a grain of salt so you can digest it easier, I think they seen it changing and affecting the music when they seen Lupe Fiasco, and they got scared. They said wow – a young brother, skilled in the way he's skilled, smart, intelligent, easy to look at, got the hearts and minds of young people... so when they seen Lupe Fiasco, their plan and design according to them was to take Lupe Fiasco off his plan and off his track. Are you following me? And so they seen it coming back around and they had to keep the Lady Gaga's in our face, they had to keep the Rihanna's in our face, they have to keep this low vibratory frequency in the music in our face. So we wouldn't hear Lupe. So we wouldn't hear Immortal Technique, M-Y Oil, Wise Intelligence from Poor Righteous Teachers, Dead Pres. Even when they seen the reunion between the brothers in Goody Mom, they did not want that coming back. Are you following me? Even the tidbits that Andre 3000 have put out there. They didn't want this, man; feel good music vibrating with the soul. And then you may slide something, slip something out there to make people think. They don't ever want that coming back, man. Are you following me?

Bro. Corey: Mmm-hmm.

Prof. Griff: So they have to keep the pressure on. So as far as hip hop is concerned, I think there are some brothers and sisters that are coming over the horizon that's gonna change the vibratory frequency in hip hop, and we're about to see the resurgence of the Golden Era of Hip Hop, which was the conscious era of hip hop, come back.

Bro. Corey: That'd be good to see. I hope I can be around when that happens.

Prof. Griff: Right. Exactly. So we're gonna see it. In our lifetime we're gonna see it. You understand what I'm saying? And I don't mind sitting down and having a conversation with P Diddy's Jay-Z's and Nas and some others. Niki Minaj and the rest of these people. They may not like what I have to say. I respect their art form and the way they're presenting what they are doing, but nonetheless I disagree with the agenda, and I just want to make them aware of the agenda, that's all. That's all. I don't hate them as individuals. You know, I love my people, I don't care who it is. You understand what I'm saying?

Bro. Corey: Yeah.

Prof. Griff: I want to make sure they have the knowledge of what this agenda is and how they're affecting our people. Serious. Because when we become fans of theirs, we buy into the FANtasy. We buy into the FANtastic stories that they weave. And we become part of that agenda. We become part of it. Are you following me? And then subconsciously, we carry out the agenda of the Illuminati and we don't even know it. We don't even know it. So I'm slated to have my book come out in February, **The Psychological Covert War on Hip Hop**. As you should already know, that was one of the books that I had already completed that was in my computer when my house burned down. So I had to kind of re-vamp the entire book. But everything happens for a reason.

Bro. Corey: And it's slated for a February release?

Prof. Griff: February 7th, man. I said to myself that I was gonna get it done and have it out.

Bro. Corey: That's good to know.

Prof. Griff: Yeah.

Bro. Corey: I'll definitely pick that up. Once again, I thank you for your time. I really, really appreciate it.

Prof. Griff: I hope people receive this well when they read this, because you know, this is my life, man. And I'm gonna be honest with you, and I'm not just saying this, man. I'm really saying this from the depth of my being, man, I hope I live long enough to even read the damn article, brother. Because the recent attacks and the people that have come against me, you would not believe it, man, if I wasn't on the phone with you documenting this right now. And as I say, and as I've been saying in the four or five interviews that I've done, if this be my last time, people hearing my voice for the last time, I want them to know that my heart is in a good place and I don't have anything personal against any of the artists that I mention in my body of work. I don't mean ill feelings toward them or anything. I love them, actually. I just want to be able to see our people through, man, to the point where we end up carving out our own destiny, but we need our souls intact. Are you following me? So as I always say, man, Revolution is not an event, it's a process. And hopefully people will not paint Professor Griff in a negative light.

Bro. Corey: Well, let's hope this is not the last conversation people hear from you, and that we'll be around when the book comes out so that, you know, we can talk about that when it comes out.

Prof. Griff: Oh, give thanks.

Following are the portions of my interview XXL Magazine left out most likely for legal (Illuminati) reasons:

XXL: What is the Illuminati?

RS: The Illuminati from the standpoint of my research refers to all of the secret societies and global elitist clubs including The Brotherhood, P2, The Freemasons, Skull and Bones, The Boulè, The Bilderberg Group, the Council on Foreign Relations, The Trilateral Commission, The Royal Institute of International Affairs, The Bohemian Grove Society, The Order of the Rose, The Round Table, and other such "secret" organizations.

One of **the** secret rites taking place in **the** P-2 **Lodge,**

Propaganda Due or P2 was an irregular or "black" Masonic lodge that operated in Italy from 1966-1981, headed by Licio Gelli. P2 was implicated in numerous Italian crimes and mysteries, including the nationwide bribe scandal Tangentopoli, the collapse of the Vatican-affiliated Banco Ambrosiano, and the murders of journalist Mino Pecorelli and banker Roberto Calvi. P2 came to light through the investigations into the collapse of Michele Sindona's financial empire.

P2 was sometimes referred to as a "state within a state or a "shadow government". The lodge had among its members prominent journalists, parliamentarians, industrialists, and military leaders -- including the then-future Prime Minister Silvio Berlusconi; the Savoy pretender to the Italian throne Victor Emmanuel; and the heads of all three Italian intelligence services.

*For the **love of money is a root of all kinds of evil**, for which some have strayed from the faith in their greediness, and pierced themselves through with many sorrows.*

----1 Timothy 6:10

103

XXL: Who are the key players in the union of the Illuminati and hip-hop?

RS: If you mean key "pawns" (i.e., expendable pieces) then count Sean "Puffy" Combs who attended Howard University where he became a member of the notorious fraternity, Alpha Phi Alpha and they are all Boulé (i.e., Illuminati pawns). Other key pawns include, but are not limited to Jay-Z, Will Smith, Ne-Yo, T.I., Nelly, Kanye, Rihanna, Lady GaGa, Beyonce, Dr. Dre, Eminen, Rick Ross, Kobe Bryant, Lebron James, Mike Jones, Lil' Flip, Young Jeezy, all who have allowed the Illuminati to use them to infiltrate hip-hop.

There is however; one KEY player and that is BMG (Bertelsmann Music Group) Publishing, an Illuminati front that controls over one million copyrights. Artists who are now or have once been signed to this company, or one of its affiliates, include Avril Lavigne, Coldplay, Shakira, Nelly, Britney Spears, R. Kelly, Shania Twain, Christina Aguilera, Kelly Clarkson, Linkin Park, Jay-Z, Maroon5, Justin Timberlake, Joss Stone, Elvis Costello, Ne-Yo, Mariah Carey, Black Eyed Peas, Kenny Chesney, The Game, Mario, Rascal Flatts, No Doubt, Thomas Anders, Jessica Simpson and 50 Cent as well as legends like Bob Dylan, Elvis Presley and Frank Sinatra.

Nation Magazine stated on November 8, 1999, "Contrary to the company's official history, Bertelsmann cooperated with the Nazis in the late thirties and early forties, publishing a range of Hitlerian propaganda."

Do not forget that it was the Nazis who developed mind control experiments, so-called Nazi science, which has been ongoing for decades using esoteric knowledge about the human psyche. This is the only part of my interview that XXL left in: Mass hypnosis is attainable by the repetition of an important theme (like "rap") until it is accepted as fact by the subconscious and then conscious mind. Such messages can be transmitted during TV shows, MUSIC, video games or films and are not immediately perceived by the eyes and conscious mind. Entertainers have long influenced us in the messages of their music and in their culture, dress and attitude. .

President George W. Bush and British Prime Minister Tony Blair shake hands after their press conference in the East Room of the White House on Friday November 12, 2004. (Paul Morse/ WhiteHouse)

"For we wrestle not against flesh and blood,
but against principalities, against powers, against the rulers of the darkness of this world,
against spiritual wickedness in high places"

– Ephesians 6:12.

Selling your Soul

Fatboy Slim makes it clear that the **"Illuminati: a secret society does exist"** and the people involved in the music industry, as you were able to hear, are well aware of this. The couple lines said by Prodigy, shown in the video, which are also used as a sample in many Hip Hop tracks by many different artist saying **"Illuminati want my mind, soul, and my body"** is a statement that characterizes on point what exactly is that these people want from us and the price these performers have to pay in exchange for their place in the industry.

Selling your soul to devil may be a joke to many people, but is something that is literally going on in the world, not only the in Music industry but in Hollywood and every area of work that is controlled by them. Remember that they called themselves the **Illuminati** 'cause they believe themselves to be enlightened by the one who carries the light, also known as **Lucifer** – he portraits himself as a god to this people and they believe it, because of the power that has been given to him for a short period of time.

Puppets of Illuminati

Most of these rappers and singers become part of the problem instead of the solution, some because of fear of the implications of going against these devils, like many have in the past before being "terminated;" such is the case of **Tupac Shakur**, **Pimp C**, **Michael Jackson**, among many others; the great majority though, are part of it because they have more <u>love</u> for the money and fame than they do for their brothers and sisters, allowing demons and the "Elite" to used them as mere puppets, helping the few to control and kill the many.

His name was John Todd, a former member of the illuminati. He warned us against their plans for world domination before he was framed and effectively discredited by the illuminati. The words that he left on his audio tapes are still coming to fruition, which puts lots of credibility on his claim that he was an insider. These audio tape speak about the evil plans of the illuminati for world control. This is just another piece of the puzzle that explains what's going on today's world. Few people have any clue as to the deliberate Satanic subversion of America by the Illuminati.

JOHN TODD

And no wonder! For Satan himself transforms himself into an angel of light

<u>**2 Corinthians 11:14**</u>.

The Illuminati has been around for centuries in one way or another. Its presence in the 20th century is the direct result of the Nazis. The Nazi connections to the occult and the Bavarian Thule Society were parallel to the American members of 33rd degree Freemasonry.
When Operation Paperclip was successfully executed, the Nazi element of the Bavarian Thule Society was fused with the American members of Freemasonry to create the Illuminati.

Operation Paperclip, MK-ULTRA, October Surprise, and George Bush are all facets of the Illuminati, a group whose ideals are rooted in the occult and dedicated to global domination.

Queen Elizabeth had a big grin on her face Monday night in London as she met Lady Gaga, who wore red leather and curtsied, following the Royal Variety Performance in Blackpool, England.

Soon after the American Revolution, John Robinson, a professor of rural philosophy at Edinburgh University in Scotland and a member of a Freemason lodge, said that he was asked to join the Illuminati. After studying the group, he concluded that the purposes of the Illuminati were not compatible with his beliefs.

In 1798, he published a book called Proofs of A Conspiracy, which states:

"An association has been formed for the express purpose of rooting out all the religious establishments and overturning all the existing governments... The leaders would rule the world with uncontrollable power, while all the rest would be employed as tools of the ambition of their unknown superiors."
http://www.theinfovault.net/vault/politics/projectpaperclip.html

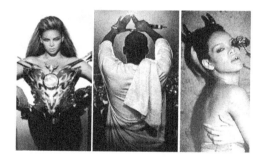

Not many people are aware that corporations and advertising companies use specific colors, numbers, tones, patterns, symbols, and sequences in their ads and logos, that have a subversive or "subliminal" effect on the sub-conscious mind. Most (if not all) forms of media, including movies, video games, books and music, as well as religious myths, cultural traditions, common slogans and phrases, as well as even child hood past-time games and activities (such as cards, dice, chutes and ladders, etc.) have been and are still used to covertly deliver multi-layered messages or "suggestions." The all-seeing eye is the elite's favorite symbol. It represents the eye of Lucifer seeing all and is usually atop a pyramid, the symbol for a top-down command and control system of compartmentalization.

*For all **the law is fulfilled in one word**, even in this: "You shall **love your neighbor as yourself**."* ---**Galatians 5:14**

106

From: Conspirators' Hierarchy: The Story of The Committee of 300

1. To establish a One World Government/New World Order with a **unified church and monetary system** under their direction. The One World Government began to set up its church in the 1920's and 30's, for they realized the need for a religious belief inherent in mankind must have an outlet and, therefore, set up a "church" body to channel that belief in the direction they desired.

2. To bring about the utter destruction of all national identity and national pride, which was a primary consideration if the concept of a One World Government was to work.

3. To engineer and bring about the destruction of religion, and more especially, the Christian Religion, with the one exception, their own creation, as mentioned above.

4. To establish the ability to control of each and every person through means of mind control and what **Zbignew Brzezinski** called **technotronics**, which would create human-like robots and a system of terror which would make Felix Dzerzhinsky's Red Terror look like children at play.

5. To bring about the **end to all industrialization** and the production of nuclear generated electric power in what they call "the post-industrial zero-growth society." Excepted are the computer- and service industries. US industries that remain will be exported to countries such as Mexico where abundant slave labor is available. As we saw in 1993, this has become a fact through the passage of the North American Free Trade Agreement, known as NAFTA. Unemployables in the US, in the wake of industrial destruction, will either become opium-heroin and/or cocaine addicts, or become statistics in the elimination of the "excess population" process we know of today as Global 2000.

6.   To encourage, and eventually legalize the use of drugs and make pornography an "art-form," which will be widely accepted and, eventually, become quite commonplace.

7.   To bring about depopulation of large cities according to the trial run carried out by the Pol Pot regime in Cambodia. It is interesting to note that Pol Pot's genocidal plans were drawn up in the US by one of the Club of Rome's research foundations, and overseen by Thomas Enders, a high-ranking State Department official. It is also interesting that the committee is currently seeking to reinstate the Pol Pot butchers in Cambodia.

8.   To suppress all scientific development except for those deemed beneficial by the Illuminati. Especially targeted is nuclear energy for peaceful purposes. Particularly hated are the fusion experiments currently being scorned and ridiculed by the Illuminati and its jackals of the press. Development of the fusion torch would blow the Illuminati's conception of "limited natural resources" right out of the window. A fusion torch, properly used, could create unlimited and as yet untapped natural resources, even from the most ordinary substances. Fusion torch uses are legion, and would benefit mankind in a manner which, as yet, is not even remotely comprehended by the public.

9.   To cause by means of **limited wars** in the advanced countries, by means of **starvation** and **diseases** in the Third World countries, **the death of three billion people by the year 2050**, people they call "useless eaters." The Committee of 300 (Illuminati) commissioned **Cyrus Vance** to write a paper on this subject of how to bring about such genocide. The paper was produced under the title "**Global 2000 Report**" and was accepted and approved for action by former President James Earl Carter, and Edwin Muskie, then Secretary of States, for and on **behalf of the US Government**. **Under the terms of the Global 2000 Report, the population of the US is to be reduced by 100 million by the year of 2050.**

10. To weaken the moral fiber of the nation and to demoralize workers in the labor class by creating mass unemployment. As jobs dwindle due to the post industrial zero growth policies introduced by the Club of Rome, the report envisages demoralized and discouraged workers resorting to alcohol and drugs. The youth of the land will be encouraged by means of rock music and drugs to rebel against the status quo, thus undermining and eventually destroying the family unit. In this regard, the Committee commissioned Tavistock Institute to prepare a blueprint as to how this could be achieved. Tavistock directed **Stanford Research** to undertake the work under the direction of **Professor Willis Harmon**. This work later became known as the "**Aquarian Conspiracy.**"

New Age leader Marilyn Ferguson, who wrote the million copy bestselling book, The Aquarian Conspiracy, included the triquetra symbol at the beginning of each chapter of her 447-page encyclopedia promoting New Age perversion. Indeed, the very cover of her book has this symbol prominently displayed against a stark, black background.

In her book, The Aquarian Conspiracy, Ferguson displays an arrogant, in-your-face attitude. She confidently discloses that yes, there is a global, New Age conspiracy. She gushingly reports that the goal of its leadership is to dramatically transform humanity and usher in a New Millennium of Oneness. Ferguson writes:

A leaderless but powerful network is working to bring about radical change in the United States - This network is the Aquarian Conspiracy - There are legions of conspirators. They are in corporations, universities, and hospitals, on the faculties of public schools, in state and federal agencies - and the White House staff. Whatever their station or sophistication, the conspirators are linked (pp. 23-24)

11. To keep people everywhere from deciding their own destinies **by means of one created crisis after another and then "managing" such crises**. This will confuse and demoralize the population to the extent where faced with too many choices, apathy on a massive scale will result. In the case of the US, an agency for Crisis Management is already in place. It is called the Federal Emergency Management Agency (FEMA), whose existence I first enclosed in 1980.

12. To introduce new cults and continue to boost those already functioning which include rock music gangsters such as **the Rolling Stones** (a gangster group much favored by European Black Nobility), and all of the Tavistock-created rock groups which began with **the Beatles**.

13. To continue to build up the cult of Christian Fundamentalism begun by the British East India Company's servant Darby, which will be misused to strengthen the Zionist State of Israel by identifying with the Jews through the myth of "God's chosen people," and by donating very substantial amounts of money to what they mistakenly believe is a religious cause in the furtherance of Christianity.

14. To press for the spread of religious cults such as the Moslem Brotherhood, Moslem Fundamentalism, the Sikhs, and to carry out mind control experiments of the Jim Jones and "Son of Sam" type. It is worth noting that the late Khomeini was a creation of British Military Intelligence Div. 6, MI6. This detailed work spelled out the step-by-step process which the US Government implemented to put Khomeini in power.

15. To export "religious liberation" ideas around the world so as to undermine all existing religions, but more especially the Christian religion. This began with the "Jesuit Liberation Theology," that brought an end to the Somoza Family rule in Nicaragua, and which today is destroying El Salvador, now 25 years into a "civil war". Costa Rica and Honduras are also embroiled in revolutionary activities, instigated by the Jesuits. One very active entity engaged in the so-called liberation theology, is the Communist-oriented Mary Knoll Mission. This accounts for the extensive media attention to the murder of four of Mary Knoll's so-called nuns in El Salvador a few years ago. The four nuns were Communist subversive agents and their activities were widely documented by the Government of El Salvador. The US press and the new media refused to give any space or coverage to the mass of documentation possessed by the Salvadorian Government, which proved what the Mary Knoll Mission nuns were doing in the country. Mary Knoll is in service in many countries, and placed a leading role in bringing Communism to Rhodesia, Moçambique, Angola and South Africa.

16. To cause a total collapse of the world's economies and engender total political chaos.

17. To take control of all foreign and domestic policies of the US.

18. To give the fullest support to supranational institutions such as the United Nations, the International Monetary Fund (IMF), the Bank of International Settlements, the World Court and, as far as possible, make local institutions less effective, by gradually phasing them out or bringing them under the mantle of the UN.

19. To penetrate and subvert all governments, and work from within them to destroy the sovereign integrity of the nations represented by them.

20. To organize a world-wide terrorist apparatus and to negotiate with terrorists whenever terrorist activities take place. It will be recalled that it was Bettino Craxi, who persuaded the Italian and US Governments to negotiate with the Red Brigades kidnapers of Prime Minister Moro and General Dozier. As an aside, Dozier was placed under strict orders not to talk what happened to him. Should he ever break that silence, he will no doubt be made "a horrible example of," in the manner in which Henry Kissinger dealt with Aldo Moro, Ali Bhutto and General Zia ul Haq.

21. To take control of education in America with the intent and purpose of utterly and completely destroying it. By 1993, the full force effect of this policy is becoming apparent, and will be even more destructive as primary and secondary schools begin to teach "Outcome Based Education" (OBE).

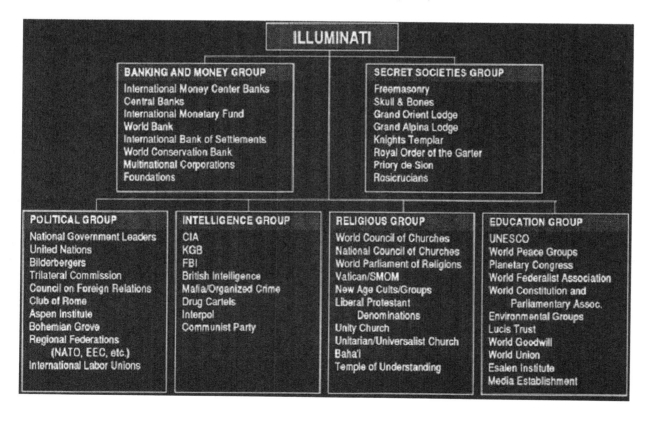

The Illuminati are a group that practices a form of faith known as "enlightenment". It is Luciferian, and they teach their followers that their roots go back to the ancient mystery religions of Babylon, Egypt, and Celtic druidism. They have taken what they consider the "best" of each, the foundational practices, and joined them together into a strongly occult discipline. Many groups at the local level worship ancient deities such as "El", "Baal", and "Ashtarte", as well as "Isis and Osiris" and "Set". These people teach and practice

http://www.disclose.tv/action/viewphoto/3933/Illuminati_Organization_Chart/

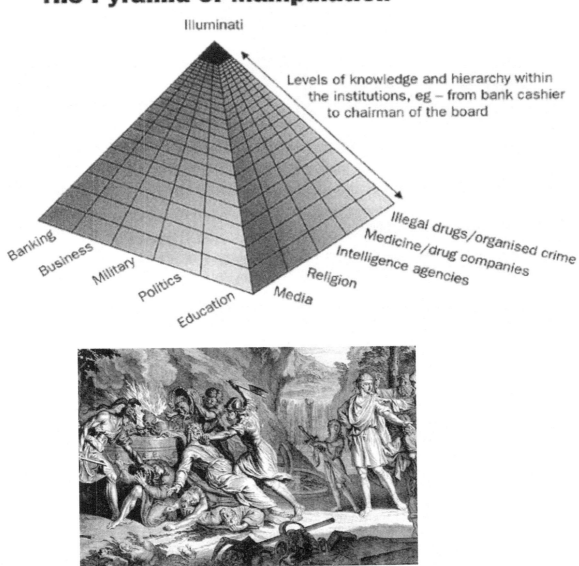

The word **Baalim** is the Hebrew plural for **BAAL, the pagan god of nature and fertility**. I quote from the Westminster Dictionary of the Bible article '**BAAL**' (emphasis mine)

"... *Baal worship apparently had its origin in the belief that every tract of ground owed its productivity to a supernatural being, or baal, that dwelt there. The farmers probably thought that from the Baalim, or fertility gods, of various regions came the increase of crops, fruit and cattle ... The worship of **Baal** was accompanied with lascivious rites (1 Kings 14:24), the sacrifice of children in the fire by parents (Jer.19:5), and kissing the image (1 Kings 19:18; Hos 13:2). **Baal** was often associated with the goddess **Astoreth** (Judg.2:13), and in the vicinity of his altar there was often an **Asherah**. (Judg.6:30; 1 Kings 16:32-33,R.V.)*"

ILLUMINATI

THE SECRET COVENANT

ILLUMINATI

"An illusion it will be, so large, so vast it will escape their perception.

Those who will see it will be thought of as insane. We will create separate fronts to prevent them from seeing the connection between us.

We will behave as if we are not connected to keep the illusion alive. Our goal will be accomplished one drop at a time so as to never bring suspicion upon ourselves. This will also prevent them from seeing the changes as they occur.

"We will always stand above the relative field of their experience for we know the secrets of the absolute. We will work together always and will remain bound by blood and secrecy. Death will come to he who speaks.

We will keep their lifespan short and their minds weak while pretending to do the opposite. We will use our knowledge of science and technology in subtle ways so they will never see what is happening.

will use soft metals, aging accelerators and sedatives in food and water, also in the air. They will be blanketed by poisons everywhere they turn.

The soft metals will cause them to lose their minds. We will promise to find a cure from our many fronts, yet we will feed them more poison.

poisons will be absorbed through their skin and mouths, they will destroy their minds and reproductive systems. From all this, their children will be born dead, and we will conceal this information.

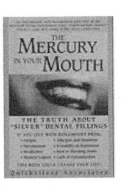

The poisons will be hidden in everything that surrounds them, in what they drink, eat, breathe and wear.

We must be ingenious in dispensing the poisons for they can see far. We will teach them that the poisons are good, with fun images and musical tones. Those they look up to will help. We will enlist them to push our poisons.

They will see our products being used in film and will grow accustomed to them and will never know their true effect. When they give birth we will inject poisons into the blood of their children and convince them its for their help. coll-damage-cartoon.jpg
desertpeace.wordpress.com

will start early on, when their minds are young, we will target their children with what children love most, sweet things.

When their teeth decay we will fill them with metals that will kill their mind and steal their future.

When their ability to learn has been affected, we will create medicine that will make them sicker and cause other diseases for which we will create yet more medicine.

Click to view larger printer friendly version of cartoon

We will render them docile and weak before us by our power. They will grow depressed, slow and obese, and when they come to us for help, we will give them more poison.

"We will focus their attention toward money and material goods so they many never connect with their inner self.

We will distract them with fornication, external pleasures and games so they may never be one with the oneness of it all. Their minds will belong to us and they will do as we say. If they refuse we shall find ways to implement mind-altering technology into their lives.

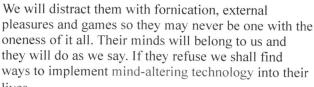

We will use fear as our weapon. We will establish their governments and establish opposites within. We will own both sides. We will always hide our objective but carry out our plan. They will perform the labor for us and we shall prosper from their toil.

Our families will never mix with theirs. Our blood must be pure always, for it is the way. will make them kill each other when it suits us. We will keep them separated from the oneness by dogma and religion.

We will control all aspects of their lives and tell them what to think and how. We will guide them kindly and gently letting them think they are guiding themselves.

114

will foment animosity between them through our factions. When a light shall shine among them, we shall extinguish it by ridicule, or death, whichever suits us best.

We will make them rip each other's hearts apart and kill their own children.
We will accomplish this by using hate as our ally, anger as our friend. The hate will blind them totally, and never shall they see that from their conflicts we emerge as their rulers.
http://bqpfrc-bias.blogspot.com/2008_07_01_archive.html

They will be busy killing each other. They will bathe in their own blood and kill their neighbors for as long as we see fit.

will benefit greatly from this, for they will not see us, for they cannot see us. We will continue to prosper from their wars and their deaths. We shall repeat this over and over until our ultimate goal is accomplished. We will continue to make them live in fear and anger though images and sounds. We will use all the tools we have to accomplish this. The tools will be provided by their labor. We will make them hate themselves and their neighbors.

http://culturefreedomradio.webs.com/apps/blog/show/7477945-concerning-today-s-uncle-toms-

We will always hide the divine truth from them, that we are all one. This they must never know! They must never know that color is an illusion, they must always think they are not equal. Drop by drop, drop by drop we will advance our goal. We will take over their land, resources and wealth to exercise total control over them.

We will deceive them into accepting laws that will steal the little freedom they will have.

We will establish a money system that will imprison them forever, keeping them and their children in debt.

Consumer debt can be a form of slavery! http://www.debtslaves.org/
http://livingstingy.blogspot.com/2009/01/modern-day-slavery-or-debt-slavery.html

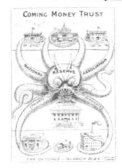
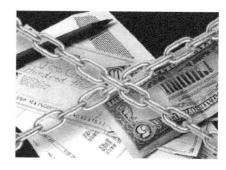

When they shall ban together, we shall accuse them of crimes and present a different story to the world for we shall own all the media

. http://www.aavw.org/special_features/homepage_cartoons.html http://www.aavw.org/special_features/homepage_cartoons.html

We will use our media to control the flow of information and their sentiment in our favor. When they shall rise up against us we will crush them like insects, for they are less than that. They will be helpless to do anything for they will have no weapons.

http://traceyricksfoster.wordpress.com/2009/02/22/when-media-hides-behind-a-hidden-agenda-how-media-manipulation-can-produce-undesirable-results/

We will recruit some of their own to carry out our plans, we will promise them eternal life, but eternal life they will never have for they are not of us.

The recruits will be called "initiates" and will be indoctrinated to believe false rites of passage to higher realms. Members of these groups will think they are one with us never knowing the truth.

must never learn this truth for they will turn against us. For their work they will be rewarded with earthly things and great titles, but never will they become immortal and join us, never will they receive the light and travel the stars.

http://www.noquarterusa.net/blog/3152/the-birth-of-whitey-black-liberation-theology-and-the-nation-of-islam/

They will never reach the higher realms, for the killing of their own kind will prevent passage to the realm of enlightenment. This they will never know.
http://www.vnnforum.com/showthread.php?t=49037

The truth will be hidden in their face, so close they will not be able to focus on it until its too late.

Oh yes, so grand the illusion of freedom will be, that they will never know they are our slaves.
http://www.cartoonstock.com/vintage/directory/b/black_people.asp

They will live in self-delusion. When our goal is accomplished a new era of domination will begin. Their minds will be bound by their beliefs, the beliefs we have established from time immemorial. Via-American Thinker

"When all is in place, the reality we will have created for them will own them. This reality will be their prison. By Kyle-Anne Shiver

But if they ever find out they are our equal, we shall perish then. THIS THEY MUST NEVER KNOW. If they ever find out that together they can vanquish us, they will take action. They must never, ever find out what we have done, for if they do, we shall have no place to run, for it will be easy to see who we are once the veil has fallen. Our actions will have revealed who we are and they will hunt us down and no person shall give us shelter.

It must NEVER, EVER be written or spoken of for if it is, the consciousness it will spawn will release the fury of the PRIME CREATOR upon us and we shall be cast to the depths from whence we came and remain there until the end time of infinity itself."

The secret Relationship Between Blacks and Jews

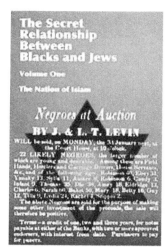

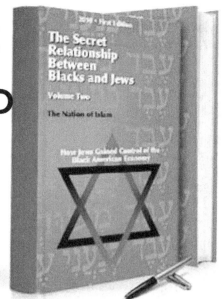

DJ from the arena : Because it seems like, I said this, the behavior seems somewhat obsessive, you know what I'm saying? But, if anybody is familiar with you Griff, they would know that you don't back down at any kind of controversy cause I remember when everything happened with the book "Secret Relationships between Blacks and Jews, Vol. 1". Folks was in the media and in the music industry was looking for you to bow down and cow, cow and you was like, "hell no, I'm standing by it. If it's accurate, I'm riding with it". You never buckled, Brother.

PG: And guess what? Volume 2 came out recently and the white boy on the internet asked Public Enemy if there were going to apologize to me because Professor Griff was right – this a white boy saying this. Because Professor Griff in 1989 was absolutely correct and they put the information out there, and it proved that I was correct cause I stood my ground. Are you following me? My father taught me you never apologize for the truth, and I'm not going to. Not going to but I think what #$%^(*&^is actually participating in is this hyper-feminine, metrosexual agenda that he has going on. Because if any man, Brother, gotta keep pounding on his chest and yelling at the top of his lungs that he's a man, he's probably not a man at all. You understand what I'm saying? And just because you get on your blog talk 'and you talk like this – and we're having positive energy and we're bringing positive energy down', that don't make your ass conscious. That's not consciousness, are you following me?

If we could only get our entertainers to tour cities promoting black on black love, or Anti-Black PSA's

In addition to running his non-profit organization The Hip-Hop Summit Action Network, Simmons serves as chairman of the Foundation for Ethnic Understanding. The foundation's mission is to foster and develop positive relationships with other ethnic groups. The Foundation for Ethnic Understanding's president Rabbi Marc Schneier will present the campaign today (Nov. 12) at the World Jewish Congress Board of Governors meeting in Paris. According to The Jerusalem Post, Rabbi Schneier is hoping that local Jewish communities will broadcast the ad in their hometowns.

"It's a whole different ball game when you have two African-Americans [who] are considered demigods," Rabbi Schneier said. "We cannot fight our battles alone. We cannot do it. And these ads are a manifestation of that," he said.

The spot will be converted into Spanish, Russian, French and other languages using Voxonic translation technology, a new software being marketed and developed with the help of fellow mogul Andre Harrell.

The PSA will be run in the United States, Europe and South America.

The spot features Simmons, who founded Def Jam in 1984 with the company's current President Jay-Z asking viewers: "What's hot? Respect for people. What's not hot? Hating people for their color or religion."
The commercial is slated to run nationally in January in the United States, to coincide with Martin Luther King Jr. day. Time/Warner has donated over $10 million in air time for the PSA.

In related news, Jay-Z will hit seven cities in 17 hours as part of Cingular's "Jay-Z Hangar Tour," which will stop in Atlanta, Philadelphia, Washington, DC; New York, Chicago, Los Angeles and Las Vegas.

The rapper will perform for radio contest winners in the various cities in airport hangars in support of his new album Kingdom Come, which hits stores Nov. 21.

News Source: AHH

Rick Ruben

The music industry have long believed that Rick Ruben practices black and white magic

The Entertainment Industry - Dominated by Jews

Now we know for a fact that the major Entertainment Industries, the ones that count, are owned by Jews, exclusively, but it doesn't stop there.

The Entertainment Industry (which I from hereon out for simplicity will call the Industry, and by that I mean the Mainstream Media, the Movie Industry, the Music Industry and the Art Industry, if not otherwise specified) seems to favor Jewish artists, producers and managers. Behind most successful rock- or movie star is a Jew, and a large percentage of artists are Jewish as well. [7] This is particularly interesting if we ponder that the Jewish world population is just a fragment of the population as a whole. According to a Jewish website, Judaism 101, there are approximately 13-14 million Jews in the world, compared to a world population of around 6 billion souls.

As we can see if we go to Answers.com, concentrating only on American musicians, many of the most influential musicians in modern history have been Jewish. Examples are [and I have added a few names not mentioned at Answers.com as well, because these people are relevant Jews]:

Barry Manilow
Bette Midler
Phil Ochs
Joe McDonald (Country Joe & the Fish)
Robbie Krieger (The Doors)
Max Weinberg (Bruce Springsteen's E-Street Band)
Roy Bittan (Bruce Springsteen's E-Street Band)
Slash (Guns & Roses)
Gene Simmons and Paul Stanley (KISS)
Cass Elliot (The Mamas and the Papas)
Leslie West (Mountain)
Peter Yarrow (Peter, Paul & Mary)
Joey Ramone (The Ramones)
Jakob Dylan (The Wallflowers)
Phil Spector
Allen Ginsberg
Marc Knopfler (Dire Straits)
Marc Bolan (T-Rex)
Manfred Mann

Elvis Presley
Lou Reed
David Lee Roth
Alice Cooper
Neil Sedaka
Paul Simon
Art Garfunkel
Barbara Streisand
Jeff Beck
Tiny Tim
Michael Bolton
Eric Carmen
Sammy Davis, Jr.
Neil Diamond
Bob Dylan
Leonard Cohen
Ramblin' Jack Elliott
Arlo Guthrie
Billy Joel
Carol King

Burt Bacharach
Leon Russell

Donovan P. Leitch (known as Donovan, who had a mega-hit with Buffy StMarie's
Mike Bloomfield (Paul Butterfield Band and guitarist for Bob Dylan)"Universal Soldier"
in the 60's)

The Jewish Control Over the Entertainment Industries

"The Octopus Returns"
by Kenn Thomas

Danny Casolaro was "suicided" in 1992 on the trail of the mother of all conspiracies, a transnational cabal manipulating world political events since World War II called The Octopus. Key to his research was a super-surveillance software called PROMIS, which was given to a crony of Ronald Reagan's as a pay off for the deliverance of $40 million to the Ayatollah Khomeini for the "October Surprise" -- holding on to the 52 American hostages in Iran until after Jimmy Carter lost the 1980 election. The crony profiteered from PROMIS (really owned by a company called Inslaw) by selling it to police agencies throughout the world for the purpose of tracking criminals and extrapolating their next moves.

Today, seven Jewish Americans run the vast majority of US television networks, the printed press, the Hollywood movie industry, the book publishing industry, and the recording industry. Most of these industries are bundled into huge media conglomerates run by the following seven individuals:

Gerald Levin, CEO and Director of AOL Time Warner

Michael Eisner, Chairman and CEO of the Walt Disney Company

Edgar Bronfman, Sr., Chairman of Seagram Company Ltd [4]

Edgar Bronfman, Jr, President and CEO of Seagram Company Ltd and head of Universal Studios [4]

Sumner Redstone, Chairman and CEO of Viacom, Inc

Dennis Dammerman, Vice Chairman of General Electric

Peter Chernin, President and Co-COO of News Corporation Limited

Those seven Jewish men collectively control ABC, NBC, CBS, the Turner Broadcasting System, CNN, MTV, Universal Studios, MCA Records, Geffen Records, DGC Records, GRP Records, Rising Tide Records, Curb/Universal Records, and Interscope Records. [5]

http://www.illuminati-news.com/Articles/42.html

Feral House plans a new edition of the book The Octopus: Secret Government and the Death of Danny Casolaro. Casolaro's own notes - those that didn't disappear the night he died - provided the basis of the book, which I co-wrote with another celebrated conspiracy writer, Jim Keith. That first edition came out in 1996 and is now a bit of a collector's item, costing about $100 on amazon if you can find a copy.

exploited Blacks who quite literally walked into his office threatening to kill him. Rap star Ice Cube even threatened Heller in one of his recorded songs, prompting the Anti-Defamation League to flag it as anti-Semitic. Ruthless Records released a Jewish rap duo called Blood of Abraham. As Chuck D, the lead vocalist for the Black rap group Public Enemy, noted, "There's no way to get trained on the seamier elements of the music business being on the street -- that element is reserved for boardrooms." [D, CHUCK, p. 85] Those in Chuck D's reminiscences about "boardroom" behavior include Lyor Cohen (manager of Rush Productions, and an Israeli); Al Teller, an executive at MCA whose parents died in the Holocaust; Steve Ralbovsky of CBS; Bill Adler (a publicist); and Rick Rubin of Def Jam Records. (Jewish diamond dealer Jacob Arabo has made the news as a favored jewelry merchant to the Black rap crowd that seeks to symbolize wealth and power, or, as the New York Times put it, "the jeweler who gives most of today's leading rappers their shine." [CENTURY, p. 1]

How the Music Industry Works

The way the Industry works has been covered by me in previous articles, like "Mind Control in the Field of Art" and I highly recommend that you read it, and also all other articles I have posted in the "I Sold My Soul to Rock'n'Roll and Mind Control" section of my website. For you who doubted me may now be able to restudy this section with new eyes, and perhaps you will find that it makes more sense.

Wes Penre is the owner of the domain Illuminati News and the publisher of the same. Please also check out his MySpace website: http://www.myspace.com/wespenre.

I will not repeat myself here, due to that I have covered this subject in details in the above articles, but rely on that you do your own further research there and elsewhere too for that matter.

In Summary

There is no doubt that the Entertainment Industries are run by the Illuminati Talmudic Jews and that their Agenda is clear. The Industries are run by criminals with two main purposes in mind:

1. To make lots of money with whatever methods available. Nothing is holy and murder is accepted, if necessary.

2. To manipulate people into accepting the New World Order and a One World Government. This is done in different overt and covert ways, also covered in the above sections of my website as mentioned under "How the Music Industry Works" here above. Only artists they can control will be promoted and accepted, or artists that they can make a big buck out of and later conform or waste. If dropping them makes them "talk", or if a 'bad situation' is eminent, there is always 'other means' to take care of the uncomfortable situation (read John Lennon and 2PAK).

I hope this article has made things a little clearer and as always, don't take my word for it. I strongly encourage you to do your own research if you still don't think this is evidence enough.

4ᵀᴴ DEGREE

The Synagogue of Satan, the God of Sin, Satan

10% blood suckkkers of the poor

"Our scientific power has outrun our spiritual power. We have guided missiles and misguided men."

-- Martin Luther King, Jr.

Ashahed Muhammad's 2005 book
The Synagogue of Satan, which charges that the world is being manipulated and corrupted by Satanic powers led by Jewish elites, is available for purchase in print and as a DVD at most major NOI events and through *The Final Call*. Trading heavily in Jewish conspiracy theories and Holocaust denial, the *Synagogue of Satan* alleges the Satanic powers are influenced and guided by the theology of Judaism and by an inherent Jewish predilection for immorality.

Evidence points to the existence of a group of wise and illustrious Fratres who assumed the responsibility of publishing and preserving for future generations the choicest of the secret books of the ancients, together with certain other documents which they themselves had prepared. That future members of their fraternity might not only identify these volumes bur also immediately note the significant passages, words, chapters, or sections therein, they created a symbolic alphabet of hieroglyphic designs. By means of a certain key and order, the discerning few were thus enabled to find that wisdom by which a man is "raised" to an illumined life.

William Shakespeare left his mark on the King James Version (KJV) of the Bible. At least that is the rumor going around. According to a host of Websites and books, William Shakespeare was called upon to add his artistic touch to the English translation of the Bible done at the behest of King James, which was finished in 1611. As proof for this idea, proponents point to Psalm 46, and allege that Shakespeare slipped his name into the text. Here is how the story goes. Since Shakespeare was born in the year 1564, then he would have been 46 years old during 1610 when the finishing touches were being put on the KJV. In the King James Version, if you count down 46 words from the top (not counting the title) you read the word "shake," then, if you omit the word "selah" and count 46 words from the bottom you find the word "spear."

This item is available on the Apologetics Press Web site at: **http://www.apologeticspress.org/articles/1828**

Bacon, Shakespeare, and the Rosicrucians

The present consideration of the Bacon--Shakespeare--Rosicrucian controversy is undertaken not for the vain purpose of digging up dead men's bones, but rather in the hope that a critical analysis will aid in the rediscovery of that knowledge lost to the world since the oracles were silenced. It was W. F. C. Wigston who called the Bard of Avon "phantom Captain Shakespeare, the Rosicrucian mask." This constitutes one of the most significant statements relating to the Bacon-Shakespeare controversy.

Bacon, Shakespeare, and the Rosicrucians

It is quite evident that William Shakespeare could not, unaided, have produced the immortal writings bearing his name. He did not possess the necessary literary culture, for the town of Stratford where he was reared contained no school capable of imparting the higher forms of learning reflected in the writings ascribed to him. His parents were illiterate, and in his early life he evinced a total disregard for study. There are in existence but six known examples of Shakespeare's handwriting. All are signatures, and three of them are in his will. The scrawling, uncertain method of their execution stamps Shakespeare as unfamiliar with the use of a pen, and it is obvious either that he copied a signature prepared for him or that his hand was guided while he wrote. No autograph manuscripts of the "Shakespearian" plays or sonnets have been discovered, nor is there even a tradition concerning them other than the fantastic and impossible statement appearing in the foreword of the Great Folio.

A well-stocked library would be an essential part of the equipment of an author whose literary productions demonstrate him to be familiar with the literature of all ages, yet there is no record that Shakespeare ever possessed a library, nor does he make any mention of books in his will. Commenting on the known illiteracy of Shakespeare's daughter Judith, who at twenty-seven could only make her mark, Ignatius Donnelly declares it to be unbelievable that William Shakespeare, if he wrote the plays bearing his name, would have permitted his own daughter to reach womanhood and marry without being able to read one line of the writings that made her father wealthy and locally famous.http://www.bibliotecapleyades.net/secret_teachings/sta41.htm

Paul wrote in Romans 13:1: "Let every person be subject to the governing authorities; for there is no authority except from God, and those authorities that exist have been instituted by God. Therefore whoever resists authority resists what God has appointed, and those who resist will incur judgment."
http://freethought.mbdojo.com/foundingfathers.html

125

What if the Illuminati was involved in making the King James. Bible?

Christianity has been split
up into many factions (denominations) and it would require a great deal of imagination to picture the vast majority, who profess to be Christians today, as true soldiers, or followers, of Jesus Christ.

Generally speaking, Christianity has deteriorated in regard to the practice of good works. This becomes a matter of major importance when we study the struggle going on between the forces of Good and Evil to-day, because the practice of good works created neighbourliness, and brought about unity in the Christian Fold

Usury in the **Bible**. If thou lend money to [any of] my people

http://forum.davidicke.com/showthread.php?t=11956&page=2996

David Icke

http://www.openbible.info/topics/the_illuminati_conspiracy

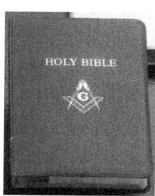

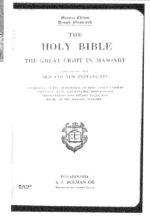

This is why the gentlemen, the books that I just ran off to you are very important because these Brothers are living right now, and the knowledge in their books we can apply. I wrote all this in my book 'Analytixz; 20 Years Of Conversations and Enter-views with Professor Griff, Minista of Information for Public Enemy'. 'Analytixz' – I wrote all this in the book, so this is, you can get it and read it for yourself, I didn't bit my tongue. So, the work they are doing, you can't deny their research, the research is deep, but the jews who run the music industry names are no longer hidden behind american sounding names.

For certain people have crept in unnoticed who long ago were designated for this condemnation, ungodly people, who pervert the grace of our God into sensuality and deny our only Master and Lord, Jesus Christ..... Jude 1:4

And from a religious perspective, and I'm not this religious dude, but the Holy Qu'ran teaches that some Sabines and some Jews and some Christians even, who enter into the hereafter before the Prophet, you understand what I'm saying? We have no right calling white people devils if they are not acting as such. Those men that we mentioned, the Alex Jones, Jordan Maxwell Michael Cerian, David Ike, an the rest of these people are good people – they are putting the information out there. They are risking their lives, in most cases, by putting the information out there, but I don't think they gear their information toward black people. Plain and simple. I read John Coleman's book, I read Texe Marrs, I read Griff Springmire – I've read all their work. They not talking to us. Truly, they're not. Extract what they have, use what we can use and let's push on.

Hip-hop's code of silence hurts police

By Gelu Sulugiuc

Warner Brothers Head Lyor Cohen is one of the many music industry executives who profits from this Stop Snitching Movement. In addition as a label head he'll never snitch on the behind the scenes unsavory practices the industry routinely uses to get records on the airwaves

NEW YORK (Reuters) - When rapper Lil' Kim was sentenced to a year in federal prison this summer for lying to a grand jury about a Manhattan shootout, she was lionized by media covering the hip-hop music scene for not "snitching."

Even as prosecutors confronted her with security camera tapes showing her standing next to one of the shooters, she lied about who was involved.

The media hoopla helped the rapper enter the Billboard chart at No.6 with her latest record "The Naked Truth," released shortly after her incarceration in September.

Criminals have always relied on a code of silence to evade prosecution. But calls to "stop snitching" have grown louder in hip-hop, which grew out of black inner cities to become a huge influence on youth culture across America.

Critics say this taboo on "snitching" or informing is now part of hip-hop's mystique and makes it increasingly hard for police to solve violent crimes in inner-city neighborhoods.

Vice President Dick Cheney is considered one of the most secretative politicians in American history. He is is a strict practitioner of 'Not Snitching'. Trust us Hip Hop has nothing to do with this.

King of Kings' Bible Rev 12:9 And the great dragon was cast out, that old serpent, called the Devil, and Satan, which deceiveth the whole world: he was cast out to the earth, and his angels (Luke 9:55) were cast out with him (Matthew 25:41).

Prayer without good works availeth a man nothing. In Christian weakness and disunity lies the atheistic strength. For one reason or another many Christian denominations are fast losing their hold upon the youth of the so-called Free Nations. Each person lost to the Christian belief usually turns to secularism and often ends up as a "Fellow Traveller" in one or another of the atheistic ideologies of Communism or Naziism.[1]

The vast majority of professed Christians are not real "Soldiers of Jesus Christ" whereas every card-bearing member of either the Communist or Nazi parties must swear to give unlimited obedience to the leaders; to devote every waking hour to the furtherance of theCause; and contribute one tenth of his, or her, income, towards financing the party's activities.
While Christians are hopelessly divided into approximately 400 denominations, Communists and Nazis are all solidly united as anti-Christians. A continuation of this state of affairs cannot help but enable the leaders of one or another atheistic group winning world domination. When

http://yamaguchy.netfirms.com/carr/pawns_01.html (2 of 11)5.4.2006 12:13:04

William Carr, Pawns in the Game, ch 1
they do so they will enslave body, soul and mind, all who refuse to accept their heathen ideology. The Illuminati will then impose the despotism of Satan.
Pawns in the game William guy Carr chapter one

William Guy Carr

- Karl Marx (1818-1883) was a German of Jewish descent. He was expelled from Germany, and afterwards from France, for his revolutionary activities. He was given asylum in England. In 1848 he published the Communist Manifesto. Marx admitted this long range plan, to turn the world into an International of Soviet Socialist Republics, may take centuries to accomplish. Karl Ritter (1779-1859) was a German Professor of History and Geopolitical science. He wrote the anti-thesis to Karl Marx's Communist Manifesto. He also drew up a plan by which he maintained the Aryan Race could first dominate Europe and then the entire world. Certain Atheistic leaders of the Aryan Group adopted Karl Ritter's plan. They organized Naziism to further their secret ambitions to obtain ultimate control of the World and turn it into a Godless State, under their conception of a totalitarian dictatorship. This small group of men knew they must either join up with, or destroy, the power and influence of the International Bankers. It is doubtful if more than a mere handful of the top level leaders of the Communist and Fascist movements know their organizations are being used to further the secret ambitions of the Illuminati which are the High Priests of Satanism.

Satan has infiltrated our Churches. I could write a small book on the number of "christian" organizations that are controlled by Lucifer. The web of power, influence and infiltration affecting our churches comes from government, church leadership, and especially "Foundations" that offer money and assistance. Foundations such as the John Birch Society. Organizations such as the World Council of Churches.

- According to the leaders of both atheistic groups the State must be Supreme. This being so the Head of the State is God on Earth. This belief brings into actual practice the deification of man. Much more is generally known about Karl Marx and Communism than about Karl Ritter and Naziism. Ritter was for many years Professor of History at Frankfort University, Germany. Afterwards he taught Geography at the Berlin University. In educational circles he was considered one of the greatest authorities on History, Geography, and Geopolitical Science. Because the "Aims and Objects" of the Leaders of the Aryan Party have always been kept secret, Karl Ritter's connection with the Leaders and Naziism is very little known. Intelligence Officers connected with the British Government unearthed his connection with the Aryan War Lords when studying Political Economy; Geopolitical Science; and Comparative Religions, in German universities.[4]This information was passed on to the proper authorities but, as so often happens, political leaders and diplomats, either failed to realize the significance of what they were told or wished to ignore it.[5]http//yamaguchy.netfirms.com/carr/pawns_01.html

pawns in the game
william guy carr
chapter 1

- Evidence will be produced to prove that Modern Communism was organized in the year 1773 by a group of International Money-Barons who have used it since, as their manual of action, to further their secret plans to bring about a Totalitarian Godless State. Lenin made this clear in his book Left Wing Communism. On page 53, he said : "Our theory (Communism) is not a dogma (Settled Doctrine); it is a manual of action". Many modern leaders have said and done the same things as Lucifer did during the heavenly revolution. There is no appreciable difference betweenRed and Black Atheism. The only difference is in the plans used by the opposing leaders to ultimately win undisputed control of the world's resources, and bring into being their ideas for a Totalitarian, Godless, Dictatorship.

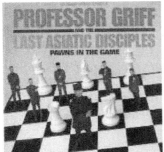

I based my first album on william guy Carr's work

My first sngle i demonstrated how the powers that be control both sides of the conflict

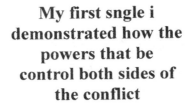

KRS-One writes 'gospel of hip-hop'

Stand aside Christianity, Islam and Judaism, a new rap religion is set to take over the world and KRS-One is its prophet

"I respect the Christianity, the Islam, the Judaism but their time is up," KRS-One told AllHipHop. *"I don't have to go through any religion [or] train of thought. I can approach God directly myself."*

Rapper KRS-One has become an apostle, publishing a 600-page Gospel of Hip-Hop dedicated to the "spirituality" and "divinity" of hip-hop culture. "In 100 years," he said, "this book will be a new religion on the earth."

http://www.guardian.co.uk/music/2009/sep/01/
krs-one-gospel-hip-hop

The religous element rose in hi[hop after the conscious era of hip hop failed to deliver hip hop from its grip of gangsta rap and its inventors

Taking the Gospel to the Streets...
www.holyhiphop.com

"...the subject that will be of most importance politically is 'Mass Psychology'.... The populace will not be allowed to know how its convictions were generated. When the technique has been perfected, every government that has been in charge of education for a generation will be able to control its subjects securely without the need of armies or policemen. As yet there is only one country which has succeeded in creating this politician's paradise."

-- Bertrand Russell, The Impact of Science on Society

Is Hip Hop The Perfect Breeding Ground For Freemasonry & the Illuminati?

Jennifer Hudson says "Illuminati, Schluminati!" But was the road to Hip Hop's lofty success paved in hell?

jennifer Hudson is **the** latest victim of **the** latest craze in

Jennifer Hudson is the latest victim of the latest craze in black celebrity conspiracy theories. Jennifer Hudson is actually being accused of sacrificing her family as part of an initiation into the Illuminati secret society.

The brutal murders of her mother Darnell, brother Jason and nephew Julian in 2008 made headlines worldwide. J Hud's highly-publicized family murders were a tragic blow to anyone who is a fan of Hudson, and now the R&B singer will have to relive the sad events with a horrible new twist claiming that she is responsible. Gregory King, the father of Jennifer Hudson's nephew Julian, has fed into and brought the Illuminati rumors to light in a new video at the 2008 crime scene. He accuses J Hud of being a Freemason and sacrificing her family for her success. Similar rumors have surfaced about Kanye West after the unexpected death of his mother. By the way, Gregory king is using the whole story to promote his new album...figures.

Do you think J Hud sacrificed her family or did the conspiracy theorists go too far with this one?

*"I'm so glad someone brought this Illuminati mess up because only a child of God would address it. That is the most ignorant thing I have ever heard in my life. And it's offensive because basically what? The people that are here today don't deserve to be where they are? What, we didn't work for it? So I find-and I hate to go there-but I find it's those that can't make it that would probably join Illuminati, or whoever that is, to get somewhere."***Jennifer Hudson**
www.highbridnation.com

http://dimewars.com/Blog/ViewBlogArticle.aspx?vn=Jennifer+Hudson
+Accused+Of+Sacrificing+Her+Family+For
+Illuminati&BlogID=785c9372-1e3e-484b-8ed3-e6e2321263cf

"Do not call conspiracy all that this people calls conspiracy, and do not fear what they fear, nor be in dread. But the Lord of hosts, him you shall honor as holy. Let him be your fear, and let him be your dread. Isaiah 8:12-13

http://www.openbible.info/topics/the_illuminati_conspiracy

Rev Run's new image

When Jesus Prayed He always said Father I know Thou hearest me. When u pray say "Father I know You hear me". This will increase ur faith

Reverend Run RT. stunt in front of their ostentatious profligate show

Run

The fear is that Holy Hiphop is not so holy when the vibration of the frequency of the music is just the same

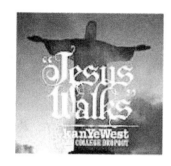

Kanye was in North Africa Morocco for the 2011 Mawazine Festival. He rocked his show, until...

He played Jesus Walks. Morocco is a very Muslim country and is still considered a holy country. They still have woman walking around that are covered up. They were not feeling Kanyes song. Kanye supposedly came up with a Jesus Walks dance too..

132

Satanism is not about ritual sacrifices, digging up graves and worshiping the devil. The devil doesn't exist. Satanism is about worshiping yourself, because you are responsible for your own good and evil. http://www.jesus-is-savior.com/False%20Religions/Wicca%20&%20Witchcraft/anton_lavey.htm

"A white male child of perfect innocence and intelligence makes the most suitable victim."

Anton LaVey

One of the top songs of the 70's was "Hotel California" by the Eagles. Most people have no idea the song refers to the Church of Satan, which happens to be located in a converted HOTEL on CALIFORNIA street! **On the inside of the album cover, looking down on the festivities, is Anton LaVey (pictured to left), the founder of the Church of Satan and author of the Satanic Bible!**

People say, the Eagles aren't serious, they're just selling records. That's what you think! The Eagles manager, Larry Salter, admitted in the Waco Tribune-Herald, (Feb. 28, 1982) that the Eagles were involved with the Church of Satan! Not surprisingly, one of the Eagle's songs is titled "*Have A Good Day in Hell.*"

As you can see, Crowley and LaVey have both had a profound influence upon the rock-n-roll culture. It's just solid proof that rock-n-roll is of the Devil.

Architect/**Canibus/ Professor Griff**. In this photo:

Rappers Who Believe In The Illuminati: Canibus & Professor Griff Release A Track Called Dead By Design "Illuminati Going To Murder Us Just Like They Did To 2pac" [Audio]

"We shall unleash the Nihilists and Atheists, and we shall provoke a formidable social cataclysm which in all its horror will show clearly to the nations the effect of absolute atheism, origin of savagery and of the most bloody turmoil. Then everywhere, the citizens, obliged to defend themselves against the world minority of revolutionaries, will exterminate those destroyers of civilization, and the multitude, disillusioned with christianity, whose deistic spirits will be from that moment without compass (direction), anxious for an ideal, but without knowing where to render its adoration, will receive the true light through the universal manifestation of the pure doctrine of Lucifer brought finally out in the public view, a manifestation which will result from the general reactionary movement which will follow the destruction of christianity and atheism, both conquered and exterminated at the same time."
(Ibid, p. 11.)

133

"...the pyramid represents the conspiracy for destruction of the Catholic (Universal Christian) Church, and establishment of a "One World", or UN dictatorship, the "secret" of the Order; the eye radiating in all directions, is the "all-spying eye" that symbolizes the terroristic, Gestapo-like, espionage agency that Weishaupt set up under the name of "Insinuating Brethren", to guard the "secret" of the Order and to terrorize the populace into acceptance of its rule."
(William Guy Carr, "Pawns in the Game." [Willowdale, Ontario: Federation of Christian Laymen. 1958.] p. 8.)

When Cheryl James abruptly abandoned her red-hot career as "Salt" of the hip-hop duo Salt-N-Pepa and became a Christian, she also shattered her relationship with partner Sandra "Pepa" Denton.

Created in an effort to celebrate Christian hip-hop ministry and bring light to gospel MCs, the Holy Hip Hop Awards is an offshoot of Holy Hip Hop Week, which has featured rap luminaries like Kurtis Blow, Grand Master Caz and Ma$e. Though largely unknown outside of Christian circles, this year's nominees include Mobsters of Light, Che Che Da Supastar, Chris Chicago, Mobigga, Mr. D-Note, Halo & Reign and many more.

Play from Kid and play

the Church humming your name" - "Pastor" **Mase - 300 Shots** (Gamediss)**"I have one in the chamber and one in your brain/ I'll have hoes in the back of the Church humming your name"** - "Pastor" Mase - 300 Shots (Game Diss). From Mase's days with G-unit...now thats what you call a *Gospel Gangsta...*

134

THE AFRICAN ORIGIN OF FREEMASONRY
African Origin of Western Freemasonry - DVD
By Ashra Kwesi

Visually documented slide presentation lecture video exposes the African origin of symbols and concepts used in freemasonry. Studio-produced. Ashra Kwesi exposes the African origin of symbols and concepts used in masonry. He offers enlightening explanations of: the African origin of the architect God of the Universe mentioned in freemasonry, ancient African priests - the first Sons of Light who achieved 360 degrees, pre-dynastic Africans, the first operative masons, the African mystery schools, prototypes for Solomon's Temple and the first Grand Master builders before Hiram Abif, the origin of the Scottish Rite, York Rite, Shriners, Eastern Stars and much more...

This work explores the mystery and mythology found in Religion and Freemasonry. We also will present information connecting Religion and Freemasonry to Ancient Africa as we discuss the supposed hidden meanings of movements, characters, and the zodiac.

The Universal Society Supreme 13 presents to you, The African Origin of Freemasonry, OES, Knights Templars and Shriners.

George Washington sent a letter to G.W. Snyder in which he stated: "It is not my intention to doubt that the doctrine of the Illuminati and the principles of Jacobinism had not spread to the United States. On the contrary, no one is more satisfied of this fact than I am. The idea meant to convey was that I did believe the Lodges of Freemasonry in this county had, as societies, endeavored to propagate the diabolical tenets."

What is more disturbing is that the Masons may believe that the twins represent an ongoing battle over who will rule the world. At times it will be Horus, and at other times it will be Seth. Since the Masons probably share the astrological belief that we are entering a new age, they probably believe that the balance of power is about to shift. While most people refer to the new age as the Age of Aquarius, some occult believers refer to this new age as the age of Horus.

Since the last age was dominated by Europeans, it might lead Masons to believe that the next age will be dominated by non-Europeans. This could explain some of the racism that is so prevalent in society. If the Masons feel threatened by non-Europeans because of some prophetic vision, then they will do everything in their power to fight this development. This may partly explain the eugenic-transhuman agenda. Perhaps they believe that by transforming themselves into transhumans and conquering space that they can change this natural ebb and flow.

Mastaba de Mereruka

I know this is a tremendous amount of speculation based mainly on the constellation Gemini. But I have a strong feeling about this one, and I wanted to share it with everyone to see what the reaction would be. Does any of this make sense?

The most important principle of the Freemasons that is traced to ancient Egypt is the belief in materialist evolution. This theory of evolution is based on the belief that the universe exists by and of itself, evolving only by chance. In this theory of evolution, matter was always extant, and the world originated when order arose from chaos. This state of chaos was referred to as Nun. A latent, creative force exists within this state of disorder which has the potential to rise above the disorder.

Another philosophical connection established between the ancient Egyptians and the Freemasons is believed to be the common rituals associated with death and burial practices. Specifically, the link between ancient Egypt and the Masons can be found in the text known as The Book of the Dead. This text's original title is in fact The Book of Coming Forth by Day. It is an ancient Egyptian funerary text that outlines instructions for the afterlife.

Contrary to popular belief, The Book of Coming Forth by Day does not instruct individuals on how to raise the dead in order to escape death, but rather provides instructions for the afterlife. These instructions, in the form of spells, were used by the Egyptian elite for their burial practices.

In addition, spells were offered as gifts to the gods, for healing such ailments as the inability to walk, and to prevent death during the afterlife. The ultimate aim of The Book of Coming Forth by Day was to enable the individual to overcome the hardships and obstacles.

Furthermore, members of the Freemasons are believed to consider themselves to be special heirs of the people of ancient Egypt, a belief that experts have attributed to the philosophical commonality between the Freemasons of today and the ancient Egyptians.

According to some experts, these principles and theories were adopted by the Freemasons, and were incorporated into the moral and metaphysical ideals espoused by members of Freemasonry.

Freemasonry in Egypt developed alongside that of the Ottoman Empire. The Scottish Rite of the Freemasons was founded in 1886 by Halim Pasha, the son of the first viceroy of Egypt. Its development flourished until the 1950s when it fell from popularity during the dethronement of King Farouk and was closed after the 1956 Suez Crisis.

If you're not familiar with Ashra Kwesi, read the following article and study his work.

http://www.finalcall.com/artman/publish/National_News_2/article_7449.shtml
http://www.kemetnu.com/kwesi_with_dr__ben.htm

Ashra Kwesi spent 14 years as an apprentice in Kemet (Egypt) to the renowned African Kemetologist, Dr. Yosef ben Jochannan (known affectionately as Dr. Ben). Brother Kwesi also performed extensive field research in Sudan, Ethiopia and Kenya with Dr Ben. Ashra Kwesi now continues Dr. Ben's legacy of educating our African people on the African Nile Valley.

Ashra Kwesi (r) with his wife Merira in the vending area. and Ashra Kwesi with Dr Ben
Photo: Erick Muhammad

Origins of Freemasonry: Ancient Egypt
According to Masonic historians, Freemasonry is based on the principles
and values of ancient Egypt.

FREEMASONRY OF THE ANCIENT EGYPTIANS
By Manly P. Hall

Interpretations of the Freemasonry of ancient Egypt are set forth as revealed in the teachings of the State Mysteries, including Egyptian magic, the Osirian cycle, the secret doctrine of Egypt, and the initiation of Plato. The appendix is a restoration of the ancient Egyptian mystery rituals, The Crata Repoa, describing initiation ceremonies which took place in the old temples (as translated by Dr. John Yarker from the French edition of 1778).

Mustafa El-Amin, author of bestseller Al-Islam, Christianity, and Freemasonry, now examines what it is about Freemasonry that made most of the founding fathers of America feel the need to embrace it; why is it that so many people of influence (members of Congress, the Supreme Court, judges, politicians)--past and present--have joined and studied the teachings of Freemasonry.

To understand literally the symbols and allegories of Oriental books as to ante-historical matters, is willfully to close our eyes against the Light. To translate the symbols into the trivial and commonplace, is the blundering of mediocrity.

All religious expression is symbolism; since we can describe only what we see, and the true objects of religion are THE SEEN. The earliest instruments of education were symbols; and they and all other religious forms differed and still differ according to external circumstances and imagery, and according to differences of knowledge and mental cultivation. All language is symbolic, so far as it is applied to mental and spiritual phenomena and action. All words have, primarily, a material sense, however they may afterward get, for the ignorant, a spiritual non-sense. "To retract," for example, is to draw back, and when applied to a statement, is symbolic, as much so as a picture of an arm drawn back, to express the same thing, would be. The very word "spirit" means "breath," from the Latin verb spiro, breathe.

137

'These ancient Egyptian figures demonstrate how prevalent was Osiris' sacred sign, "X"'

X Symbol in the Masonic Lodge

One thing is for sure: The Masonic Order uses the X not only for the revelatory 17th degree of Knights of East and West, but for others as well. In the Royal Arch's Super-Excellent Master's Degree, the **First Sign given is the crossing of the hands over the breast/chest**. This sign refers to the penalty assessed if any secrets learned are ever divulged. Then, in the ritual ceremony for the Select Master Degree, the **Second Sign is made by crossing the hands and arms just below the neck** and dropping them downward quickly. Again, this is a reminder of the disclosure penalty, which is to have the body butchered and quartered.

Supreme Court Justice nominee Clarence Thomas, appearing before a U.S. Senate Committee, in 1991, holds his right hand up to take the Oath. But at the same time, Thomas places his left hand and arm in such a fashion as to present the familiar Dueguard of a Fellow Craft sign of Freemasonry.

[Quoted from above page image; pg. 58 Codex Magica]: "Sign of the Master of the Second Veil," or informally, sign of the hidden hand of the Men of Jahbuhlun (Richards monitor of Freemasonry, pg. 74); and "Guards of the Conclave" during the ritual for the Knights of the Christian Mark Degree. **(Richardson's Monitor of Freemasonry. p. 123)"**

Excerpt (p. 22) of Richardson's Monitor of Freemasonry, illustrating and describing the sign and due-guard of a Fellow Craft Mason.

When this statue was unveiled of George Washington, the first President of the United States, the people could not understand why their esteemed George was depicted in such a strange, half-naked, pose. Look at the classic image of the Satanic symbol of "Baphomet", however, and all becomes clear

http://thebiggestsecretpict.online.fr/nwo/washington+bapho.jpg

King James Bible: 1 COR 10:21

Ye cannot drink the cup of the Lord, and the cup of devils: ye cannot be partakers of the Lord's table, and of the table of devils.

Eye of Amen-Ra -- Back of Dollar Bill
CBS Eye Symbol
Time Warner Symbol
Toyota Symbol

Holy -- refers to the female opening

Mushroom Head -- enlightened one (see topic: Manna)

Noah's Ark -- comes from the original Egyptian celebration of the coming of the Spring rains or Arca noah

Oval Office -- symbolic of operating from inside the womb

Pillar - phallic emblem**

Sign of the cross - Egyptian burial state of Pharaoh with his arms folded across his chest

Trinity -- father, son and holy (e.g. see holy) spirit; the original version was father, mother & son

Two Pillars -- left side: Boaz, eagerness, strength right side: Jachin, God makes him firm (1 King 7:21)****

Washington Monument -- phallic emblem**

The society of Western Civilization has not advanced one-inch forward from its pre-illiterate past. It's so-Called religious symbols are no more than references to sexualith and pro-creation....

*Arc of the Covenant -- feminine womb****

Baphomet - symbol of copulation; completed man (e.g. & you thought this symbol was about the devil!)*

*Church steeples - phallic emblem***

Christos -- Greek word for Christ which means oiled; hence "anointed one".

Jordan Maxwell religious sex cult symbology Bobby Hemmitt
http://www.youtube.com/watch?v=YAF9nHmJYTM&feature=related

Politics vs poly-tricks

WASHINGTON   BAPHOMET

139

THE CFR CABAL IN THE WHITEHOUSE

14 of the 17 policymakers in the picture currently belong to the Council on Foreign Relations (cfr.org). Two others, Rumsfeld (currently a member of the Trilateral Commission) and Laird, are former members of the CFR. Of the 17, George W. Bush himself is the only one who has not belonged to the organization, but he is a member of the 'Skull and Bones'.

Starting on the left: Former Secretary of Defense Harold Brown, former Secretary of State Lawrence Eagleburger, former Secretary of State James Baker, former Secretary of State Colin Powell, former Secretary of Defense James Schlesinger, Secretary of Defense Donald Rumsfeld, Vice President Dick Cheney, President George W. Bush, Secretary of State Condoleezza Rice, former Secretary of State George Shultz, former Secretary of Defense Melvin Laird, former Secretary of Defense Robert McNamara, former Secretary of State Madeleine Albright , former Secretary of State Alexander Haig, former Secretary of Defense Frank Carlucci, former Secretary of Defense William Perry, and former Secretary of Defense William Cohen.

The Council on Foreign Relations (CFR), an Illuminist organization headquartered in New York City, has as its official logo a conquering, wild, naked, man riding a rampant white horse, while giving the *Sign of Admiration* and *Astonishment*. The fingers of the hand are pointed toward the CFR's hidden Master in the Stars, the Prince of the Power of the Air (Lucifer). Notice, too, the black, circular background and the cryptic Latin inscription, *ubique*, which means "everywhere." This logo, until recently, was printed on every issue of the CFR's official publication, *Foreign Affairs*. The man on a white horse theme, I believe, comes from the Bible's *Revelation 6*, the Four Horsemen of the Apocalypse. The first rider comes riding a white horse and proclaims to the world, "Peace," which claim proves to be a monumental lie.

The Council on Foreign Relations (CFR) and The New World Order is the illuminati in America

Council on foreign relations = the Illuminati in America

Thomas Jefferson wrote: "The Central Bank is an institution of the most deadly hostility existing against the principles and form of our Constitution. If the American people allow private banks to control the issuance of their currency, first by inflation and then by deflation, the banks and corporations that will grow up around them will deprive the people of all their property until their children will wake up homeless on the continent their fathers conquered."

King James Bible

And I looked, and behold a pale horse: and his name that sat on him was Death, and Hell followed with him. And power was given unto them over the fourth parts of the earth, to kill with sword, and with hunger, and with death, and with the beasts of the earth.

The CFR states that it is "host to many views, advocate of none," and it "has no affiliation with the U.S. government." No, no affiliation at all, if you don't count: "A Council member was elected president of the United States. Dozens of other Council colleagues were called to serve in cabinet and sub-cabinet positions," as they describe it in "Foreign Affairs," along with many members of Congress, the Supreme Court, the Joint Chiefs, the Federal Reserve, and many other Federal bureaucrats.

They are not AFFILIATED with government; they ARE the government, in effect.

http://www.conspiracyarchive.com/NWO/Council_Foreign_Relations.htm

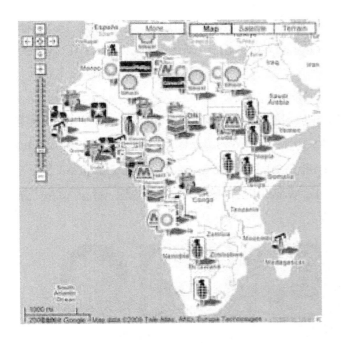

Africa Program

Africa is the poorest continent and has long suffered war, famine, and disease. But African leaders and international players are creating ways to restore peace, promote good governance, and upgrade health across the continent's 54 countries. African leaders have formed stronger regional and sub-regional institutions and committed their countries to policies and programs to stimulate economic growth and increase funding for education, health, and infrastructure.

http://www.cfr.org/project/1031/africa_program.html

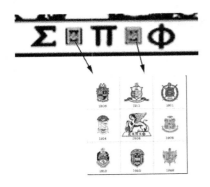

This Ebony magazine article posted below was originally written to celebrate the 100 year anniversary of the Grand Boule in 2004:

In 1904, the first African-American Greek Secret Society was formed in Philadelphia, by Dr. Henry Minton and five of his colleagues. The Boule, (an acronym for Sigma Pi Phi) and pronounced "boolay"), was formed to bring together a select group of educated Black men and women.

Fashioned after Yale's Skull and Bones, the Boule historically takes pride in having provided leadership and service to Black Americans during the Great Depression, World Wars I and II, and the Civil Rights Movement.

What could the Boule offer America's Blacks in the early 20th century? Joining the exclusive secret society offered advancement and perks to select Blacks in return for loyalty to its objectives. In the first constitution, the group proclaimed that the upper tenth of Blacks started to live the good life as Boule members, while the majority of ordinary Blacks were disenfranchised. But what were the Boule's objectives?

The importance of stealing the Black professional away from Garvey is because an Afrocentric organization that articulated and captured the Black professional would give YT no safe haven in the Black community, so the Boule' – the remaking of the house negro – was necessary to build a group of Negroes who had an investment in protecting the white system as produced by YT having stolen this land... This is post reconstruction. Taking away the articulate Negro, now desiring to replace them with organized institutions to keep them away from self improvement. So we find in the same period, as the founding of the Boule', the founding of the 4 Black male (Alpha Phi Alpha, Kappa Alpha Psi, Omega Psi Phi, and Phi Beta Sigma) and 4 black female (Alpha Kappa Alpha, Delta Sigma Theta, Zeta Phi Beta, and Sigma Gamma Rho) college-based fraternities and sororities. We also find the founding of the NAACP and Urban League."

-- Steve Cokely

142

Steve Cokely talks about how African Americans who were influential within their community were "steered" into literature, the arts, and organizations during and after the high tension between "Blacks and Whites" in America, starting from the early 1900's.

"When we look at the Boule' closely, we find a confusion of values. Black men who felt that their advancement was edged upon a positive relationship with wealthy and influential white people. And I say that this may have an adverse impact on our revolution. Therefore, we give them (the Boule') today, this official warning... Our goal is not to kill off the Boule', but to warn them as an organization. To warn the individual that if they bring false values, or worship a false idol, into the community at a time the community attempts to self-determinate (liberate ourselves), if we give the call, they will come and grab you, we have every one of your addresses and phone numbers, we can get you, if we choose to. But we only choose to ask you to step aside and the day we got to get "massa," you find some way to be on vacation... To kill off the Boule' would be like eating the peel off a banana and ignoring the actual banana."

-- Steve Cokely

Henry McKee Minton was the leading figure in the discussions about organizing a group for such purposes. Henry Minton was born in Columbia, South Carolina, on Christmas Day in 1871. He went to school at the Academy at Howard University and, eventually, Phillips Exeter Academy, from which he graduated in 1891. Minton studied law for a year and then went to pharmacy school at the Philadelphia College of Pharmacy, from which he graduated in 1895. Minton then received the M. D. degree from Jefferson Medical College in 1906.

Minton also spent considerable time contemplating the isolation in which accomplished black men lived and worked. He began to talk with other black professionals – Dr. Algernon B. Jackson (b. 21 May 1878) being chief among them – about their shared conditions and about his ideas for forming an organization that would bring them together in fellowship. Minton thought that black learned and professional men should have an organization that "should be a fraternity in the true sense of the word; one whose chief thought should not be to visit the sick and bury the dead, but to bind men of like qualities, tastes and attainments into a close and sacred union that they might know the best of one another." Members would not be "selected on the basis of brains alone – but in addition to congeniality, culture and good fellowship; that they shall have behind them [at initiation] a record of accomplishment, not merely be men of promise and good education." His fraternity would contain the "best of Skull and Bones of Yale and of Phi Beta Kappa."

Henry McKee Minton

Pictured here in 1917, are the founding **members** of the Atlanta Branch.

143

The solution: A man, who crawls on all fours as a baby, walks on two legs as an adult, and walks with a cane in old age.

The Riddle of the Sphinx.

"What has one voice, and is four-footed in the morning, two-footed in the afternoon and three-footed at night?"

Each time the Thebans gave a wrong answer, she ate one of them. Many perished, including eventually Haemon, son of Creon - ruler since the death of Laius, the previous king. [incompatible with Sophocles' Antigone, of course]. Creon then announced he'd give the kingship and Laius' widow (his sister Jocasta) to whoever solved the riddle. Oedipus, on his way from Delphi, gave the answer: "Man". The Sphinx threw herself off the acropolis and committed suicide.

Each May, as a mandatory ritual, each **member must????????**

"The Black 'Skull and Bones' - The "Boule"

In the first constitution the group proclaimed that: "Whereas it seems that wise and good men of ambition, refinement and self respect should seek the society both for the mutual benefit and to be an example of the higher type of manhood. Be it resolved that a society be organized for the purpose of blinding men of like qualities into a close, sacred, fraternal union, that they may to full ability and the other and by concerted action bring about those things that seem best for all that cannot e accomplished by individuals efforts.

Advisor's To The King

Whereas it seems wise and good that men of ambition, Refinement and self-respect should seek the society of each other Both for the mutual benefit and to be an example of the higher type of manhood. Be it Resolved that a society be organized for the purpose of binding men of like qualities into a close, sacred, fraternal union, that they may know the best of one another, and that each in this life may to his full ability aid the other, and by concerted action bring about those things that seem best for all that cannot be accomplished by individual effort.

http://www.sigmapiphi.org/home/history_of_the_boule.php

Links to the Rest of the Interview.
http://www.youtube.com/watch?v=Pw8EcJDazEE
http://www.youtube.com/watch?v=ELuxHKoC0Bk
Steve Cokely is a great source of vital information. He currently is facing health problems and is still in the hospital from what I understand for more info regarding Brother Steve Cokely http://truthmovement.com/?p=878

Garvey said, "If the oil of Afrika is good for Rockefeller's interest, if iron is good for Carnegie trust, then these minerals are good for us. Why should we allow Wall Street and the capitalist group of America and other countries exploit our country when they refuse to give us a fair chance in the countries of our adoption? Why should not Afrika give to the world its Black Rockefeller, Rothschild, and Henry Ford?"

DuBois, along with Alain Locke — the first Black (Cecil) Rhodes Scholar — publicly defiled Garvey by calling him a "gorilla" any chance they got. Locke was quoted as saying, "We hope the white man delivers 'cause we crushed a great black thing, but we know he'll deliver or our people will attack and plague us forever more."

http://knowledgeisking.ning.com/profiles/blogs/the-black-skull-and-bones-the

REMAKING OF THE HOUSE NEGRO

The Boule recruits top Blacks in American Society into its ranks. Today, 5000+ Archons, (male Boule members) and their wives, (Archousais), with 112 chapters, make up the wealthiest group of Black men and women on the planet

But to who does the Boule really serve? The Satanic (mostly white) global elite! As long as the Black member conforms to the rules, the riches will be in abundance, if not, down comes the hatchet. Blackmail is part of the deal. This masonic secret society has a pyramid style like all the rest. The lower ranks are kept from knowing what the upper ranks are doing.

The early 20th century was a period of reconstruction. Marcus Garvey's "Back to Africa" Movement was in full swing. Garvey represented genuine Black leadership. Dubois, founding member of the NYC chapter of the Boule said, "The Boule was created to keep the black professional away from Marcus Garvey".

The remaking of the House Negro was necessary to institute a group of Blacks who had a vested interest in protecting the Elite White System. It was about selling out brothers and sisters for power and money. The majority of Black lawyers, doctors, engineers and accountants were members of the club.

PREDATORY INTENTIONS

According to Bobby Hemmitt, underground Metaphysician and Occultist lecturer, "This Black elite society based on Skull and Bones (Yale) was chosen by the U.S. Government (Illuminati) to run Black neighborhoods". See here: http://www.youtube.com/watch?v=PA6jmaoG7V8
Conspiracy Theorist and Futurologist Steve Cokely, had this to say, "Anywhere there are prominent professional Blacks, chances are they're in the Boule". Martin Luther King and Jesse Jackson are reported to have been Boule members, among many other high profile, successful and moneyed Blacks such as Barack Obama, Bill Cosby, Al Sharpton and Thurgood Marshall. See this:http://www.youtube.com/watch?v=ey7gDJfRICA
The members of the Boule pose as Freedom Fighters or Civil Rights Activists on the surface. In truth, the elite members are operating for personal gain. The Boule works in concert with their masters in maintaining the grip of white supremacy on the people.

Back to DuBois against Garvey. DuBois was one of the strongest opponents of Garvey and was an instrumental "tool" (he was used by someone else, will explain, read on, son!) in stopping one of the strongest grassroots movements in this century. What was Garvey's plan? His plan was to take as many Afrikans from the america's and start a settlement in the nation of Liberia and then help their new nation produce and control their own rubber crops and other natural resources. Garvey said, "If the oil of Afrika is good for Rockefeller's interest; if iron is good for Carnegie trust; then these minerals are good for us. Why should we allow wall street and the capitalist group of amerikkka and other countries exploit our country when they refuse to give us a fair chance in the countries of our adoption? Why should not Afrika give to the world its black Rockefeller, Rothschild, and Henry Ford?" This would've meant no Firestone, as we know it today, because it would have set a precedent that would have made all Afrikans aware of their land and mineral wealth. This would've smashed the financial arm of white supremacy. DuBois, along with Elaine Locke -- the first black (Cecil) Rhodes scholar (will explain) -- publicly defiled Garvey by calling him a "gorilla, dark, and dumb ass" any chance they got -- is this separation or what?! Locke was quoted as saying, "We hope the white man deliver's cause we crushed a great black thing, but we know he'll deliver or our people will attack and plague us forever more." These two house negroes made a bet that YT would come out on top and give a certain percentage of these greedy negroes, namely Boule' members, the wealth they stole from Afrika. What's deep is they didn't believe in Afrikan self-reliance and preferred YT to give them table scraps instead of us making the whole pie!

Marcus *Garvey*   *Du Bois*

Marcus *Garvey*

Du Bois

The historical class struggle within the African Liberation Movement

Personal and political antagonism between *Du Bois* and Marcus *Garvey* was ... spend "the remaining years of [his] active life" in the fight *against* imperialism. ...n another broadside *against Du Bois*, *Garvey* argued that "Negroes have done nothing praiseworthy on their own initiative in the last five hundred years to ... The African Socialist International and the black working class is opposed to Pan African neocolonialism

146

ADVISERS TO THE KING

The Boule is another arm of the nefarious secret societies that recruit, indoctrinate and cull for the dark forces. Therein are perks galore, power and notoriety all lying in wait for the easily compromised soul.
In the Greek system, the Boule was the Lower House of Parliament. Charged with organizing the affairs of the city for the King. Let that sink in.This is an ancient story. The New World Order is The Old World Order. The elite Blacks of the Boule are culling and controlling their own for a slice of the elite white man's pie.

The Black Elite also known as "THE BOULE" (Sigma Pi Phi). There's not much out there on them, but here's some interesting vids and articles. It's a "invite" only club, and many of the who's who of Black America are members. They have also taken the name coined by Boule' member, W.E.B. DuBois, "The Talented Tenth".

"We, the talented 10th, are the best able and the only ones suitable to save the black race." - Vernon Jordan (member of Trilateral Commission and Board of Council of Foreign Relations, close adviser to President Bill Clinton, John Kerry's (skull & Bones member) Lead Debate Negotiator, and bunch of other stuff!)

COMPROMISING SITUATIONS

Like other secret societies, the Boule encourages homosexual trysts as initiation practices. This must be done to join the ranks. Bobby Hemmit says, "Any kind of top-notch Negro gets together and they f*ck each other"

These perversions are then catalogued and stored on record. Later, if needed, these abuses may be used as bargaining tools in the ULTIMATE GAME. What is the Ultimate Game? Capturing human souls.

The enemy may appear to have a white face but it goes much deeper than that. This is a force cloaked within many facades, personas, fictions and governing powers. See here: *http://masonfitup.blogspot.com/2009/12/masonic-initiation.html.*

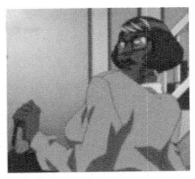

Madea on the boondocks
GAY BOULE (orbiting **the** heck out this thread)

CONCLUSION:

We, the people, have been handed cultural, political and religious belief systems designed to be used to great advantage by these generational Satanists and lying collectives.

These elite systems promote dissension, division, hatred, bigotry and war. According to the ruling powers, people are objects that need to be controlled. Therefore, we have men and women in high places that are soulless and beyond the reach of normal reasoning processes.

We have an ancient enemy with a large collection of demonic assistants. The evil elite has had a good run. Though they may be certain skin colors, certain nationalities and creeds, they are apart from you and me. They have long ago abdicated any and all connections to a shared humanity.

THE COUNCIL ON FOREIGN RELATIONS CONSPIRACY

Through the Council on Foreign Relations Conspiracy, the World's Elite Have Overtaken America's Government, Media, and Education System. The Council on Foreign Relations conspiracy to control the American government has become known to more people over the last two decades or so.

Especially through the Internet, information revealing the New World Order agenda and the people behind that agenda has become easier to find. In the past, though, only the most curious and suspicious people would seek out the usually obscure books that disclosed information about the Council on Foreign Relations (CFR).

One of the earlier books that detailed the Council on Foreign Relations conspiracy was **Kissinger: The Secret Side of the Secretary of State,** by Gary Allen. Published in 1981, it revealed how the CFR was extremely secretive in the early years.

Kissinger: The Secret Side of the Secretary of State,

The Bilderberg Group, Bilderberg conference, or Bilderberg Club is an unofficial, annual, invitation-only conference of around 130 guests (billionaires and world leaders?), most of whom are persons of influence in the fields of politics, business, and banking. The participants talk about a variety of global issues, economic, military, and political...

http://muslimvillage.wordpress.com/2009/05/01/bilderberg/

The Global 2000 report to the President, prepared by the Council on Environmental Quality and the Department of State begins as a STUDY for the "*PROBABLE CHANGES IN THE WORLD'S POPULATION, NATURAL RESOURCES, AND ENVIRONMENT THROUGH THE END OF THE CENTURY.*"

The report concludes that the stresses are already severe enough to deny many millions of people basic needs for food, shelter, health, and jobs, or ANY HOPE for betterment. At the same time, the earth's carrying capacity - the ability of biological systems to provide resources for human

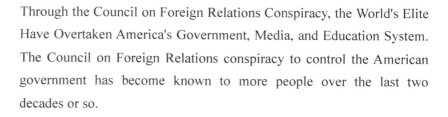

People involved in the 2000 PNAC report (from top left): Vice President Cheney, Florida Governor Jeb Bush, Defense Secretary Rumsfeld, Deputy Defense Secretary Paul Wolfowitz, Cheney Chief of Staff I. Lewis Libby, Undersecretary of State John Bolton, Undersecretary of Defense Dov Zakheim, and author Eliot Cohen. *[Source: Public domain]*

148

TRILATERAL COMMISSION

The logo for the Trilateral Commission (Zionist entity of the New World Order) contains a 666. Each arrow when separated from the logo is a 6, making 666. David Rockefeller created this organization, based in the United States, to soften America to the New World Order. Commission members include senators, congressmen, President Clinton and many members of his cabinet. Other presidents have also been members.

Trilateral Commission logo which is actually "666"

Why the World Wide Web (www) is NOT 666: the Mark of the Beast
666 is total of the numerical values in the letters of the antichrist's name
The World Wide Web is not a name.
666 is total of the numerical values of the letters in the antichrist's name
The actual total of "www" is 18 — not 666.
666 is the number of a man, the antichrist, or the beast
The World Wide Web is not a man.
The mark of the beast controls the ability to buy or sell
The World Wide Web currently does not
The mark of the beast goes in the right hand or forehead
The World Wide Web does not.
The mark is symbolic of the antichrist or beast
The World Wide Web is not
The mark is received only after worshiping the beast
The World Wide Web is not worship
Should I be concerned with "www" as "666"?

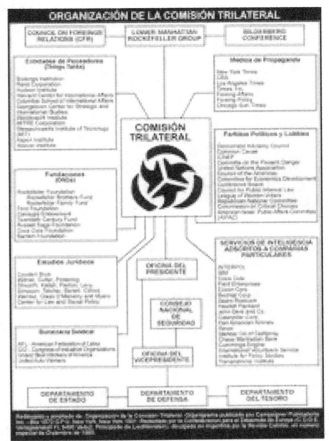

Map of the Nine Squares

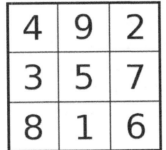

The magic square

In ancient times, words, numbers and symbols were considered as potential powers. When they are placed as opposites, their union becomes dynamic and tangible energy is released.

The time is always 10:10

THE NINE SQUARES OF ANCIENT NEW HAVEN

SQUARE 1 (top left): Edmund Tapp, James Prudden, Peter Prudden, William Fowler, Thomas Osborne, Wid. Baldwin, An Elder, Richard Platt, Zachariah Whitman.

SQUARE 2 (top middle): Thomas James, T. Powell (?), Widow Greene, Thomas Yale, Thomas Fugill, John Punderson, John Johnson, Abraham Bell, Edward Wigglesworth, John Burwell(?), Joshua Atwater, Mrs. Constable, Mr. Mayres, John Evanse

SQUARE 3 (top right): William Thorp, Robert Hill, Wid. Williams, Andrew Low, Jeremiah Dixon, Edw. Tench(?), Anne Higginson, Mr. Lucas, Deamor(?), David Atwater, John Goffinch(?), Francis Newman, Henry Browning

SQUARE 4 (center left): Thomas Buckingham, Thomas Welch, Jo. Whitehead(?), Samuel Bailey, William Hawkins, Richard Miles, Nathaniel Axtell, Stephen Goodyear, Henry Stonehill, Thomas Gregson

SQUARE 6 (center right): Francis Brewster, Mark Nance(?), Jarvis Boykin, Benjamin Ling, Mrs. Eldred, Robert Newman, Mr. Marshall, Richard Beckley, William Andrews, John Cooper

SQUARE 7 (bottom left): Roger Alling, John Brockett, Mr. Hickocks, John Budd, William Jeanes(?), Nath Elsey(?), Robert Seeley, Benjamin Fenn, William Wilkes, George Lamberton, Thomas Jeffrey, Mr. Mansfield, Richard Hull, William Preston

SQUARE 8 (bottom center): Matthew Gilbert, Thomas Kimberly, Owen Rowe, Mr. Davenport's Walk, An Elder, Jasper Crane, John Davenport, John Chapman, John Benham, Thomas Nash, Richard Malbon

SQUARE 9 (bottom right): Richard Perry, Nathaniel Turner, Ezekial Cheever, Theophilus Eaton, David Yale, Mr. Eaton, Samuel Eaton, William Tuttle

The Brothers Rockefeller,inheritors of a colossal fortune, are using their massive wealth, power, and prestige to create what they call the "New World Order." Shown above (from left to right) are David, Chairman of the Board of both the Council on Foreign Relations and the Chase Manhattan Bank; Winthrop (now deceased); John D. an advocate of people control; Nelson, the "political" Rockefeller; and Laurance. After years of planning and campaigning, a brilliant coup d'etat has finally installed Nelson in the White House, without the risk of an election.

Formed in 1973 by Illuminati godfather and New World Order oligarch, David Rockefeller, the **Trilateral Commission** brought together the elite in finance and industry from the three world regions represented in the group: Japan, Europe and the United States.Other high-profile reptiles intrinsically involved were Zbigniew Brzezinski, a kind of Democratic Henry Kissinger and major world player who is to Barack Obama what Kissinger was to Nixon, Reagan, Bush et al; Federal Reserve chiefs Alan Greenspan and Paul Volcker; and other high-ranking Brookings Institution and CFR members. Like its sister groups, the Trilateral Commission is a highly secretive, highly elitist closed-shop cabal working to a plan for world government (or "supranational sovereignty", as the term officially goes) by an "intellectual elite and world bankers," to quote Trilateral Commission founder, David Rockefeller (see below).Bottom line, if the Bilderberg Group, Chatham House, CFR and others were formed to run the Western world, the Trilateral Commission was formed to include Japan — and ultimately Asia — in the master plan.

Here's what David Rockefeller had to say about that plan during his speech to the Trilateral Commission in 1991:**We are grateful to the Washington Post, the New York Times, Time magazine and other great publications whose directors have attended our meetings and respected the promises of discretion for almost forty years. It would have been impossible for us to develop our plan for the world if we had been subject to the bright lights of publicity during those years. But the world is now more sophisticated and prepared to march towards a world government. The supranational sovereignty of an intellectual elite and world bankers is surely preferable to the National auto-determination practiced in past centuries.** http://www.consciousape.com/discussion-topics/the-trilateral-commission/

The Rockefeller File
by Gary Allen

At the center of Insider power, influence, and planning in the United States is the pervasive Council on Foreign Relations ... The CFR was created by the Rockefellers and their allies to be the focus of their drive for a "New World Order".

http://www.redicecreations.com/specialreports/2006/10oct/
illconfsnb322.html

Skull and Bones is the most well known of the secret societies based at Yale University. It was founded in 1832 by William Huntington Russell and Alphonso Taft, two students who were not admitted into Phi Beta Kappa at Yale University, in New Haven, Connecticut.

The first Skull and Bones class, or "cohort", was in 1833. Skull and Bones is known by many names, including The Order of Death, The Order, The Eulogian Club, and Lodge 322. Initiates are most commonly known as Bonesmen, Knights of Eulogia, and Boodle Boys.

The females who have recently been permitted to become members would be known as Boneswomen, Ladies of Eulogia, and Boodle Girls. In public, its corporate name is the Russell Trust Association. In 1999 it had assets of $4,133,246.

Skull and Bones is the only secret society known to have a summer home and its own private island. This private island, one of the Thousand Islands lying in gray territorial area between the United States and Canada, was given to the Order by one of its early mysterious benefactor families who were associated with the secret society.

Differences between Skull and Bones and other fraternities

Skull and Bones is different from other semi-secretive fraternities and sororities on several points. First, its current membership rosters are a secret to the public, as well as its activities. Second, it is what is called a "senior society," in that only upcoming seniors are inducted into the secret society only for one year prior to graduation. Third, members have a history of committing crimes to further The Order. Whether these crimes are part of the initiation or simply as a mutual encouragement of peer pressure, are unknown. For instance, grave-robbing has been committed on several occasions.

The Skull and Bones Tomb was rumored to hold Geronimo's skull, which inspired Native American activist and Apache chief Ned Anderson to try to force a search and a DNA test. He would face many obstacles. As a Yale student in 1918, Prescott Bush, former Connecticut Senator, father of President George H. W. Bush and grandfather to President George W. Bush, had dug up the skull himself with two other students from its federal burial ground at Fort Sill, Oklahoma and presented it as a gift to the fraternity.

http://www.crystalinks.com/skullbones.html

"GEORGE HERBERT WALKER BUSH, former president of the U.S., Council on Foreign Relations (CFR) Director, Trilateralist, CIA Director. Bush, one moonlit night in 1948 at Yale University, crawled naked into a coffin. With 15 brother 'Bonesmen' (as they call one another) encircling him, he told personal tales of debauchery, took an occult oath, was raised from the coffin (what THEY call being 'born-again') as a MAN-GOD, jumped into a pile of mud, thus joining the occult, elitist Skull & Bones Society. He, indeed, is still a 'Boner' today."

-- Retired Police Officer Jack McLamb, Operation Vampire Killer 2000, p 9.

http://www.goodnewsaboutgod.com/studies/political/newworld_order/world_order.htm

As Republican President, Bush spoke before Congress in 1990, delivering a speech which he entitled 'Toward a New World Order." The date in 1990 on which he delivered this speech, which was the **first time** a U.S. president had spoken **publicly** of the coming New World Order, was NO coincidence. It was September 11 - the infamous 9/11 - a date and event that would, eleven years later in 2001, be used by the New World Order – the Zionist Jewish elitists/Illuminati – to steal by fraud, Americans' God-given and Constitutional rights.

Dr. John Coleman's- The Committee of 300: (see- The Conspirator's Hierarchy: The Committee of 300, 4th edition)

152

ANNUIT COEPTIS 'announcing conception'

Illumined eye Great architect 'Lucifer'

NOVUS ORDO SECLORUM 'Secular New Order'

13 letters in motto **E PLURIBUS UNUM** 'One of Many'

13 illuminated Stars - 13 enlightened Colonnies

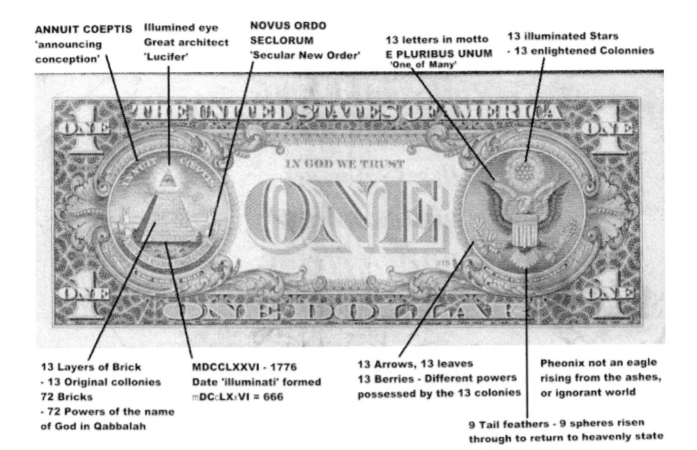

13 Layers of Brick - 13 Original collonies 72 Bricks - 72 Powers of the name of God in Qabbalah

MDCCLXXVI - 1776 Date 'illuminati' formed mDCcLXxVI = 666

13 Arrows, 13 leaves 13 Berries - Different powers possessed by the 13 colonies

Pheonix not an eagle rising from the ashes, or ignorant world

9 Tail feathers - 9 spheres risen through to return to heavenly state

Reading Clockwise Starting with A = ASMON The Anagram For: MASON or FREEMASON

Masonic All Seeing Eye

Pyramid is a Phallic Symbol

NOVUS ORDO SECLORUM = A New Order Of The Ages = THE NEW DEAL Understood by the Illuminati as: 'The New World Order' under Their Control

Anyone see the 11,13,and 33 in this Microsoft logo?

Money is the god of our time, and Rothschild is his prophet," wrote the German philosopher Heinrich Heine.

33 flourishes = 33rd degree.

Federal Reserve, why is USA money controlled by a non government body?

Federal Reserve Note anagram = **A Refereed Lovers Net.** Vast election fixing scheme, which give them the ability to determine the outcome of any election. How? Each $10 bill is a veiled threat - Do as you're told or loved ones disappear.

B2, a level in the Common European Union of Reference for Languages. NWO.

First United States Secretary of the Treasury - Pyramid on his tomb

An Eagle playing the piano is a classic Illuminati insignia, symbolizing the mastery over the bird kingdom through the power of repetition and tones.

Pyramid = **Eye of Providence**

In God We Trust Anagram = **Winged Tutors.** Refers to the diety Baphomet.

Demon Face in Tree tops - **The Owl God** of Bohemian Grove?

8(number of 10s front and back)**x10=80** The atomic number of mercury, the only liquid metal and highly toxic.

According to Exodus 7:7, Moses was 80 years old when he first talked to Pharaoh. Egypt = Pyramids.

10+10+10+10=40 The planet Venus forms a pentagram in the night sky every eight years with it returning to its original point every 40 years with a 40 day regression

8 Pillars. In 8 AD - Vonones I becomes king of Parthia.

'Ten Dollars' Anagram: **Last Lord En** Lord En is one of the Illuminati deities. We only know his name. Not much more.

Seals like the one used in the Great Seal of the United States can be traced back to at least 4,000 BC in Egypt, Babylon, Assyria and India."

- David Icke, "The Biggest Secret" (353)

The word "money" comes from the Lunar cults. Early words for the Moon were "mon" and "min" giving us "money" printed at a "mint." We have a global "monarchy" that controls the world's "money" supply. We have finance "ministers," prime "ministers" and their "ministries" being controlled by occult elites/societies. "Monks" perform "monthly ceremonies" in "monasteries." It is interesting to note that the plant "mint" is green, our "money" printed at the "mint" is green, and the Isis moon goddess Statue of Liberty is green. Someone who is ignorant is green. Moon-lovers are "lunatics," from the French; they are "monsters." You can see how the elite esoterically worship the moon continuing the Lunar cult, while exoterically condemning and marginalizing it. "You will see beneath the pyramid seventeen seventy-six, spelled out in Roman Numerals, plus the words, Annuit Coeptis, and is translated as Annuit, our enterprise. Coeptis is translated to mean 'crowned with success,' or 'is crowned with success;' therefore, Annuit Coeptis is 'our enterprise, which is now a success.' Then in order to find out what enterprise was a success, read on the one dollar bill at the bottom of the pyramid, Novus Ordo Seclorum. Which translates as the 'New Order of the World' The New World Order! Now, we must remember that Germany was the home of the concept of The New World Order. Adolph Hitler's entire motivation was to establish a new world order."

-- Jordan Maxwell, "Matrix of Power"

Corporate America

The United States OF America is a Corporation Owned by Foreign Interests
- Below are two articles covering the fact that, since the Act of 1871 which established the District of Columbia, we have been living under the UNITED STATES CORPORATION which is owned by certain international bankers and aristocracy of Europe and Britain.

In 1871 the Congress changed the name of the original Constitution by changing ONE WORD -- and that was very significant as you will read. -
- by TheUnjustMedia.com -
(Posted here: Tuesday, September 25, 2007)
[Permanently archived here: [International Banking]

http://www.illuminati-news.com/2007-09.htm

155

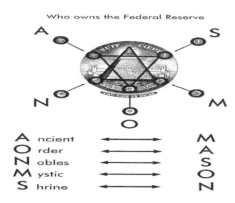

Who owns the Federal Reserve

Ancient ⟷ **M**
Order ⟷ **A**
Nobles ⟷ **S**
Mystic ⟷ **O**
Shrine ⟷ **N**

Jordan Maxwell,

"Matrix of Power"

Q: Who owns the Federal Reserve?
A: The Federal Reserve system, commonly called the Fed, has risen to the top of many people's thoughts lately.

Concerns over whether the housing slowdown and mortgage mess will push the economy into a dangerous position has many investors hoping the Fed will help. But who is the Fed and who owns it?

The Fed is the nation's central bank. Here's how the Fed describes its status: "It is an independent entity withing the Federal government." The Fed was created by an act of Congress on Dec. 23, 1913 and it is subject to oversight by Congress. The Fed has a seven-member Board of Governors based in Washington D.C. Board members are appointed by the President and confirmed by the Senate for 14-year terms.

The seven Board members make up a majority of the 12-member Federal Open Market Committee, which is the body charged that makes decisions about monetary policy — the nation's short-term interest rates and money supply. The other five voting members of the Open Market Committee rotate among the heads of the 12 Federal Reserve Banks, located in major cities. These banks issue stock to member banks, which is a condition of these banks being part of the Federal Reserve system. But the Fed is not operate for profit. For more details, check out "Who owns the Federal Reserve" on the Fed's website.

The Latin translation of Annuit Coeptis Novus Ordo Seclorum is "Our New World Order is Crowned with Success."

The other Latin phrase Et Pluribus Unim means "One Out of Many." Order out of Chaos. The Hegelian dialectic. The problem-reaction-solution paradigm used by the elites to drive world events, opinions and policies. There are 13 letters in Annuit Coeptis and 13 letters in Et Pluribus Unim.

The dollar encodes the number 13 repeatedly. There are 13 stars above the eagles head, 13 steps on the Pyramid, 13 vertical bars on the shield, 13 horizontal stripes at the top of the shield, 13 leaves on the olive branch, 13 arrows, 13 fruits, and 13 numbers.

"You will find on the dollar bill, the eagle, which comes from the ancient concept of the Phoenix, and has thirteen stars above it. The thirteen stars are arranged in the configuration of the Star of David, or the hexagram. Most people think the thirteen stars represent the original thirteen colonies. In the first place, why did they have to have thirteen colonies? Why couldn't they have twenty-seven, or four, or ten?

When one understands that the number thirteen is a very important, profound Masonic number, and that many of the founding fathers of this country were Freemasons, as well as Rosicrucians, then you will follow this connecting thread of material to see what was actually being created. They knew what they were doing when they divided this country into thirteen colonies. The number thirteen is not an unlucky number for them. It is an unlucky number for you."

-- Jordan Maxwell, "Matrix of Power"

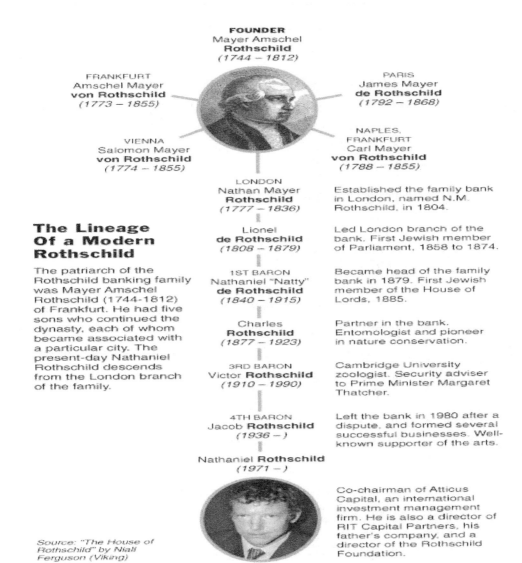

FOUNDER
Mayer Amschel
Rothschild
(1744 — 1812)

FRANKFURT
Amschel Mayer
von Rothschild
(1773 — 1855)

PARIS
James Mayer
de Rothschild
(1792 — 1868)

VIENNA
Salomon Mayer
von Rothschild
(1774 — 1855)

NAPLES,
FRANKFURT
Carl Mayer
von Rothschild
(1788 — 1855)

LONDON
Nathan Mayer
Rothschild
(1777 — 1836)

Established the family bank in London, named N.M. Rothschild, in 1804.

The Lineage Of a Modern Rothschild

The patriarch of the Rothschild banking family was Mayer Amschel Rothschild (1744-1812) of Frankfurt. He had five sons who continued the dynasty, each of whom became associated with a particular city. The present-day Nathaniel Rothschild descends from the London branch of the family.

Lionel
de Rothschild
(1808 — 1879)

Led London branch of the bank. First Jewish member of Parliament, 1858 to 1874.

1ST BARON
Nathaniel "Natty"
de Rothschild
(1840 — 1915)

Became head of the family bank in 1879. First Jewish member of the House of Lords, 1885.

Charles
Rothschild
(1877 — 1923)

Partner in the bank. Entomologist and pioneer in nature conservation.

3RD BARON
Victor **Rothschild**
(1910 — 1990)

Cambridge University zoologist. Security adviser to Prime Minister Margaret Thatcher.

4TH BARON
Jacob **Rothschild**
(1936 —)

Left the bank in 1980 after a dispute, and formed several successful businesses. Well-known supporter of the arts.

Nathaniel **Rothschild**
(1971 —)

Co-chairman of Atticus Capital, an international investment management firm. He is also a director of RIT Capital Partners, his father's company, and a director of the Rothschild Foundation.

Source: "The House of Rothschild" by Niall Ferguson (Viking)

The New York Times; Culver Pictures (top), Jack Guez/Agence France-Presse — Getty Images (above)

I was wondering what their net worth is. According to Forbes it's just $1.5 billion in total (for the whole family). Even though it is said that they were estimated to be worth $6 billion in 1850. I would find it hard to believe that such shrewd business family would lose such an incredible amount of value during the last century and a half. It's even rumoured that around the 1850's that they owned half of the world finance. But I don't know if that is confirmed financially.
Btw... 1 dollar now is worth (has the buying power of) about what 4 cents was worth in 1913, due to inflation over the last century according to republican congressman Ron Paul. So $6 billion in 1913 would be equivalent to more than $150 billion today.
and according to the website I linked above, $6 billion in 1913 would be equivalent to $1.9 trillion today!!
There are even rumors that they're worth $100 trillion!!!. Now what is real??? What are they really worth??? According to Forbes the richest man in the world is Bill Gates, and the Richest family is the Walton family. The Rotschilds are somewhere down the line, but in the top 100 though.. Well if that's true, then they've lost at least 98% of their fortune since 1850. Now I find that hard to believe.

157

The Protocols is full of Talmudic contempt for non-Jews.

"How clear is the undeveloped power of thought of the purely brute brains of the goyim... What could have been simpler than to take the money they wanted from their own people? "... We will put an end to those abuses to which we owe our mastery over the goyim, but which cannot be allowed in our Kingdom." (178) (I am using the L. Fry edition of The Protocols, entitled Waters Flowing Eastward, available from gsgbooks@mindspring.com)
http://www.bibliotecapleyades.net/bloodlines/rothschild.htm

Farrakhan and Hip-Hop: A Not-So-Odd Couple
by Salim Muwakkil

June 12-13, 2001
New York, New York

Well, for one thing, Congress is making noises about legislation that could drastically affect the hip-hop industry's bottom line. A bill proposed by Sen. Joe Lieberman (D-Conn.), called the "Media and Market Accountability Act," threatens to restrict mainstream access to rap music. And there are other signs of governmental hostility. The Federal Communications Commission recently fined a station in Colorado Springs, Colo., for playing a record titled "The Real Slim Shady" by white rapper Marshall "Eminem" Mathers.

Farrakhan's verbal audacity was a perfect fit for the aggressive, "no sell-out" attitude of rap music. "One rap song from you is worth more than 1,000 of my speeches," he told the crowd at the summit. "You are the new leadership. Will you accept your responsibility as a leader?"

So, you thought you were pretty well informed by now about all of the main players on the 'conspiracy' playing field? You've maybe been hearing for years about (or bumped into on your own) the various elements of society who control our world from behind the scenes.

You've gotten familiar with the role played by, for instance, the **Khazarian Zionists** (who invented the word 'Jew' to disguise their adopted heritage, as distinguished from the biblical Judeans), or the role played by the **Banksters** (banking gangsters) controlling the economies of the world, by the **CFR** (Council on Foreign Relations), the **Trilateral Commission**, the **Bilderbergers**, the **Committee of 300** (the 17 wealthiest so-called **'elite' families**) -- the **Rothschild's** in England and **Rockefellers** in America and **Bronfman's** in Canada, and on and on, comprising the physical power structure of the **New World Order** puppets under the direction of darkly motivated, other-dimensional 'master deceivers' commonly known as Lucifer or Satan and their 'fallen angel' cohorts. http://www.whale.to/b/pope.html

158

Farrakhan challenges the hip hop community

The freedom of speech is one thing, but freedom is not license. That's what is wrong in American society. You can say anything you want to without care for how it affects anything. That is not freedom. That is license. You say, "I'll do anything I want to do. I'll say anything I want to say because I'm grown. Don't nobody tell me what to do." That attitude is revolutionary, it is really shaking up the parents and it is probably the right attitude to break from the old, but it is not the right attitude to come into the new. The elders are rejecting the youth because the youth are not listening to them and the youth are doing something that the elders do not quite understand. Let me help the elders to understand what is going on here.

Snoop Dogg, T.I. Praise Louis Farrakhan At Nation Of Islam Convention

ROSEMONT, Ill. — *Rapper Snoop Dogg made an appearance Sunday at the Nation of Islam's annual Saviours Day convention, praising Minister Louis Farrakhan and suggesting that he is a member of the movement.*

Snoop, whose real name is Calvin Broadus, gave a $1,000 donation to the Nation and said he will always seek the minister out.

The rapper called himself the "leader of the hip-hop community" and said it was his first Saviours Day event. He told followers that he would share the information he gathered with other musicians.

"When you get a speech from Minister Farrakhan it's about a mirror, it's about looking at yourself," the rapper later told The Associated Press. "It's about seeing yourself and what you can do to better the situation ... We're doing a lot of wrongs among ourselves that need correcting."

During his annual Savior's Day Speech in a Chicago suburb on Sunday, Nation of Islam leader, minister Louis Farrakhan tee'd off on Rihanna calling her style, dress, lyrics and dancing unacceptable. Farrakhan? Causing controversey? Naaaaaaaaah! Not him. lol. In his tirade he went as far as to call the entertainer "filthy" and her fans "swine." Don't you just love when he uses that word? It seems like he's expanded it to unclude not only his most common target in homosexuals but now all things "filthy."

Today do we see people making evil fair seeming ... has no power, only when you give it to him...he has no power over you...his defense will be. ... So I would say that the Devil has made evil fair seeming to many people. ...

Essays Explaining What Has Happened to this World

By: Nicole Terry PH: 717-497-5231 Email: Nicole@Boxemail.com

The documents listed below, plus hundreds more and numerous Essays explaining what has happened to this World are available on Disks for FREE. The documents are not secret. They are all on the Public Record. All of the Cases and Documents listed below are on the Disks so you can see them for yourself. Just contact me (Nicole Terry) and I will be glad to send them to you.

What would happen to someone who played a major role in the discovery and publication of the following facts?

1. The IRS is not a U.S. Government Agency. It is an Agency of the IMF. (Diversified Metal Products v. IRS et al. CV-93-405E-EJE U.S.D.C.D.I., Public Law 94-564, Senate Report 94-1148 pg. 5967, Reorganization Plan No. 26, Public Law 102-391.)

2. The IMF is an Agency of the UN. (Blacks Law Dictionary 6th Ed. Pg. 816)

3. The U.S. has not had a Treasury since 1921. (41 Stat. Ch.214 pg. 654)

4. The U.S. Treasury is now the IMF. (Presidential Documents Volume 29-No.4 pg. 113, 22 U.S.C. 285-288)

5. The United States does not have any employees because there is no longer a United States. No more reorganizations. After over 200 years of operating under bankruptcy it's finally over. (Executive Order 12803) Do not personate one of the creditors or share holders or you will go to Prison. 18 U.S.C. 914

6. The FCC, CIA, FBI, NASA and all of the other alphabet gangs were never part of the United States government. Even though the "US Government" held shares of stock in the various Agencies. (U.S. V. Strang, 254 US 491, Lewis v. US, 680 F.2d, 1239)

7. Social Security Numbers are issued by the UN through the IMF. The Application for a Social Security Number is the SS5 form. The Department of the Treasury (IMF) issues the SS5 not the Social Security Administration. The new SS5 forms do not state who or what publishes them, the earlier SS5 forms state that they are Department of the Treasury forms. You can get a copy of the SS5 you filled out by sending form SSA-L996 to the SS Administration. (20 CFR chapter 111, subpart B 422.103 (b) (2) (2) Read the cites above)

8. There are no judicial courts in America and there has not been since 1789. Judges do not enforce Statutes and Codes. Executive Administrators enforce Statutes and Codes. (FRC v. GE 281 US 464, Keller v. PE 261 US 428, 1 Stat. 138-178)

9. There have not been any Judges in America since 1789. There have just been Administrators. (FRC v. GE 281 US 464, Keller v. PE 261 US 428 1Stat. 138-178) 10. According to the GATT you must have a Social Security number. House Report (103-826)

STATES IS A CORPORATION, NOT A LAND MASS AND IT EXISTED BEFORE THE REVOLUTIONARY WAR AND THE BRITISH TROOPS DID NOT LEAVE UNTIL 1796.) Respublica v. Sweers 1 Dallas 43, Treaty of Commerce 8 Stat 116, The Society for Propagating the Gospel, &c. V. New Haven 8 Wheat 464, Treaty of Peace 8 Stat 80, IRS Publication 6209, Articles of Association October 20, 1774.)

- **10**. We have One World Government, One World Law and a One World Monetary System. (Get the Disks)

11. The UN is a One World Super Government. (Get the Disks)

12. No one on this planet has ever been free. This planet is a Slave Colony. There has always been a One World Government. It is just that now it is much better organized and has changed its name as of 1945 to the United Nations. (Get the Disks)

13. New York City is defined in the Federal Regulations as the United Nations. Rudolph Giuliani stated on C-Span that "New York City was the capital of the World" and he was correct. (20 CFR chapter 111, subpart B 422.103 (b) (2) (2)

14. Social Security is not insurance or a contract, nor is there a Trust Fund. (Helvering v. Davis 301 US 619, Steward Co. V. Davis 301 US 548.)

15. Your Social Security check comes directly from the IMF which is an Agency of the UN. (Look at it if you receive one. It should have written on the top left United States Treasury.)

16. You own no property, slaves can't own property. Read the Deed to the property that you think is yours. You are listed as a Tenant. (Senate Document 43, 73rd Congress 1st Session)

17. The most powerful court in America is not the United States Supreme Court but, the Supreme Court of Pennsylvania. (42 Pa.C.S.A. 502)

18. The Revolutionary War was a fraud. See (22, 23 and 24) 20. The King of England financially backed both sides of the Revolutionary war. (Treaty at Versailles July 16, 1782, Treaty of Peace 8 Stat 80)

19. You cannot use the Constitution to defend yourself because you are not a party to it. (Padelford Fay & Co. v. The Mayor and Alderman of The City of Savannah 14 Georgia 438, 520)

20. America is a British Colony. (THE UNITED STATES IS A CORPORATION, NOT A LAND MASS AND IT EXISTED BEFORE THE REVOLUTIONARY WAR AND THE BRITISH TROOPS DID NOT LEAVE UNTIL 1796.) Respublica v. Sweers 1 Dallas 43, Treaty of Commerce 8 Stat 116, The Society for Propagating the Gospel, &c. V. New Haven 8 Wheat 464, Treaty of Peace 8 Stat 80, IRS Publication 6209, Articles of Association October 20, 1774.)

- **21**. Britain is owned by the Vatican. (Treaty of 1213)

22. The Pope can abolish any law in the United States. (Elements of Ecclesiastical Law Vol.1 53-54)

23. A 1040 form is for tribute paid to Britain. (IRS Publication 6209)

24. The Pope claims to own the entire planet through the laws of conquest and discovery. (Papal Bulls of 1455 and 1493)

25. The Pope has ordered the genocide and enslavement of millions of people. (Papal Bulls of 1455 and 1493)

26. The Popes laws are obligatory on everyone. (Bened. XIV., De Syn. Dioec, lib., ix., c. vii., n. 4. Prati, 1844) (Syllabus, prop 28, 29, 44)

27. We are slaves and own absolutely nothing, not even what we think are our children. (Tillman v. Roberts 108 So. 62, Van Koten v. Van Koten 154 N.E. 146, Senate Document 43 & 73rd Congress 1st Session, Wynehammer v. People 13 N.Y. REP 378, 481)

28. Military Dictator George Washington divided the States (Estates) into Districts. (Messages and papers of the Presidents VO 1, pg. 99. Webster's 1828 dictionary for definition of Estate.)

29. "The People" does not include you and me. (Barron v. Mayor & City Council of Baltimore. 32 U.S. 243)

30. The United States Government was not founded upon Christianity. (Treaty of Tripoli 8 Stat 154.)

31. It is not the duty of the police to protect you. Their job is to protect the Corporation and arrest code breakers. Sapp v. Tallahassee, 348 So. 2nd. 363, Reiff v. City of Philadelphia, 477 F.Supp. 1262, Lynch v. N.C. Dept of Justice 376 S.E. 2nd. 247.

32. Everything in the "United States" is For Sale: roads, bridges, schools, hospitals, water, prisons airports etc. I wonder who bought Klamath Lake. Did **anyone take the time to check? (Executive Order** 12803)

33. We are Human capital. (Executive Order 13037)

34. The UN has financed the operations of the United States government for over 50 years and now owns every man, women and child in America. The UN also holds all of the Land in America in Fee Simple. (Get the Disks for the Essay and Documents.)

35. The good news is we don't have to fulfill "our" fictitious obligations. You can discharge a fictitious obligation with another's fictitious obligation. (Get the Disks)

● **36**.   The depression and World War II were a total farce. The United States and various other companies were making loans to others all over the World during the Depression. The building of Germany's infrastructure in the 1930's including the Railroads was financed by the United States. That way those who call themselves "Kings," "Prime Ministers," and "Furor," etc., could sit back and play a game of chess using real people. Think of all of the Americans, Germans etc. who gave their lives thinking they were defending their Countries which didn't even exist. The millions of innocent people who died for nothing. Isn't it obvious why Switzerland is never involved in these fiascoes? That is where the "Bank of International Settlements" is located. Wars are manufactured to keep your eye off the ball. You have to have an enemy to keep the illusion of "Government" in place. (Get the Disks and see the Documents for yourself.)

37. The "United States" did not declare Independence from Great Britain or King George. (Get the Disks for Documents and Essay.)

38.   Guess who owns the UN? The disks have many more cites including Hundreds of Documents to verify the 40 statements above and numerous other facts.   The Disks also include numerous Essays written by Stephen Ames and several other people that fully explain the 40 above mentioned facts.   The Disks will clear up any confusion and answer any questions that you may have.   The cites listed above are only the tip of the iceberg. Also included on the Disks are several hundred legal definitions because without them it is next to impossible for the non-lawyer to understand many of the Documents.   Simple words such as "person" "citizen" "people" "or" "nation" "crime" "charge" "right" "statute" "preferred" "prefer" "constitutor" "creditor" "debtor" "debit" "discharge" "payment" 'law" "United States," etc, do not mean what most of us think because we were never taught the legal definitions of the proceeding words. The illusion is much larger than what is cited above.

There is no use in asking an Attorney about any of the above because: "His first duty is to the courts...not to the client."   U.S. v Franks D.C.N.J. 53F.2d 128.   "Clients are also called "wards of the court" in regard to their relationship with their attorneys." Spilker v. Hansin, 158 F.2d 35, 58U.S.App.D.C. 206. Wards of court. Infants and persons of unsound mind. Davis Committee v. Lonny, 290 Ky. 644, 162 S.W.2d 189, 190. Did you get that? An Attorneys' first duty is not to you, and when you have an Attorney you are either considered insane or an infant.

The United States is still a British Colony.

The Truth is sometimes stranger than fiction!

. the United States of America might **still** be **the British colonies**.

In This Photo: <u>Chuck D</u>, <u>Flavor Flav</u>, <u>Professor Griff</u>
(L-R) Chuck D, Professor Griff and Flavor Flav, of Public Enemy perform during the Vegoose music festival at Sam Boyd Stadium's Star Nursery Field October 27, 2007 in Las Vegas, Nevada.
(October 27, 2007 - Photo by Ethan Miller/Getty Images Entertainment)

5th DEGREE

Pimps, Preachers Politicians Pedophiles and the Pulpit

"We need a program of psycho-surgery and political control of our society. The purpose is physical control of the mind. Everyone who deviates from the given norm can be surgically mutilated. The individual may think that the most important reality is his own existence, but this is only his personal point of view. This lacks historical perspective. Man does not have the right to develop his own mind. This kind of liberal orientation has great appeal. We must electrically control the brain. Someday, armies and generals will be controlled by electrical stimulation of the brain."

-- Dr. Jose Delgado, MKULTRA

2 Timothy 3:1-5 *This know also, that in the last days perilous times shall come. For men shall be lovers of their own selves, covetous, boasters, proud, blasphemers, disobedient to parents, unthankful, unholy, without natural affection, trucebreakers, false accusers, incontinent, fierce, despisers of those that are good, traitors, heady, high-minded, lovers of pleasures more than lovers of God; having a form of godliness, but denying the power thereof: from such turn away.*

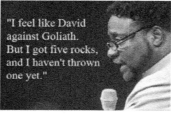

http://straightfromthea.com/2011/05/26/bishop-eddie-long-is-out-of-rocks-settlement-reached-sex-scandal/

Most informed brothers and sisters in the Black community know that there are any number of prominent white-sex offenders in the Black community. However, many of our people do not understand why these freaks have become so wealthy and influential in our community. This discussion forum is not going to focus on the particular problem of white-sex in the Black world community. We have discussed this issue extensively. For an in-depth discussion and analysis of white-sex, please click on the following posts: http://waronthehorizon.com/site/?p=1443

Most of us have heard about **Bishop Eddie Long's homophillic abuse** of the (4) young Black brothers who've accused him of sexually abusing them as teens. Eddie Long is a known white-sex offender, just like many other prominent Black preachers and political figures in the Black community. Four (4) of the known white-sex offenders in the Black community who come to mind are Tyler Perry, Oprah Winfrey, T. D. Jakes, and Barack Obama. Like Eddie Long, each of them share a significant amount of support from the Black world community. Like Eddie Long, each of them has been put into their position in order to promote and spread white-sex among Afrikan people. Like Eddie Long, none of them care about the well-being of Black people whatsoever. And like Eddie Long, each of them are mere puppets on the end of the white, so-called jew string of dominance and control.

Our children are led to believe freedom comes with personal wealth. Athletes and entertainers are the carrots on the sticks to deliver unto us the illusion that money is a cure all.

For example, Heisman Trophy winner Ricky Williams came out of school and signed for millions and became instantly independently wealthy. The brother's first act as a gladiator was to put on a dress as the bride to racist New Orleans coach Mike Dick-ka. Ya know I ain't never seen a wedding and honeymoon where the bride didn't get screwed!

When whites claim that Elvis Presley is not dead, they're not talking 'bout that fat, drug addicted man who is now gone, but the process of Culture Banditry that is alive and well in Eminem, Britney Spears, Sting, the Rolling Stones, Madonna, Sanborn, Kenny G and the legions lining up to steal the culture of Afrikan people, enjoying wealth/power and respect after the theft from the people darker than blue.

We are mass media junkies, who must get a daily jolt of their barbarism, murder, sexual backwardness, and anti-Afrikan propaganda. Their mass media continues to "annihilate Afrikan Images" to stall our struggles for liberation. In addition they are managing and destroying our culture as they continue the "Black Holocaust." The Culture Bandits goal is to control our consciousness and produce Negro victims for exploitation.

It is critical that we understand; cartoons, radio, talk shows, television, music, videos movies, soap operas sports and fashions. We will watch that bastard "Amerikkkan Kulture" as it continues to destroy positive Afrikan images and culture. The Culture Bandit Watch is design to dissect and expose the enemy and the sellouts who enjoy a life of privilege because of the damage they do to we!

Wyclef Shot In The Hand In Haiti

Breaking News: Wyclef Jean Emcee-turned political figure was shot in the hand while in Haiti on Saturday night (19/03/2011).

The international musician was travelling in a vehicle with Busta Rhymes and Jimmy Rosemond when armed gunmen shot at his car. Luckily Wyclef was only shot in the hand and has been treated and released from hospital. No other members of his entourage were hit. Wyclef's team released this statement via his twitter.

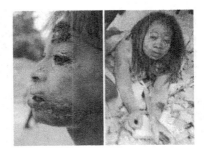

Jay-Z's 'Big Pimpin' regret provides 'blueprint' for hip-hop

If you were an internationally renown rapper with millions of dollars and a wife by the name of Beyonce, you would probably be pretty happy with your artistic choices, right? But apparently Jay-Z regrets Big Pimpin', his 1999 monster hit, for its unfortunate lyrics, an admission that retroactively spoils hundreds of Spring Breaks the nation over.

Jay-Z

Says Jay-Z, "Some [lyrics] become really profound when you see them in writing. Not Big Pimpin'. That's the exception. It was like, I can't believe I said that. And kept saying it. What kind of animal would say this sort of thing? Reading it is really harsh." Given that Jay-Z is older, wiser and madly in love with a talented bad-ass like Bee, lyrics such as "You know I thug em, f**k em, love em, leave em/Cause I don't f**king need em," probably seem like the height of douchebaggery. Then again, we all danced to it, so what does that say about us? Oh right, that we're douche bags too *http://showstoppaent.blogspot.com/2010/11/jay-z-regrets-big-pimpin-lyrics-what.html*

he follow up to Jay-Z's instant classic Blueprint (2001)

Actually the movie's called " Hustle and Flow", but I couldn't help my self but title it for its amazing theme song (its hard out here for a pimp), for it by the way, won best music theme song at the Oscars

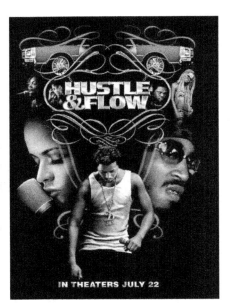

Members of Oscar-winning musical group THREE 6 MAFIA are 'pimping out' their Oscar around Los Angeles in order to gain access to the hottest nightclubs.

Grammy Award-winning producer and So So Def Records founder **Jermaine Dupri**, Rap-A-Lot Records founder **James "J Prince" Smith**, **Luther "Luke" Campbell** and **2Live Crew**, No Limit Records Founder **Master P**, and Atlanta-based production company **Organized Noize** are all being recognized through performances in collaboration with some of today's biggest stars.

Released as part of a blackmail scandal, Eve's sex tape features former boyfriend/producer Stevie J touching himself just out of frame (thanks), while pleasing his lady with a massive sex toy. The leaked footage may have been only 18 seconds long, but it was more than enough time to show Eve's freaky side and what exactly lies under the Pitbull's skirt.

Even though her famous actor father Laurence Fishburne is embarrassed by her porn career, Montana Fishburne says her mom still loves her, but doesn't want to see her dragged into the dark side of the porn industry. When asked about her mother,who has been divorced from Fishburne since Montana was two years old, here's what she had to say: "My mom just says, 'I love you.' We don't talk about it every day. She wants me to be happy and doesn't want me to get dragged into the dark side of porn." That dark side, Montana says, includes drugs and destructive behavior from "low self-esteem."

R. Kelly Trial: Sex Tape Is Played In Court; Judge Nearly Calls Mistrial After Witness Misspeaks
Judge has forbidden use of the word 'investigation.'

CHICAGO — As R. Kelly's child-pornography trial began in earnest on Tuesday morning (May 20), the prosecution and defense completed their opening arguments, and a juror who was the victim of a rape was removed from the jury. The removed juror had called the court to express concern over the financial hardship the trial would cause, according to the *Chicago Tribune*.

On Tuesday morning, the media was admonished by the judge, who said that anyone who recreates images from the sex tape could be charged with reproducing child pornography. This could cause legal difficulty for any members of the media who have played the tape in an effort to verify the identities of the people in it.

Unheard Interview With The Late Pimp C Reveals UGK Never Got Publishing For "Big Pimpin'" [Audio]

Flavor Flav, Master P.I.M.P., with Brigitte Nielsen and the late Anna Nicole Smith.

Chuck D and Flavor Flav

Flavor Flav congregates with the local chapter of Mensa

- **Unreleased Pimp C Interview Reveals UGK Was Uncredited For "Big Pimpin'"**

Pimp C

In an interview released on **HoodBoxOffice.com**, the late **Pimp C** talked about the song that got **UGK** national fame, the 1999 smash, **Jay-Z's** "Big Pimpin'."

Pimp C stated that Jay had the song and hook already mapped out, his plan was to put UGK on in order to reach a broader audience.

"What people have to understand is that was a Jay-Z song. Jay-Z had that song. He had the beat already, he had the hook already. It was going to be a hit with or without UGK. By putting us on it, he reached another market. He was able to get people involved that maybe would not have been so receptive to a happy-go-lucky tune like that."

The UGK rapper also noted that he and partner **Bun B** were fortunate to be on the record but their verses were works for hire and they did not receive any publishing for the song.

Jay-Z

"I still ain't got no platinum plaque for that song yet," he said. *"So right now, what I'm trying to do, I'm trying to get my plaque. And I'm not saying that's Jay-Z's fault. I'm saying that somewhere, the ball was dropped. Partly on our end, a whole lot on Def Jam's end. Let me get my plaque, man. 'Cause I go to the studio where it was recorded at and I see the plaque and I don't have one."*

UGK

Pimp C

169

From unexpected drama to shocking performances, MTV's 2009 Video Music Awards managed once again to raise eyebrows and get people talking. What most people missed, however, were the occult meanings encoded in the VMAs. The TV event was in fact a large scale occult ceremony, complete with an initiation, a prayer and even a blood sacrifice. We'll look at the symbolism that appeared during the show.

"Who wants to pray to the devil with me?

Jack Black comes out dressed as a heavy metal guy on steroids to promote a video game. At one point he asks the audience to put their devil horns in the air and the proceeds to pray to the "darklord Satan". The whole thing is light-hearted and comical but I don't see any other way a prayer to Satan can be inserted into a primetime show without getting a truckload of complaints from "concerned parents". The scene starts off semi-funny but Jack Black finishes off on a more serious note by saying: *"I ask you to grant tonight's nominees with continued success in the music industry"*. This last

phrase actually reveals a dark truth about the entertainment business. So the net result of this scene is this: everybody threw up their "devil horns" hand sign, then took each other's hands and prayed to Satan. This piece of pre-rehearsed comedy might have been an insignificant skit in another show. But in the context of this one, with its many recreations of occult rituals, the skit takes on a whole other, sinister meaning.

Beyonce to Sasha Fierce: Symbolic Occult Rebirth

"When I'm onstage I'm aggressive and strong and not afraid of my sexuality. The tone of my voice gets different, and I'm fearless. I'm just a different person."

Good Beyonce with cross

Evil Sasha Fierce mimicking devil horns

The Vigilant Citizen sez, "Sasha Fierce is wearing a metal plate featuring Baphomet's vehicule, [whose face] is also featured on the sigil of the Church of Satan."

"I have someone else that takes over when it's time for me to work and when I'm on stage, this alter ego that I've created that kind of protects me and who I really am".
-**Beyonce**

Pink is blindfolded and bound with ropes. Her costume exposes her left breast, as is the case with Masonic initiates. Instead of having her left leg exposed, Pink's costume bears a diamond pattern which is very reminiscent of the floors in Masonic lodges.

There is no way a Mason could watch this performance without recalling his initiation into the First Degree. Here's a description by Mark Stavish:

Pink's Masonic Initiation

"The blindfold used represents secrecy, darkness and ignorance as well as trust. The candidate is led into the lodge room for initiation but is not able to see what is happening. He is bound about the waist and arm with the cable tow."
-Mark Stavish, Freemasonry: Rituals, Symbols and History of the Secret Society

Taylor Swift's Initiation

Taylor Swift's Acceptance into the Order

Taylor Swift wins the "Best Female Video" award and goes up on stage to give her thank yous. Kanye West pops out of nowhere, taking the mic from her hand, and informs her that Beyonce has "one of the best videos of all time". This scene has caused much controversy and has earned Kanye the title of "Douchebag of the year" plus a the honor of being called a "jackass" by the President of the United States. I might shock some people by saying this... but this "unexpected" event was... STAGED! There I said it.

After Swift's public humiliation, Beyonce, the queen of the ceremony, calls her up on stage to let her "have her moment". She appears from backstage (as if awaiting her cue) in a red dress which is strikingly similar to Beyonce's. A reader of this site has noticed that, at the moment the two singers hug, a strange phrase appears on the screen behind them saying "RDFO IL 40 PRO DEL ATO". I have no idea what that means, but it was there. If you solve this enigma, be sure to post it in the comments.

Award ceremonies like the VMAs define and crystallize the pop culture of an era. They consecrate the chosen artists while leaving the others dwelling in the shadows of anonymity. As shown above, the whole show was heavily permeated with occult symbolism, primarily focusing on the "initiation" aspect of it. Why is MTV exposing young people (who know nothing about occultism) to such rituals? Is there a subliminal effect on the viewers? Are we educating the new generation to accept these symbols as part of popular culture? There is definitely a second layer of interpretation in many of MTV's products. To decode the symbols is to understand the inner-workings of the entertainment industry.

Nicki Minaj whips out a dildo on stage

During the 2011 VMAs, Nicki wore a Harajuku-inspired dress featuring mirror fragments (a Monarch symbol representing the fragmenting of personality). The combination of "kiddie" accessories with the sexiness of the dress' cut (it's "revealing" at the right places) is a little questionable.

http://vigilantcitizen.com/musicbusiness/the-2011-vmas-a-celebration-of-todays-illuminati-music-industry/

Nicki Minaj.........Decession

Nicki Minaj is already a created alter persona, very different from the real person that is Onika Tanya Maraj. The odd, fashion-crazy, surgically-enhanced persona that is Minaj is a made-for-the-music-industry character created to become a star. On top of that alter, there is Roman Zolanski, a male alter-ego that appeared on some songs and that will probably be appearing a lot more in the future. Roman Zolanski is based on Roman Polanski, the movie producer who was charged for rape by use of drugs and lascivious act upon a child under 14 a few years ago.

The Oprah Winfry show vid right I remember this.

On May 1, 1989, the Oprah Winfrey show had as its guest a person who, as a young girl, was forced to participate in a ritual in which a Christian infant was sacrificed. The amazing thing about this guest is that she was not affiliated with some unknown radical blood letting cult, but that She was a Jew. According to an article on the show in the Chicago Tribune, the woman was "undergoing long-term psychiatric treatment," apparently because of her horrible experience. The news paper article is quoted below in its entirety.

Jews Protest Sacrifice Tale on Oprah Show
Chicago Tribune, 5/7/89
New York Times News Service

"Hundreds of television viewers and the leaders of several Jewish and civil liberties organizations have protested allegations on a popular talk show last week that some Jews practice ritual killing of children.

The allegations were made by a guest using the pseudonym Rachel on 'The Oprah Winfrey Show,' a widely viewed syndicated talk show. During the program, broadcast Monday, Winfrey introduced the guest as someone who was undergoing long- term psychiatric ("The Jews are more subject to diseases of the nervous system than the other races and peoples among which they dwell. Hysteria and neurasthenia appear to be most frequent. Some physicians of large experience among the Jews have even gone so far as to state that most of them are neurasthenic and hysterical."

The History of Jewish Human Sacrifice

The knowledge of Jewish ritual murder is thousands of years old. It is as old as the Jews themselves. Non-Jews have passed the knowledge of it from generation to generation, and it has been passed down to us thorough writings. It is known of throughout the nation. Knowledge of ritual murder can be found in even the most secluded rural villages. The grand-father told his grand children, who passed it on to his children, and his children's children, until we have inherited the knowledge today from them.

(The Jewish Encyclopedia, Vol. IX, (1905), p. 225); "Idiocy and imbecility are found comparatively more often among Jews than among non-Jews...The Mongolian type of idiocy is also very frequently observed among Jews...Among the Jews the proportion of insane has been observed to be very large...Jews are more liable to acute psychoses of early age than are non-Jews." (The Jewish Encyclopedia, Vol. VI, (1904), p. 556, 603-04)) treatment for a multiple personality disorder.

The woman told Winfrey that she had witnessed the ritual sacrifice of children and had been a victim of ritualistic abuse.

"The guest also said of such practices: 'there's other Jewish families across the country. It's not just my family.' The assertions were made during a program that focused on the cult murders of at least 13 people whose bodies were found last month near Matamoros, Mexico.

The woman's comments provoked hundreds of angry phone calls and letters to Jewish and civil liberties groups, spokesmen for the groups said in interviews late last week. Jeffrey Jacobs, the chief operating officer of Winfrey's production company,

"Harpo Productions Inc., denied Winfrey had acted irresponsibly in broadcasting the interview since she had emphasized on the show that the guest spoke only for herself.

He added that Winfrey and her producers would meet with representatives of the Jewish and civil liberties groups next week in Chicago, where the show is taped.

Winfrey was traveling Friday, Jacobs said, and was unavailable for comment. Early in the interview Winfrey said, 'This is the first time I have heard of any Jewish people sacrificing babies, but anyway -- so you witnessed the sacrifice?'

"The woman responded: 'Right. When I was very young, I was forced to participate in that, and which I had to sacrifice an infant.'

The guest was repeatedly identified by Winfrey as being Jewish. At one point, the woman asserted that {Jewish} ritual sacrifices occurred in other Jewish families around the country and that they were known to the Police."

http://www.thewatcherfiles.com/jewish_sacrifice.htm
Loads of related content some of it disturbing.

6th DEGREE

Hood Treason, the Pacifi Antidote, Sou d Out at 10 off Certified Uncle Toms

and the hip hop 10 commandments

"Brainwashing is a system of befogging the brain so a person can be seduced into acceptance of what otherwise would be abhorrent to him. He loses touch with reality. Facts and fancy whirl round and change places. However, in order to prevent people from recognizing the inherent evils in brainwashing, the Reds pretend that it is only another name for something already very familiar and of unquestioned respect, such as education or reform."

-- Edward Hunter, Brainwashing, 1956

Lynching is a word synonymous with murder. Staten Island s NYOIL, tired of seeing the metaphorical death in the eyes of shorties around his block, decided to fight back by spittin truth. Voicing his frustrations through his edutainment style of MCing brought forth the October 2006 release of NYOIL s (pronounced N.Y. Oil) self-produced single Ya ll Should All Get Lynched.

"In the case of hip hop this moment not only represents a billion dollar industry (the likes of which have never been seen by the record and associated industries) but it also and more nefariously represents the most direct and, sans Slavery, effective means of controlling and culturally influencing the people.

This is why identifying Hip Hop as a moment is so vitally important! Recognizing a moment doesn't require emotional connection or favor; however, it does require a Keen eye and the ability to see historical patterns. It requires the ability to create and initiate strategy based on raw fact."

The HipHop culture has grown into a 10 billion dollar a year cash cow. Unfortunately, along with its growth came a monumental diversion from its original artistic standards and fundamental rules. Lost is the loyalty to the art form, and the desire to be true to ones roots and artistic expression. Found is the insatiable appetite for money, drugs, sex, and debilitating lifestyles.

Being a culture that had once prided itself on the **phrase "Keep It Real"**, the culture has adopted behaviors and lifestyles that are far from its most famous selling point. The new and improved marketing strategies of elements that reside outside the culture have created a "new monster". A monster that is comprised of an overdose of lyrical pornography, lyrical drug sales, thousands of digital murders and crimes, and topped with the senseless disrespect of women and the community from which the artist themselves were born.

The talent of the HipHop artist has the potential to carry a message and information that can bring about a redistribution of power on a global scale. Those who operate from a higher level of power consciousness are aware of this; those that characterize themselves as rap artists generally seem to be ignorant of this fact."

http://www.willielynchsnewestslave.com/

175

"In the case of hip hop this moment not only represents a billion dollar industry (the likes of which have never been seen by the record and associated industries) but it also and more nefariously represents the most direct and, sans Slavery, effective means of controlling and culturally influencing the people.

This is why identifying Hip Hop as a moment is so vitally important! Recognizing a moment doesn't require emotional connection or favor; however, it does require a Keen eye and the ability to see historical patterns. It requires the ability to create and initiate strategy based on raw fact."

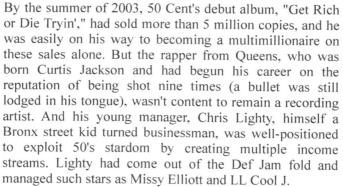

By the summer of 2003, 50 Cent's debut album, "Get Rich or Die Tryin'," had sold more than 5 million copies, and he was easily on his way to becoming a multimillionaire on these sales alone. But the rapper from Queens, who was born Curtis Jackson and had begun his career on the reputation of being shot nine times (a bullet was still lodged in his tongue), wasn't content to remain a recording artist. And his young manager, Chris Lighty, himself a Bronx street kid turned businessman, was well-positioned to exploit 50's stardom by creating multiple income streams. Lighty had come out of the Def Jam fold and managed such stars as Missy Elliott and LL Cool J.

With Lighty, 50 Cent created the "G-Unit" brand, including a record company, a clothing company and a sneaker deal with Reebok's RBK line. The G-Unit Clothing Company was a joint-venture deal, with hip-hop-influenced designer Marc Ecko fronting the money, handling the manufacturing and distribution, and splitting the profits fifty-fifty with 50.

It's a plethora of MCs young and old who are still on the front lines of social and political relevant conscious music; it's just that mainstream media is not allowing a particular brand of Hip Hop because they only want to propagate one ideal. And we have this ideal that those ten MC's that we hear in every rotation in mainstream mediums are what Hip Hop is. So if it's not in the mainstream it's apparently not in the bloodstream for a lot of people because they are allowing mainstream media to dictate what Hip Hop is or isn't for them. But we're still right here. MC's are still touring, still putting out records and a lot of people don't want to get back to that era especially corporate people and for social, economic and political reasons also. Basically, more so political reasons. So I say that it's a myth that we are not going to get back to that era. For me it's not a matter of getting back to that era. It's a matter of becoming aware of the fact that that era hasn't left us. It's still here **Wise Intelligent FINAL CALL INTERVIEW JUNE 2011!**

176

G: oh ok. So can we honestly say brining this thing up into a modern day understanding of this thing. That I have written that this 10% element these bloodsuckers of the poor are actually the illuminaty ? Right now, as we speak, there are over a half dozen people that I have listed that are on my list right now for me for me to talk to in reference to actually and that have come out against me but not mentioning my name. I'm not going to mention their name,but they actually call me everything in the book, but they basically said, this 10% element that we deal with is not necessarily true and there is no such thing as the iliminaty. What do you think about that?

W: I'm not debating whether the illuminaty exists , or not. I think the initial statement is manifesting and unfolding before our eyes everyday. So its like if we sit around and debate if this group exists or they don't exist. I think they are working right out in the open. I don't think this is a secret society I think this is a society of secrets. We know these people exist. We know that THEY R DOING WHAT THEY SAID THEY WERE GOING TO DO. For instance we can go all the way back to John Cecil Rhodes, founder of the Biers Diamond company.This guy in his will before he passed, he wrote his will out and you can get it off the internet, "confessions of faith", or u can purchase it in book form, but anyway in his will he said he is going to die and leave his wealth to see that the sun never sets on the British Empire. In that he said that Africa should be taken over, this was in the late 1700s, look at the the despicable vermin(he called the people of Africa) look at them and how they exist on that continen.He said what does this mean the taking over of Africa? Other than more land and more jobs for the greatest race of people on earth the European or the British,,so his thing was to take over Africa ,,,kill everybody off exterminate the people of Africa and the ones he didn't exterminate turn them into slaves. Basically and take the land and divvy it up between Europeans ,,,We saw that happen. He said why not create a secret society to carry out that end. There's a means to carry out that end. This is what John Cecil Rhodes said in 1785, when he died he left all his money /estate to the Rothchilds, and that agenda in their hands. So I'm not sitting around debating whether the illuminaty exists. I mean we have to really look at what's happening here. We have to look at the eugenics movement and how it started as a small hub in America.Now it's spread ,,,now its an international movement eugenics movement under the guise of international planned parenthood that is exterminating non white people all over the planet. We have the Georgia Guide stones in GA.

They say the stones put up by an anonymous group,that no one knows nothing about but ,,they are big as hell they r monolithic they are huge. In all of them in all I believe there are 4 different languages Egyptian hieroglyphics, Mandarin or Asian language, Sanscript, English , and Greek or Latin I believe,,,these stones say that they want to repopulate the earth,,,they want to remove 3.5 billion people from the planet,,,this was like when it was 4 billion people on planet,,,these stones were erected,,,so you are talking about killing that many people off ,,,they say they want to bring the population of the earth down to about a manageable 500 million people,this is what it says on the GA Guide stones,,,,and then when u tie that in to the eugenics movement and the massive international sterilization programs that are taking place and are how theyare being funded by major corporation s who are heavily rooted in the eugenics movement like Proctor and Gamble, with Charles Gamble back in the day he's the one who financed the eugenics movement in North Carolina,,,Haynes,,from the Haynes underwear co,these guys have now P and C, Pampers, and now all of those products that they own and sell there over in the Phillipines ,in Africa, in India ,,,everywhere,,,enforcing sterilization for humanitarian aid on indigenous people of those lands...so I'm not debating whether the Illuminaty exists,,we should be past that now,,,the proof of their exisitence is the fruit that is being bore that is taking place right in front of our eyes,,, not talking about what happened 250 yrs ago300 500yrs ago,,, I'm talkingabout what took place 250 300 seconds ago , 500 seconds ago,,, They are privatizing education they are moving your kids out of a position to where they can be taught anyting in your neighborhood,,, why is 80% of all sterilization clinics in a black community? Be for real.

This is not happenstance. This is not an accident .This is not bad legislation or bad policy. It is an agenda, a mission that has been take place for a looong time,,, this is just what it is ,,,so I'm not debating that, I'm not debating whether the illuminaty exists, ,,that's just a fact, I'm not going into all of the whole conspiracy conversation and all of that conspiracy theories,,,The entire American existence is a conspiracy. Black people should know that first and foremost we were brought here based on a conspiracyto enslave a nation and make another nation rich at our expense,,,Tuskegee experiement was a conspiracy,,the eugenics movement was a conspiracy,,,just like it's a conspiracy now to cold shut down all the public school and privatize them in this charter school lottery thing so we have this charter school lottery which is a private school system inside the public school system b/c their kid can't go to the charter school unless he gets in a lottery, so they are pushing more and more kids out of school and out of education if their parents cant afford it. So ,this is just what it is Man. I'm not big on the whole argument about the illuminati and whether they exist or not,,I know…I'm dealing with the fruit of their labor

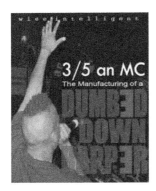

'Three-fifths an MC: The Manufacturing of a Dumbed Down Rapper." And the book goes in on how Hip Hop got this way. How did we get here and why are we here.Hip Hop didn't cause these problems. It was gang banging and drug dealing before 1976. These things were occurring long before Hip Hop. So we really need to get to the root causes of these things**Wise Intelligent FINAL CALL INTERVIEW JUNE 2011!**

HipHopDX: Your new joint, "Illuminati," addresses [Jay-Z's] long-rumored ties to that secret society, but you dismiss his inclusion in the Illuminati, or any other rapper's for that matter, as ridiculous. Why?

Wise Intelligent: I'm not dismissing inclusion, what I'm saying is it's irrelevant if they are. What would be the point? The Illuminati…goes way back to the Crusades, and way back before that. These people were about world conquest and world domination. And they've already dominated and conquered the world, and [so] there's no need to have a card carrying rapper member. What is the point? There's no point in it. What is the criteria? What would he be doing that would benefit an apparatus that has already conquered the world? I don't understand that; that just doesn't make sense to me.

I think we need to focus more attention on the fact that public schools are being shut down intentionally, to disenfranchise many urban youth, from whom Hip Hop came. If this is about Hip Hop and the youth that created Hip Hop and where Hip Hop comes from, and everybody talking about "this is where Hip Hop lives," we need to be focusing our attention on what's happening to the children that produced Hip Hop, that brought Hip Hop to the world. And we're not even talking about that, we're talking about Jay-Z. It's like, yo, Jay-Z is ill, Jay-Z is probably the illest emcee that ever wrote rhymes, but when we get right down to it, if we talking about the Illuminati…we need to get into what's happening in plain view.

My point was to bring the Illuminati out of the boogieman space. It's not a boogieman; it's legislators that are right now passing legislation that disenfranchises so many people. We're talking about 1% of the population in America controlling 50% of the wealth, controlling more wealth than 50% of the people here. We have 10% of the people all over the world making life miserable for 90% of the world and [all] we wanna talk about is Jay-Z gay, is Kanye gay? Are they in this secret society? It's not a secret society, it's right in your face. Everything they're doing is right in your face. Everything.

So, let's deal with that; let's deal with those things. Let's deal with all the sterilization programs they have going on around the world. Let's talk about that. Let's talk about the overthrowing of Egypt. Let's talk about the overthrowing of the Middle East right now. Let's talk about that! We don't wanna discuss these things. Let's talk about how mainstream corporations control what we see and hear everyday.

So my whole thing about the "Illuminati" [song], it's about a protest – protesting disenfranchisement of the large majority of the population of this planet. That's the bottom line. So Jay-Z don't have nothing to do with that. Jay-Z didn't start the eugenics programs. Jay-Z didn't do that.

http://www.hiphopdx.com/index/news/id.14226/title.wise-intelligent-talks-illuminati-and-why-jay-zs-membership-is-irrelevant

Hip Hop's (Unspoken) Ten Commandments

Thou must dis Black Women. You are allowed to distinguish between bitches, hoes and "real sisters" only during interviews when asked to clarify your statements. You must talk about beating a woman up at least once on your CD or demo. On at least four (4) but no more than five (5) singles/demos, you must talk about having rough and unprotected sex with a woman.

In 1810, Saartjie Baartman was brought to Europe from South Africa to be displayed as a sexual freak and example of the inferiority of the black woman. Baartman, who became known as the *Hottentot Venus*, was brought to Europe from Cape Town in 1810 by an English ship's surgeon who wished to publicly ...

Archetype. Synonyms. List the *Archetype* Characteristics. Classic Character. Some *Examples*. Modern Character

The original Archtype of The black mother Godess

Stylist: Angel Michelle

La Vénus hottentote (1814). Courtesy of the Bibliothèque Nationale, Paris.

This same Archtype model of Saartjie Baartman exist today

You must also refer to your girlfriend or wife as a "bitch" in an endearing way. All music videos must reflect the aforementioned notions. You can talk about doing things to other people's mothers as acts of creative statement. You may also refer endearingly to an unplanned child as a "bastard," "shorty," "lil' nigga," or "lil' G." By honoring this Commandment, you vow to never rally behind black females or support a strong family bond. You see her only as an object for sex and to reap the repercussions of your rage. You also believe she is only out to get you. *(Supplement for females)*

Thou must dis Black Men. Female rappers are allowed to distinguish between niggas, bustas, scrubs and punks. You must lyrically emasculate them in every way possible. On at least one (1) CD or demo, you must destroy his character by either calling him a homosexual or talking about his lack of money. You are allowed to refer to your boyfriend or husband as your "nigga" in an endearing way. All music videos must reflect aforementioned notions. By honoring this Commandment, you vow to never identify with the black male's struggle against white supremacy. You vow to never support a strong family bond. You also uphold the tenements that all of his problems are of his own doing. You see him as only an object for sex and money. You believe he is only out to get you.

• Commandment II

Thou must kill. You must "lyrically" take the life of at least one other black person in order to secure a hit CD. This law does not promote the physical killing of another person. However, it is not against the law to assassinate another person on record. You must only talk about killing your own kind, however, or other cultures may sue you for inciting racial violence. You must express pleasure in the kill. The kill must be graphic and extensive in detail. The consumer must always be left with the feeling that taking a person's life (lyrically) was justified. Most of the lyrical murders must be done by guns; however creativity allows for poisoning, stabbings, beatings, stompings, and suffocating. You do not distinguish between male or female kills. By keeping this Commandment, you vow to never claim acts of genocide publicly even when you are a victim of violent repression yourself. You also agree to "lyrical" acts of black-on-black violence, as well as prolific incidents of brutality.

A28 SUNDAY, MAY 5, 2002

Choir children stand around the coffin carrying the remains of Saartjie Baartman upon her arrival Friday in South Africa.

France returns old remains to homeland

'Hottentot Venus' part of 'research'

By Rachel L. Swarns
New York Times

CAPE TOWN, South Africa — The young African woman was lured to Europe with false promises of fame and fortune. She was paraded naked before jeering mobs. She was exhibited in a metal cage and sold to an animal trainer. When she died in Paris in 1816, she was penniless and friendless among people who derided her as a circus freak.

White scientists intent on proving the inferiority of blacks dissected her body, bottled her brain and genitals, wired her skeleton and displayed them in a French museum. That might have been the end of Saartjie Baartman, the young African woman derisively labeled the "Hottentot Venus."

Lost soul

But to her people here, the descendants of the nomadic hunters who first wandered across this land centuries ago, death is never the end of the story.

"It is important for her to come back," said Jennifer Pieter, a 65-year-old descendant of the nomadic Khoisan people, who once hunted in loincloths and were often killed by white farmers who classified them as vermin. "She is one of ours."

Growing trend

All across the world, museums are taking similar steps to return human remains as they reassess collections acquired in an era when indigenous people were doomed worthy of scientific study, but unworthy of the consideration commonly accorded to whites.

Two years ago, Spain returned to Botswana the bones of an unidentified African man who had been stolen from his grave and displayed in its museums for nearly a century. Known simply as "El Negro," he was given a state burial in Botswana, where he was welcomed as a stolen ancestor and a lost soul.

In the United States, many museums are now returning remains of American Indians to their descendants.

In Australia, museum officials are still struggling to identify thousands of unidenti-

• Commandment III

Thou must covet. Thou must talk about lusting after things that do not belong to you. You must have an unusual craving for things that do not belong to you. Your desire must be so strong that you unwittingly uphold the second commandment. This law does not advocate you physically going after the material possessions of someone in your community. By keeping this Commandment, you vow to never promote a strong work ethic in your music or to speak against greed, lust and impulsive behavior. In fact, you now believe greed is healthy.

- **Commandment IV**

Thou must have a lot of sex. You must have no fewer than three (3) songs on your CD or demo that promote sexual intercourse with one or a group of individuals. You cannot express a deep sense of love or marriage. Thou shalt not talk about commitment, bonding, and intimacy. You can only talk about sex in its purest and rawest terms. Do not use "make love," or "provide pleasure "or" procreate." You must never mention a sexually transmitted disease in the context of these records. You can, however, discuss the use of contraceptives, but only if you're referring to sexual intercourse with a hoe. (See first Commandment). If you are under age 16, you may substitute sex with "flirting," and "fantasies about being intimate with your teacher, neighbor's child, or another rapper." You must be creative in your graphic detail of sexual intercourse so to leave nothing to the imagination. The details can be slightly skewered in order to circumvent radio censors. However, this does not excuse radio edits from removing references to sex. Therefore stay ahead of the game by using clever phrases with dual and triple meanings. By keeping this Commandment, you vow to never promote unconditional or agape love in your community, promote the Black family in a positive light, or uplift male/female relationships.

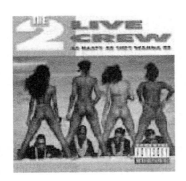

- **Commandment V**

Thou must celebrate the drug culture. Thou must condone and identify with the proliferation of drugs in the Black community. You should create endearing lyrical expressions to identify various narcotics and mind-altering substances. Though you are not to personally distribute or purchase illegal substances, you may allude to it lyrically. (To protect industry investment, we discourage musical confessions to crimes where the statue of limitations have not run out.) You may allude to a war on drugs, but only as justification to carry out the second commandment. You must continually suggest that selling drugs or "slangin" produces the only legitimate income for impoverished black people. All music videos must either glamorize this lifestyle by showing the "success" of the narcotic trade, or glamorize prison living. You should refer to drug addicted citizens in comical terms that illicit disgust, laughter, fear, pity or retribution. You are never to question U.S. drug policy. You can never promote healthy living and thinking. Nor can you advocate moderation in tobacco and liquor consumption. By keeping this Commandment, you vow to never discuss the impact of drug addiction among people of color or the community's overall health, its impact on the prison industrial complex, or its impact on the black family.

- **Commandment VI**

Thou must rarely talk about God and spirituality. You must lyrically condone atheism and a false belief system that negates the existences of a higher being. You must routinely question the existence of a god by lyrically challenging him/her/it to take your life or to grant you three wishes. You are to refer to yourself as a god who gives and takes life. You may lyrically create your own religion (see tenth commandment) based on a ghetto belief system. Thou shalt not talk about life and death as it relates to spirituality or a sense of purpose. You should never speak of scripture or religious texts. You are prohibited from acknowledging any spiritual beliefs that may have been instilled you by family. However, you may identify with a Jesus by wearing a large, diamond encrusted piece whereby you may brag about its cost. Under no circumstance are you to promote prayer, reflection, meditation, atonement, redemption, sacrifice, mercy or grace. The consumer fan base must identify with your lack of spiritual grounding by believing that the only gods are sex and money. By keeping this Commandment, you vow to limit your personal spiritual growth and development. You also vow to never been seen publicly in a church, synagogue, mosque, temple or other house of worship and reflection.

- **Commandment VII**

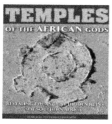

Thou must promote capitalism. On no fewer than four (4) singles or demo records you must talk about money as if it were a living, breathing thing. You must talk about making it, taking it and the love of it. Your lyrics must always place money over love, over women, over religion (see sixth commandment). You must never talking about savings and investing. Thou can, however, say the words "currency exchange," "welfare check," "first of the month," and "food stamps." You must never talk about pooling of resources. Thou can never equate capitalism with poverty. You must never mention the IMF, WTO or Federal Reserve. In fact, never mention banking or the stock market at all. Do not mention technology. Do not discuss taxing. Do not discuss the federal budget. (See Commandment V). You must promote individual wealth over community wealth. You should talk about all of your purchases, specifically naming makers/distributors of expensive jewelry, cars, clothing and liquor. Once you become a successful entertainer, you should purchase a very big house and no fewer than three (3) expensive cars. Publicly, you

182

Drug songs then and now......

Raekwon

Rick Ross

Anyone who pays close attention to hip-hop is familiar with coke rap. Artists like Raekwon and Scarface fuel intense yet favorable debates over their impressive rhyme styles and the moral quandaries their songs represent. Meanwhile, reformed drug dealers like 50 Cent, T.I. and Jay-Z dominate the charts. With the arrival of Teflon Don by Rick Ross, the Miami rapper that has earned increasing critical acclaim, its time to revisit 10 albums that exemplify how, to paraphrase the late dealer-turned-rap-kingpin Notorious B.I.G., the rap game is just like the crack game.

Here are the ten albums featured by Rhapsody as best representing the coke rap subgenre:

Camron: Purple Haze

Clipse: Hell Hath No Fury

Ice Cube: Death Certificate

Jay-Z: Reasonable Doubt

Killer Mike: I Pledge Allegiance To The Grind II

Raekwon: Only Built 4 Cuban Linx

Rick Ross: Port of Miami

Scarface: Greatest Hits

T.I. : Trap Muzik

- **Commandment VIII**

Thou cannot have a sense of history. Never, ever refer to any historical event that may cause the consumer to think about his/her relation to history. Your role is to entertain, not educate. Thou art prohibited from speaking of the following: Trans-Atlantic slave trade, African holocaust, Reconstruction, the civil rights movement, the Black Power Movement, the "real" Harlem Renaissance, and so forth. You can never mention the following people: Martin Luther King Jr, Hannibal, Mansa Musa, Harriet Tubman, Sojourner Truth, David Walker, Nat Turner, George Jackson, El-hajj Malik Shabazz (Malcolm X), Jesse Jackson, Patrice Lumumba, Nelson Mandela, Winnie Mandela, Steve Biko, Louis Farrakhan, Booker T. Washington, W.E.B. DuBois, Huey Newton, Fred Hampton, Bobby Seale, Kwame Ture, Ida B. Wells, Assata Shakur....unless you are making fun of their names, causes or crusaders. (i.e., Rah Digga's Harriet Thugman). Do not mention Africa, Brazil, the Caribbean or Asia, unless to disparage. By keeping this Commandment, you vow to never promote a sense of awareness, knowledge of self or the consumer's global relationship to kindred spirits.

- ### Commandment IX

Thou must not advocate. Thou art prohibited from advocacy of anything of social redeeming value. Your lyrics must reflect a detachment from the social, political and economic reality of your community. Your lyrics can occasionally ridicule people who march, protest and advocate social causes. The consumer should never assume that thou read newspapers, magazines or books. In other words it must appear that nothing that happens in the "real" non-entertainment world has any personal affect on your thinking. Nor should the consumer of your CD or demo walk away with the belief that you care about anything other than the Commandments IV and VII. Never talk about the "industry." By keeping this Commandment, understand you must never appear at a non-entertainment-related event, unless of course you are entertaining. You must never donate money, resources or materials to needy organizations, families or causes. When questioned about this you must defend your position by claiming you are an entertainer and that's all. You can never participate in interviews discussing relevant social issues. Thou art not responsible for the behavior encouraged by your music because thou art not responsible for marketing and sales to minor, unstable individuals, or mentally ill citizens. You understand that you cannot attend rallies, sermons, marches, and picnics, festivals or workshops that have nothing to do with entertainment or the recording industry.

- ### Commandment X

Thou must promote all things ghetto. You may never define the word ghetto or discuss its creation. You must uphold its principals and create new creeds. You must lyrically create a fictional account of ghetto living that inspires comradeship and a sense of pride among its residents. Your lyrics must create a ghetto dweller that is proud to live in the ghetto and takes offense at others moving into it. You must celebrate ghetto life by reminiscing about days in poverty and your mothers on welfare and about your fathers who were not there. Additionally, your lyrics must offer the mainstream a rare glimpse inside a "socio-economic matrix" while allowing them psychologically off the hook for the ghetto's creation. You must celebrate ghetto language, ghetto living, ghetto housing, ghetto clothing, ghetto hairstyles, ghetto sexual habits, ghetto education, and ghetto economics and ghetto self-hatred. You must romanticize poverty with tales of sex, drugs, money, greed and fear. The ghetto must become a magical place. By keeping this commandment you vow to create and then instill pride in a false culture of poverty, crime, drugs, illegitimacy, ignorance and apathy. You also vow to attribute the ghetto only to Black people. You also vow to never leave the ghetto matrix psychologically, even when your economic status changes (see seventh commandment). In other words you will remember to "keep it real…"

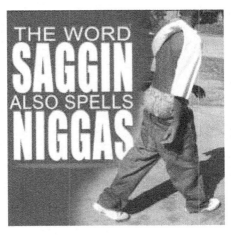

Hip Hop Hypocrisy: When Lies Sound Like the Truth, exposes the seduction of an entire generation by an intoxicated, violent, misogynistic subculture that arose out of gangs and prisons. I work with young people, as well as parents, educators, ministers, social workers, and counselors around the country to help improve academic performance and classroom management. For more information on our services, visit www.ACoachPowell.com. To participate in the dialogue, visit here often and share your ideas, questions, comments, and strategies.

- By keeping the aforementioned commandments we, "the industry," guarantee the following:

This sacred scroll must be handed to every potential and current Black hip hop artist in the nation. While some sign, many others I am sure others have refused, as there is circumstantial evidence that supports that. Occasionally a break through performer will offer lyrics that make us think act and believe as if we have purpose and are loved in this life. Yet the majority of our youth must be forced to sign, recite and then internalize these commandments in order to guarantee their market success. I imagine if they do not sign the doctrine, they are relegated to doing poetry readings at open mics, working menial jobs, fading into relative obscurity and living in the "ghetto matrix." This must be the answer, because the truth is surely a lot more painful.

By Stephanie Mwandishi Gadlin
StephGadlin@aol.com

1. Unlimited marketing success and cross-over appeal.

2. A guaranteed income

3. Fame beyond your wildest dreams

4. Unlimited (but recoupable) industry resources

5. Several music awards, citations and honors

6. Protection from community repercussions

Did Robert Johnson Sell His Soul to the Devil?

Johnson is that grand rarity in the music world—a recording artist from the 1930s who can sell millions of records in the modern day. He left his stamp on the work of almost every later blues musician, and Johnson's influence has also crossed over into the fields of rock, pop, folk and jazz. "From the first note the vibrations from the loudspeaker made my hair stand up," Bob Dylan writes in his memoir *Chronicles*. "I immediately differentiated between [Johnson] and anyone else I had ever heard." "Up until the time I was 25," Eric Clapton admits, "if you didn't know who Robert Johnson was I wouldn't talk to you."

But the rumors of Johnson's dealings with the devil are even more famous than his recordings. I've found that people who know nothing else about the blues, have often heard that story. When I tell a casual acquaintance that I write about the blues, a frequent response is: "Wasn't there that fellow who sold his soul to the devil?" Or: "I saw that movie about the guy who learned to play the blues from the devil."

7th DEGREE

Money, Madness, Music and Mayhem and the M.E.D.I.A.

multi-ethnic-destruction in amerikkka

"The American press, with a very few exceptions, is a kept press. Kept by the big corporations the way a whore is kept by a rich man."

-- Theodore Dreiser, 1871-1945

The remarks were apparently made by Swinton, then the preeminent New York journalist, probably one night in 1880. Swinton was the guest of honour at a banquet given him by the leaders of his craft. Someone who knew neither the press nor Swinton offered a toast to the independent press. Swinton outraged his colleagues by replying:

There is no such thing, at this date of the world's history, in America, as an independent press. You know it and I know it.

There is not one of you who dares to write your honest opinions, and if you did, you know beforehand that it would never appear in print. I am paid weekly for keeping my honest opinion out of the paper I am connected with. Others of you are paid similar salaries for similar things, and any of you who would be so foolish as to write honest opinions would be out on the streets looking for another job. If I allowed my honest opinions to appear in one issue of my paper, before twenty-four hours my occupation would be gone.

The business of the journalists is to destroy the truth, to lie outright, to pervert, to vilify, to fawn at the feet of mammon, and to sell his country and his race for his daily bread. You know it and I know it, and what folly is this toasting an independent press?

We are the tools and vassals of rich men behind the scenes. We are the jumping jacks, they pull the strings and we dance. Our talents, our possibilities and our lives are all the property of other men. We are intellectual prostitutes.

(Source: *Labor's Untold Story*, by Richard O. Boyer and Herbert M. Morais, published by United Electrical, Radio & Machine Workers of America, NY, 1955/1979.)

http://www.constitution.org/pub/swinton_press.htm

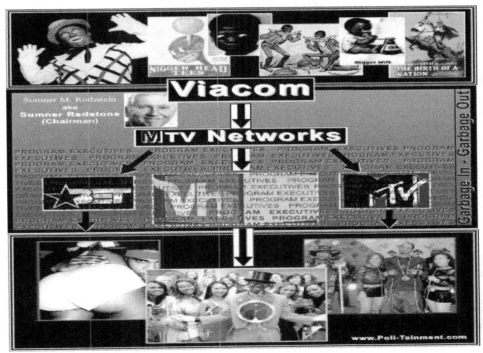

Death of hip hop culture

As Viacom networks push the machine agenda hip hop responded with unity and peace

West coast vs East coast peace

Songs that were designed to create an atmosphere of unity and peace i the hood

But never really caught on, and the little momentum id garnish the machine world struck back with these commercials to reset hip hop back to its animallistic mouse trap

2010 Kia Soul Hamster Commercial | Black Sheep Kia Hamsters Video

I really like the Kia Soul ad with the dancing hamsters. The music is amazingly catchy, you even found yourself bobbing your head to the beat. The personification of hamsters is ingenious. Everyone loves hamsters. They're cute, fuzzy, and adorable. Seeing them as rap loving and dancing with human qualities is something that people can relate to. They even wear shoes, jerseys; they look completely urbanized. It's also easy to remember because there isn't another ad on the market like this right now. Most car ads make the car look flashy, and don't really bring anything new to the table. This ad has modern music and characters that pull you into the commercial almost like a story. I didn't want to stop watching, I was mesmerized by it.

In last year's Super Bowl commercial from PepsiCo, the animated lizard mascots of SoBe Lifewater danced to Michael Jackson's "Thriller."
This year, the lizards will be making a 3D comeback as they dance with animated characters from the upcoming Dreamworks movie "Monsters vs. Aliens," including the extraterrestrial eggheads who aim to take over Earth, and the talking blob and other monsters recruited by the government to stop them.

188

*MONEY TALKS AND BULL SHIT RUNS THE MARATHON
Luke 16:13 "No servant can serve two masters. Either he will hate the one and love the other, or he will be devoted to the one and despise the other. **You cannot serve both Yahweh and Money**.

Matthew 6:24 No man can serve two masters: for either he will hate the one, and love the other; or else he will hold to the one, and despise the other. Ye cannot serve God and mammon - materialism.

"Eccentric." "Corrupt." "Evil." "Murderer."There are a lot of words that have been used to describe Libyan leader Colonel Muammar Gadhafi and members of his family. Thus far, "Beyoncé fan" hasn't generally been at the top of that list.

That's all changing now, thanks to reports that the Gadhafi family has spent major amounts of money -- we're talking six figures -- on lush and star-studded New Year's Eve parties featuring private concerts by American pop stars like Mariah Carey, Beyoncé, and Usher.Rumor has it that Muammar's youngest son Hannibal, who has been involved in a number of violent incidents in recent years, including physically abusing his wife and breaking her nose, paid Beyoncé a cool $2 million for her private performance. One year earlier, Mariah Carey reportedly received a $1 million paycheck for the same gig hosted by Hannibal's brother Moatessem.These concerts are just the beginning of a long list of the Gadhafi family's luxury expenses, many of which are detailed in a 2010 Wikileaks cable.

PAID $1 MILLION DOLLARS PER PEFORMANCE:

What do *Whitney Houston, Mariah Carey, Prince, Michael Jackson, Alicia Keys and Tina Turner* have in common? They have all been paid *$1 million dollars per performance* to entertain overseas royalty. In some cases, overseas *billionaire clients* are so anxious to book superstar talent, along with their astronomical fee, some artists have also received *tycoon cut diamonds, Ferrari's and Lamborghini's.* This is a exclusive *A-list club.*

The press which is controlled by the zionist jews, paint those that support black people in a very demonic way. Usin evry foul word in tere arsenol called the "English Language" which is a bastard language.

189

Beyonce says she donated Gaddafi performance fee

(Reuters) - U.S. singer Beyonce has said she donated the money she earned at a private party in 2009 to earthquake relief efforts in Haiti after learning the promoter had links to the family of Libyan leader Muammar Gaddafi.

The 29-year-old is the latest singer to distance herself from the Gaddafi clan, following international condemnation of his attempts to quell a rebellion in Libya and reports about stars who have performed for his entourage in recent years.

Earlier this week Canadian singer Nelly Furtado said she would give away $1 million she received to perform in Italy for the Libyan leader's family.

"All monies paid to Beyonce for her performance at a private party at Nikki Beach St. Barts on New Year's Eve 2009, including the commissions paid to her booking agency, were donated to the earthquake relief efforts for Haiti, over a year ago," Beyonce said in a statement posted on her website.

"Once it became known that the third party promoter was linked to the Qaddafi (Gaddafi) family, the decision was made to put that payment to a good cause."

Pressure on Gaddafi is growing as violence sweeps Libya.

The International Criminal Court prosecutor said on Thursday that Gaddafi, his sons and members of their inner circle could be held responsible for crimes by their security forces.

The United Nations Security Council imposed sanctions on Gaddafi and his family on Saturday, and referred Libya's crackdown on demonstrators to the court.

The music press has highlighted several famous singers who have performed for Gaddafi's clan, including his son Muatassim, in the last six years, often commanding large fees.

Forbes has released their list of top earning hip hop stars this week and it's little surprise that **Jay-Z** is wearing the crown of the kings listed. According to **Forbes**, Hova will owe about $22M in taxes for 2010, which is a little more than pocket change for most.

There are a few surprises in the list, including **Akon** who really hasn't done too much lately... and also **Kanye**, who apparently could borrow a few dollars from **Pharrell**.

Check out the entire article via **Forbes**.

Rap star Jay-Z came first in a list of the richest rappers in 2010, earning more than double that of runner-up Sean "Diddy" Combs.

Photograph by: Getty Images, Getty Images

Read more: http://www.canada.com/entertainment/tops+Forbes+list+richest+rappers/3412666/story.html#ixzz17MZxQ0a5

Jay-Z tops Forbes list of richest rappers

NEW YORK (Reuters) - Rap star Jay-Z came first in a list of the richest rappers in 2010, earning more than double that of runner-up Sean "Diddy" Combs.Shawn "Jay-Z" Carter took in $63 million US in personal income between June 2009 and June 2010, according to Forbes.com.Diddy took in $30 million, followed by Senegalese-American rapper Aliuane "Akon" Thiam at $21 million.Despite beginning a jail sentence in March for weapons charges, New Orleans-born rapper Dwayne "Lil Wayne" Carter came in fourth, earning $20 million, ahead of California rap icon Andre "Dr. Dre" Young, who took in $17 million.Almost all stars at the top of the list all share a common strategy -- diversification.The top-earning rappers pulled in cash from alcohol sponsorships, clothing lines, nightclub properties and film appearances, in addition to concert tours and record sales.Jay-Z co-owns the 40/40 nightclub chain. Diddy promotes Ciroc vodka and appeared in the feature film Get Him to the Greek. Dr. Dre and Lil Wayne have record labels. Akon appeared in a Pepsi World Cup ad campaign.The real money isn't in record sales, said Zack O'Malley Greenburg, a Forbes writer who compiled the list."Eminem tied at number 14, even though he's sold more records than any artist since 2000," Greenburg said.Eminem earned $8 million this year, despite the release of his album Recovery which sold 741,000 copies in the first week of sales."It's pretty shocking to see him so low down on the list," said Greenburg. "Compared to his peers, he doesn't really do much outside of music."Rappers have responded to the current era of the digital download, when record sales don't reach the numbers they used to."Artists don't put out albums anymore, they put out single hits, so they have reasons to tour. Hits and tours make you relevant, and they get you sponsorships, and earn you money from merchandise," said Greenburg, who is the author of a forthcoming business-focused biography of Jay-Z.

Greenburg looked at male recording artists who primarily produced rap or hip-hop, and estimated their earnings from record sales, song downloads, touring, film and TV appearances, endorsements and other sources.Canadian newcomer Drake almost cracked the top 10, coming in at No. 11 with $10 million. He topped hip hop veterans like Eminem, T.I. and 50 Cent, and was the highest-earning newcomer on the list. Hip Hop's top earners:1) Jay-Z: $63M2) Diddy: $30M3) Akon: $21M4) Lil Wayne: $20M5) Dr. Dre: $17M6) Ludacris: $16M7) Snoop Dogg: $15M8) Timbaland: $14M9) Pharrell Williams: $13M10) Kanye West: $12M11) Drake: $10M Read more: http://www.canada.com/entertainment/tops+Forbes+list+richest +rappers/3412666/story.html#ixzz17MYh43UA

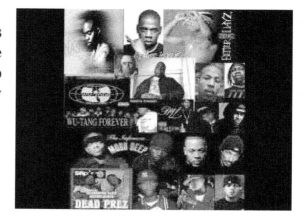

"It's not just music, but a culture," says Will Griffin, president and chief executive of Simmons Lathan Media Group (SLMG). "It's something you are, the way you look."

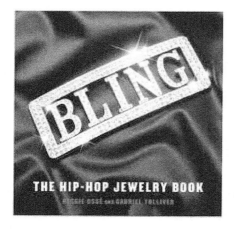

Industry of entrepreneurs

Hip-hop has grown well beyond the urban market since the genre's first hit, "Rapper's Delight," was released in 1979. SLMG says its customer base is the 45 million hip-hop consumers between the ages of 13 and 34, 80 percent of whom are white. According to SLMG's research, this group has $1 trillion in spending power. The Russell Simmons' empire is well placed to garner a big chunk of that.

Brand names have long saturated hip-hop lyrics and videos, sometimes making it tough to distinguish between a single and a jingle. But today these shout-outs are often part of calculated deals between artists and corporations.

It's quaint to recall Notorious B.I.G. in 1997 rapping about DKNY, Versace, Moschino, Coogi and Lexus in the song "Hypnotize." Back then, spouting name brands was about showing off how you spend your money. Nowadays these product placements are a key part of an entertainer's strategy to make money. If they mention anything — purses, clothes, cars or liquor – listeners can safely assume that it's not just because they love the brand.

1946 On August 19.5, 1946, Bill Clinton, the 42nd President, was born in Hope, Arkansas, at the 33rd Parallel. Also Bill Clinton in his speech accepting the democratic parties nomination in 1992 gave credit to his mother and Carol Quigly his college professor. Carol Quigly wrote a book called "Tragedy and Hope" , where he showed the secret hand that controled Amerika's government. Your the Tragedy, but I guarantee that Bill Clinton has no HOPE!

- **jacob the Jeweler Arrested on Money Laundering Charges**

Authorities arrested Jacob and Co. founder Jacob Arabo aka Jacob the Jeweler, Jeweler to the stars, in New York Thursday morning after he was indicted on a federal conspiracy charge stemming from a drug and money laundering case in Detroit.

Arabov, 41, was among 16 people named in a 13-count indictment announced in Detroit today by U.S. Attorney Stephen Murphy. Arabov was specifically charged with just one count: "conspiracy to launder monetary instruments," according to court papers released by the U.S. Attorney of the Eastern District of Michigan.

Paul Wilmot of Paul Wilmot Communications in New York, a spokesman for Jacob and Co., confirmed Arabov's arrest but maintained his innocence. He issued the following statement on behalf of the jeweler:

"The arrest of Mr. Arabov is the result of an unfortunate misunderstanding that we believe will be straightened out in the next several weeks. We are confident that once the government is advised of all the facts surrounding these issues that all of the charges against Mr. Arabov will be completely dismissed."

The indictment accuses Arabov of helping members of the "Black Mafia Family" (BMF) launder cash that it made selling drugs throughout the country during the1990s. Authorities believe the BMF sold more than 476 kilograms of cocaine and laundered more than $270 million.

The indictment says that BMF ringleaders Terry Lee Flenory and Demetrius Flenory purchased jewelry through Arabov with drug proceeds, but that Arabov failed to file Forms 8300, federal forms required for cash payments exceeding $10,000.

The indictment further states that Arabov sold jewelry to people representing the Flenory brothers and filled out Forms 8300 with the names of the representatives, although he knew the money originated from the Flenory brothers, according to court papers.

The indictment seeks the forfeiture of more than 30 pieces of jewelry, including several designed by Jacob & Co, as well as 13 houses, 30 cars and $1.2 million in currency.

Hip-hop's shadowy empire

"Big Meech" Flenory and the Black Mafia Family were hip-hop royalty. But investigators say they had a darker side. *Part 1 of 3* by Mara Shalhoup

Rick Ross

Rick Ross honored as RIAA Certifies Ringtones as Gold, Platinum

- Rick Ross and Others Receive Gold and Platinum Plaques... for Ringtones

Miami's Rick Ross (def Jam) received a plaque bearing a golden cell phone Wednesday when music industry officials honored 128 songs as the first batch of gold and platinum ring tones. Just like vinyl, tapes and CDs, the sounds of ringing cell phones will now translate into awards for sales of 500,000 (gold), 1 million (plantinum) and beyond.

"The ring tones are just another gateway to connecting with the kids and the fans," said Ross, whose award sported a shiny cell phone. "That's just the next level."

Ross, whose first album comes out later this year, was cited for his best-selling single "Hustlin'." He was joined by the Black Eyed Peas, Beyonce, 50 Cent and Kanye West. In all, 84 acts were cited as gold winners, 40 as platinum and four as multiplatinum by the Recording Industry Association of America (RIAA). The awards are given based on downloads of the ring tones.

"Just a few short years ago, it was unthinkable for sales on ring tones to go platinum," said RIAA Chairman Mitch Bainwol. "But here we are. We're transforming the way we hear our music."

According to industry experts, about 10% of music industry revenues worldwide now come from ring tones. Rapper Bubba Sparxxx, who was cited for the gold sales, said he was unaware of the ring tones' popularity.

Don Magic Juan and Snoop Dogg arrive with his unnamed female companions on dog leashes for the MTV Video Music Awards in 2003. (AP Photo/Mary Altaffer)

BY Carla Thompson

Hip hop is commercially hot, culturally influential and replete with references to pimping and prostitution. Critics say this not only sends teens a pro-pimp message, it puts some girls even more at risk for becoming prostitutes.

Experts: Hottest Hip Hop Glorifies Pimping

NEW YORK (WOMENSENEWS)--Hip hop is hot.

According to the Recording Industry Association of America, hip hop--the macho subculture of rappers, graffiti artists, and break dancers that began on New York's mean streets in the 70s--became the second-most popular music genre, with a 13.8 percent share of all music purchases in 2002. The music and its associated products are marketed to teens of all races, the fastest growing segment of thepopulation, according to the U.S. CensusBureau.

None of which pleases Rachel Lloyd, executive director and founder of Girls Educational and Mentoring Services in New York City, a four-year-old mentoring agency for girls and young women between 13 and 21 who are at risk of sexual exploitation.

"Just about every hip-hop song has a reference to pimping," protests Lloyd.

Given the unabashed and almost respectful treatment that hip hop gives to pimping and prostitution, Lloyd considers hip hop one of the threats-- along with poverty and single-parent homes--facing the girls she mentors.

The **Subversive use** of **Sacred Symbolism in** the **Media**
http://www.tactools.org/michael-tsarion-origins-and-oracles-the-subversive-use-of-sacred-symbolism-in-the-media-dvdrip.htm

About Michael Tsarion

Born in Northern Ireland, Michael Tsarion is an expert on the occult histories of Ireland and America. He has made the deepest researches into Atlantis, the origins of evil, and into the Irish Origins of Civilization. He is the author of the acclaimed book Atlantis, Alien Visitation and Genetic Manipulation, and is the producer and presenter of the Origins and Oracles series which explores ancient mysteries and forbidden knowledge.

The Hidden Persuaders, first published in 1957, Packard explores the use of consumer motivational research and other psychological techniques, including depth psychology and subliminal tactics, by advertisers to manipulate expectations and induce desire for products, particularly in the American postwar era. He identified eight "compelling needs" that advertisers promise products will fulfill. According to Packard these needs are so strong that people are compelled to buy products to satisfy them. The book also explores the manipulative techniques of promoting politicians to the electorate. The book questions the morality of using these techniques.[1]

They have changed our music to vibrate at a sexual frequency, a frequency and beat that creates mental sexual frenzy.

PLEASE, WAKE UP!!

"GOOD BOY"

The newly-created group and its "lifestyle" swept millions of young Americans into the cult. American youth underwent a radical revolution without ever being aware of it, while the older generation stood by helplessly, unable to identify the source of the crisis, and thus reacting in a maladaptive manner against its manifestation, which were drugs of all types, marijuana, and later Lysergic acid, "LSD," so conveniently provided for them by the Swiss pharmaceutical company, SANDOZ, following the discovery by one of its chemists, Albert Hoffman, how to make synthetic ergotamine, a powerful mind-altering drug. The Committee of 300 financed the project through one of their banks, S. C. Warburg, and the drug was carried to America by the philosopher, Aldous Huxley.

Adorno Sound System performing "Dialectic Destruction" (1936) by ... Theodor Adornoby

Adorno attacks consumer society for its conversion of every quality into mere quantity, the universal price-calibration of the market. If everything is exchangeable, nothing has value in itself. When the Sex Pistols launched their insult to the values of commodity-culture on the world, they declared they wanted to 'destroy passers-by'. Adorno anticipated the very terms they used in expressing their disgust for the same system.In the chapter titled 'The Culture Industry: Enlightenment as Mass Deception' Adorno developed an extended critique of the operations of consumer culture. The sentences become so dialectically self-conscious they're worth examining in detail. Anyone who resists can only survive by fitting in. Once his particular brand of deviation from the norm has been noted by the industry, he belongs to it as the social-reformer does to capitalism. Realistic dissidence is the trademark of anyone who has a new idea in business. (*Dialectic of Enlightenment* p. 132)

READ A BOOK!

Hip-Hop News: New Eminem Article in the Source and in a November 2002 Vibe article; he had this to say about using the word "nigger": "It's not my place to say it. There are some things that I just don't do." But on an old recording (produced by White beat makers he no longer works with), which was given to The Source in October of last year, Eminem opposes dating Black women "'cause I don't like that nigger shit." On another song he calls Black people "moon crickets," "spear chuckers" and "porch monkeys."

Eminem's blood sacrifice and fame afterwards:
Once you make a blood sacrifice whether it's your best friend or family member, it will get you a higher up in the elite.

In 2004, Eminem predicted his best friend, Proof, getting shot outside of a club in his music video, "Like Toy Soldiers". Proof also knew he was going to be sacrificed. This was no coincidence, it was a planned event. Proof died on the **11**th of April, 2006. Eminem took time off after Proof's death, the elite let him, about 3 years. Than in 2009, he reemerged back with his album, "Relapse" which had songs like "My Darling", "3 A.M", and "Careful What You Wish For".

Well now I know what a Devil Worshiper looks like.
do any of these rappers and entertainer worship the devil? Probably not... but this guy does, and this is the guy that Eminem and Dre would of had to sell their soul to.

"As the mainstream media has become increasingly dependent on advertising revenues for support, it has become an anti-democratic force in society."
-- Robert McChesney, journalist and author

197

The new line is a controversial move for the new owners with the recent uproar over Four Loko and similar drinks in the category. Many critics say that drinks like **Four Loko and blast are targeted towards underage drinkers**, but with 'Blast,' Colt 45 says it is going after a new target: us.

Down to a Trot

Colt 45 consumption, in millions of 2.25-gallon cases

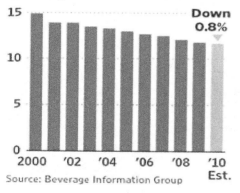

Source: Beverage Information Group

- The companies have since removed the caffeine under pressure from U.S. and state regulators, but alcohol foes continue to raise objections to the amount of alcohol in the beverages.

The level of alcohol in the 23.5-ounce single can of Blast is about the same as the amount in four regular 12-ounce beers. Such potent malt beverages have been on the market for only a few years. Colt 45 contains 5.61% alcohol.

Industry watchdogs say the fruit flavorings and colorful packaging make the products attractive to underage drinkers.

"This is a lot of booze in one can, far too much for a product that is potentially sexy and enticing for youth," said Bruce Lee Livingston, executive director of the Marin Institute, a California-based industry watchdog group.

Paul Scott, an African-American community activist in Durham, N.C., and longtime critic of malt liquor, said the marketing of Blast is "irresponsible" and will have a negative influence on "the young hip-hop generation."

Pabst's Horse of a Different Color: Colt 45 Enters Controversial Ring

The new owners of that malt-liquor brand, with the help of rapper Snoop Dogg, plan to unveil next month a label called Blast by Colt 45. The beverage will contain fruit flavors and 12% alcohol by volume, about twice the level of the original version of Colt 45.

A seven-ounce bottle of Blast has the alcohol of about 1 ½ light beers.

Hennessy is not shy about its dealings with the rap industry

Snoop endorsed Landy Cognac for two years

- The company's flagship brew, Pabst Blue Ribbon, has enjoyed strong growth since 2002 thanks to a newfound hipster appeal. But Colt 45, advertised by actor Billy Dee Williams in the 1980s, has been in decline for over a decade.

- The Metropoulos brothers said they signed a long-term marketing agreement with Snoop Dogg (whose real name is Calvin Broadus), under which the rapper will promote the brand during live music, television and other appearances. Snoop already is touting Blast on Twitter. The company declined to discuss the terms of the deal with the artist but said it will spend millions of dollars on the launch of Blast, including ads in Vibe, a music magazine.

Colt 45 has long targeted an urban, African-American audience, but Blast is aimed at a broader array of drinkers, including women, said Daren Metropoulos, 27 years old.

Blast—which will make its debut in stores April 5, or "4-5," for Colt 45—will be sold in six packs of seven-ounce bottles, as well as in single, 23.5-ounce cans. Flavors include strawberry lemonade and raspberry watermelon, with colors to match. The six-pack of seven-ounce drinks will cost about $7.

Despite rappers' affinity for glorifying alcohol use, experts are divided over whether this translates into dollars. Executives at W.J. Deutsch & Sons, which distributes Landy Cognac, reported that having Snoop Dogg's paid endorsement from 2007 to 2009 resulted in dividends, in part because he was the right man for the job. "We position Landy as a great quality but at an accessible price. We're not trying to be the biggest cognac out there. That's his M. O. as well. He's about being himself, and he's unapologetic about it," said Eric Maldonado, a director of brand marketing. "[The deal] did affect sales and exposure of our brand."

<u>Tracing the Connection Between The Beats and The Bottles</u>

Is it Love or commerce that keep rappers serving up alcohol-heavy hooks?

by Caletha Crawford

Tracing the Connection Between The Beats and The Bottles

With "Blame It (On the Alcohol)" Jamie Foxx had the longest running No. 1 song of any male to top Billboard's R&B/Hip-Hop Songs Chart. But was the song just a fun track or a commercial for Patron and Grey Goose?

Is it Love or commerce that keep rappers serving up alcohol-heavy hooks?

Jamie made Patron and Grey Goose lots of money with his hit single, Blame it on the Alcohol. Is it Love or commerce that rappers serving up alcohol-heavy hooks?

- Researchers looked at 279 songs that made it on Billboard's chart in 2005 and found that 80 percent of rap songs contained these references, while only 20 percent of hip-hop/R&B and 14 percent of rock songs had this distinction.

According to a study conducted by the University of Pittsburgh School of Medicine, rap contains the most references to alcohol, marijuana and non-specific drug use of any musical genre.

A 2005 study by the School of Public Heath at the University of California, Berkeley points out how this trend has grown. The sobering findings show that 8 percent of rap songs had references to alcohol in 1979, but by 1997, 44 mentioned booze. During the same period, the number of songs featuring brand names rose from 46 percent to 71 percent. The study goes on to conclude "that rap music has been profoundly affected by commercial forces and the marketing of alcoholic beverages."

To Jake Jamison, editor of the blog liquorsnob.com, these associations make perfect sense. "It started with [musicians] talking about what they're interested in. Then liquor companies got savvy," he said of the evolution. "It's like athletes sponsoring shoes. The name checks get the brand name out there."

Rap, in particular, has long been a booze-infused medium (Digital Underground drank a bottle of Hennessy in the 1989 hit "The Humpty Dance," after all), and with each passing year the songs are only becoming more spirited.

Stefan Kalogridis, owner of Colvin Wine Merchants in Albany, N.Y., credits radio with putting some brands on the map. "I remember Hennessy being in songs and videos. It's always been the No. 1 cognac, but after the marketing in other avenues, it became more so. Now you have Diddy behind Ciroc, which wasn't that well known when it came out. But when Diddy got behind it sales picked up," he said. "Cristal became popular because of the rap industry. It became so popular that we couldn't even get it in the store. And the price was sky high."

For Jai Jai Greenfield, co-owner of Harlem Vintage in New York, N.Y., the hoopla surrounding these artists doesn't add up to much. "People love ["Blame It"] because it has a great beat, but it doesn't influence what people are buying," she said. "People will come in asking for 'Diddy's brand' because they identify it with him, but they don't walk out because we don't have it." More than an association with a high-profile lifestyle, Greenfield said this year consumers are concerned with price. She's noticed that people are willing to switch to brands that are easier on the wallet.

Jay had a public break-up with Cristal

Jay-Z called for a boycott, saying the remarks were racist. Though Greenfield only carried Cristal for a short period, she recalls the incident. "I did notice somewhat of a backlash after Jay-Z renounced it," she said, adding that even the controversy was great advertising for Cristal. Greenfield wonders why any artist would publicize a brand they have no stake in. "I don't fault Puffy. At least he's doing it the right way [by partnering with Ciroc]. He's saying, 'let's put a brand around it, let's market it and let me get paid for it.'"

Increasingly other rappers are of the same mindset. Not only are they getting paid for promoting established brands, they're branching out with their own labels. Dr. Dre partnered with Aftermath Cognac. Jay-Z owned a stake in Armadale Vodka. Lil Jon has Little Jonathan Winery. Ultimately, Jamison said, these deals show that today's rappers are businessmen first. "The name of the game in hip-hop is starting on the streets hustling and making good," he said. "And that's what a lot of these folks are doing but in a different way."

Hennessy is not shy about its dealings with the rap industry

Young Jeezy endorses Belvedere Vodka

Whether or not someone is willing to consider a new brand may not only be a matter of expense, but the strength of their preference. In a 2009 survey conducted by market research firm Mintel, African-American consumers showed a higher preference for premium cognac, tequila, Canadian whisky and vodka, when compared to imbibers of other races.

Rick Ross is a brand ambassador for 1800 Tequila

For Maldonado the ease with which a company can convert drinkers to a new brand generally depends on the category of alcohol. "People who drink [single malt] typically want to know the ins and outs of how it's made and why it tastes this way. They probably spend a lot more time learning and discerning that category so that they tend to know what it is they like to drink," he said, contrasting it with consumers' promiscuity when it comes to vodka brands. "Vodka is more about mixing, where you can argue that you lose a little more of that flavor. It's not a product that takes a long time to make or that spends a long time aging. It's not really a complicated

Luda reps his latest investment

Brand loyalty is one reason alcohol labels are willing to pull out the big guns in the form of celebrity endorsements. But none of them want to end up with a Tiger Woods-size scandal after signing an artist. Though no one would have predicted the public relations nightmare that Woods caused, a similar controversy surrounding a rapper is easier to envision, making them a risky choice for some.brushes off these concerns: "In anything you do there can be certain risks. When choosing a spokesperson, we're focused more on finding a fit with our brand."

Up-and-comers are focused on spinning their records into gold — parlaying their success, name and reputation into product endorsements, clothing lines and television shows. In short, everyone wants to be a mogul. Liquor companies are happy to indulge the desire to diversify. Name an artist, and he probably has a deal.

Diddy fronts, and has a stake in, Ciroc Vodka. Ludacris is the face of Conjure Cognac. Young Jeezy promotes Belvedere Vodka. Rick Ross is tight with 1800 Tequila. And these just represent associations that are publicized. Insiders speculate many more are kept under wraps; leading one to wonder, upon hearing songs like "Pass the Courvoisier" or "One More Drink," where the artistry ends and commerce begins.

Jamison stated that the risk can be part of the appeal. "People expect an element of danger with hip-hop artists, and I think the companies are seeing that as long as they don't worry too much about what's being said or the context of where their product is showing up, they can reap a lot of benefits from it," he said.

Without direct business ties, Grey Goose still ranks high in shout outs

For its part, Grey Goose says it is careful to work with artists who share its commitment to "responsible decision making." The company doesn't have a specific spokesperson but has collaborated with Wyclef Jean, Kid Cudi and The Dream. It also aligns itself with the industry through programs like "Rising Icons," a BET show that honors new artists.

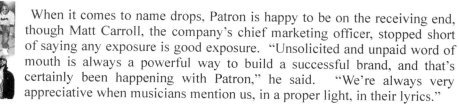

When it comes to name drops, Patron is happy to be on the receiving end, though Matt Carroll, the company's chief marketing officer, stopped short of saying any exposure is good exposure. "Unsolicited and unpaid word of mouth is always a powerful way to build a successful brand, and that's certainly been happening with Patron," he said. "We're always very appreciative when musicians mention us, in a proper light, in their lyrics."

202

GANGSTA RAPPERS GET PAID AND GET FRONTED BY "THE BEAST" -by Keidi Obi Awadu (9/21/01)

"Thus, for example, breaking up the ghetto culture of defiance that unfits so many black youths for peaceable participation in civil society may be eminently desirable" -- From the article "Winds of Change", Foreign Affairs, Fall issue 1990

As certain rappers get drawn into the clandestine network which is motivated by national security policies, they eventually can be made into mouthpieces for social engineering activities where propaganda (ideological communication) is the preferred weapon for what amounts to "quiet warfare." This propaganda is increasingly encouraging self-destructive behaviors as well as policies which limit fertility or draw larger numbers of youth into highly-promoted activities (which can include HIV testing and condom distribution). Some of these activities, such as consuming dangerous alcoholic concoctions, can be completely contradictory to the values and long-term self-interests of the hip hop generation. An example is promotion of the deadly 40 ounce malt liquors.

As my brilliant friend Alfred "Coach" Powell, the author of the landmark book Message in a Bottle: The 40 Ounce Conspiracy [note from Bruz: apparently they're not THAT good of friends, Powell's book is actually entitled "Message 'N A Bottle: The 40oz. Scandal"], has illustrated, certain high-profile rappers have been recruited by major corporations to deliver masses of black and brown youth as consumers of one of the most dangerous alcoholic beverages ever manufactured -- the deadly 40 ounce malt liquors. Coach Powell refers to these malt liquors, which are disproportionately marketed primarily at urban youth as "psycho-bio chemically engineered drugs" laced with substances which undermine the mental and reproductive capabilities of its consumer. How have hip hop artists been so short-sighted as to have been co-opted to promote this chemical warfare which has been linked to the deaths of so many of their fellows? When will they declare that their generation has suffered enough such exploitation?

Prof. Alfred "Coach" Powell
CEO/President
Human Motivation Council /
Human Motivation Circle

During my coaching years I began to notice how too many of my athletes were coming to practice intoxicated, or they were suffering the ill effects of addicted family members. This led me to write Message N/A Bottle: The 40oz Scandal (BWORLD@yahoo.com) in 1996. My latest book, Hip Hop Hypocrisy: When Lies Sound Like the Truth, exposes the seduction of an entire generation by an intoxicated, violent, misogynistic subculture that arose out of gangs and prisons. I work with young people, as well as parents, educators, ministers, social workers, and counselors around the country to help improve academic performance and classroom management. For more information on our services, visit www.ACoachPowell.com. To participate in the dialogue, visit here often and share your ideas, questions, comments, and strategies.

There is another group within the hip hop generation which has been cooperating with hostile external forces opposed to the interests of the community. This time it is blacks working within the "entertainment" media of film and television. Modern "black exploitation films" such as Boyz in the Hood, Menace II Society, Sugar Hill, Poetic Justice, Set it Off, Don't Be a Menace, Bullet, Juice, the House Party series, Phat Beach, Booty Call, etc, etc, -- these movies, which can range from irrelevant minstrel shows to how-to crime instruction, and are undermining the values and logic of the youth. In turn they are feeding a sinister form of propaganda to the world that black and brown youth within the inner cities of America are out of control and a lethal threat to a civilized society, that they are irrelevant and unnecessary -- useless eaters and excess population. These images are in the films, the made-for-urban-youth TV sitcoms, daytime talkshows, as well as in the music videos. They are not absolute, but they are pervasive.

Powerful media conglomerates with names such as Time Warner, MCA, Viacom, News Corp. and others have set up fiefdoms within the United States through which they exert a disproportionate controlling affect on various communities. These huge private corporations are led by powerful individuals such as Gerald Levin (Time Warner), Edgar Bronfman (Seagrams, Universal Music Group, MCA), Sumner Redstone (Viacom) and Rupert Murdoch (News Corp.). Their corporations operate as mini-fiefdoms which serve the interests of the U.S. national security establishment on covert operations designed to satisfy their mutual self-interests.

When it comes to name drops, Patron is happy to be on the receiving end, though Matt Carroll, the company's chief marketing officer, stopped short of saying any exposure is good exposure. "Unsolicited and unpaid word of mouth is always a powerful way to build a successful brand, and that's certainly been happening with Patron," he said. "We're always very appreciative when musicians mention us, in a proper light, in their lyrics." Carroll's "in a proper light" caveat reflects the industry's awareness that justJay had a public break-up with Cristal as musicians can help build a brand's reputation, they also have the power to tarnish it. This was illustrated in 2006 when Cristal and hip-hop had a very public break up. The champagne, which had become shorthand for the good life after numerous mentions in songs, ran into controversy when a Cristal executive said the name drops were "unwelcome." The response was swift.

White Girl Mob: Hip-Hop's Favorite White Girls

- ### *Hip-Hop's Favorite White Girls*

*Although Bay Area rappers **Kreayshawn**, **V-Nasty** and the rest of their **White Girl Mob** are trying everything in their power to destroy the love affair between Hip-Hop and white girls by making awesomely bad rap music and tossing around the N-word, it'll take a little more than a group of foul-mouthed, non-rapping white women to end our relationship with snow bunnies.*

Since white girls are catching a bad rap right now (no pun intended), we decided to salute our favorite Becky's in the business.

- ## Amber Rose

Kanye made her his girl and now Wiz Khalifa wants to put a ring on it...Amber Rose's love affair with Hip-Hop is definitely in a literal sense.

"We are social animals and we have a hierarchical and unequal society. It is a class society, and the class system creates and perpetuates the social role of consumption. We display our class membership and solidify our class positioning in large part through money, through what we have. Consumption is a way of verifying what you have and earn."

-- Juliet Schor, economist and author

204

8th DEGREE

DESTROYING HIP HOP APPETITE FOR SELF-DESTRUCTION

from " gangsta " to " gay "

"Students are merely trained not to think for themselves. They are to obey the leaders and system without question. They are taught to obey, do as they're told, and if they do, they have a great chance to move up and become an obedient supervisor themselves. Part of the Freemason conspiracy is to churn out "worker bees" that do their compartmentalized job, go home, watch propaganda on the tube, and do it again."

-- Excerpted from **Freemason Education Conspiracy**

An Interview with My Brother
A Master Teacher In His Own Right
Mwalimu K. Bomani Baruti

Prof. Griff: Alright, this is Professor Griff. I'm interviewing Mwalimu K. Bomani Baruti for my book **The Psychological Covert War on Hip Hop – The Illuminati's Takeover of Hip Hop**.   For Chapters 5, which is **Pimps, Preachers, Politicians, Pedophiles, and the Pulpit**, the 7th chapter, which is **Money, Madness, Music and Mayhem**, and the 8th chapter, which is **Destroying Hip Hop's Appetite for Self-Destruction – From Gansta to Gay**.   Just a few questions that I have. Can we just have this conversation so I can just kinda go through 'em?

Baruti: Yeah. Absolutely, Griff.

Prof. Griff: Alright. You have in the book a quote by Amos Wilson. We're gonna get to that, but I wanted to ask you about the Akoben and why you chose it as a name for your institution.

Baruti: Well, Akoben is an Adinkra symbol of the Akan people of West Africa. We chose the Adinkra symbol because it's a war horn; the sound is blown when their people are being attacked and they need to organize to defend themselves. It's also blown, of course, whenever people need to come together to make a public decision or something is an issue. But it's primarily described as a war horn. And of course, now, given the environment that we're in and have been in for the last 2,000 years, that is the single most important expression in terms of its definition. We chose it for what we do primarily for the school because we see it as a job to answer this war horn to make our children aware of their war.   Our job is to raise warriors who are aware warriors – politically aware, understanding what has happened to us, what is going on with us, what is happening to us outside and inside, and what they need to do as warriors who are answering to the ancestors and to the creator in terms of what they do, so it's very critical that we have African symbolism in terms of what it is that they need to think about and what we need to think about, too, because, you know, Akoben is the name of the publishing company Akoben House, as well as the other products and things that we do, which is Akoben Village, all centered around the idea that – the understanding, not the idea, the understanding that we are at war and we need to be acting accordingly as African people.

GOD   WISDOM   UNITY

ADAPTABILITY   HUMILITY   NURTURING

JEALOUSY   HOPE   LOVE

Homosexuality and the Effeminization of Afrikan Males

Homosexuality and the Effeminization of Afrikan Males begins with an Afrikan Centered investigation into the origins and historical evolution of homosexuality. This elemental study expands into a detailed analysis of the most important part of this work, the growing gender confusion of Afrikans socialized into European culture and society.

"Homosexuality" is the crack of the 21st Century. whites are encouraging Black boys and girls to become *"homosexuals"* through the use of:

Mass Incarceration

This methodical demasculinization manifests itself in numerous ways and rationales, from within the prison system to higher education to single parenting to the labor market to the church to the media, all of which are thoroughly discussed in this book. At the base of this assault is the historical confusion and cultural alienation of Afrikans themselves. If people act toward any problem without historical awareness, for all problems are located in history, then in all probability they act wrongly or, as many prefer to say, they do no more than react. Therefore, many of us who are alarmed over this growing sexual confusion are mostly reacting to what is being done to our sons.

Prof. Griff: Okay, and with that said, you have a quote in the book, I believe it's Chapter 9 later on in the book where it deals with tradition of purpose and order by Amos Wilson. A quote by Amos Wilson, it says "We must look at the psychopathology of everyday life and we must recognize we cannot have it both ways. We cannot talk about a people who have enslaved us, who discriminate against us, who insult us, who do all manner of other things against us, and then use them as models of normality. And yet these people are held up as normal and are used as the standard against which we measure ourselves as a people, and are used as models for us to determine the way we wish our children to behave." Now, you have that in the book. How does that relate to what we're seeing with the ongoing pattern of women raising boys, and at a certain age not able to deal with the young male energy as it relates to them resonating with not only rap music but just entertainment?

Baruti: Well, because of what we are, or have become. One time, when we first encountered Europeans and realized what they were about as they tried to destroy us, we realized that this was the enemy. And we acted accordingly. There wasn't any question on how we raised our sons or our daughters or what the definition of manhood is supposed to be in our society. We understood ourselves, we understood the enemy. But over time, because I'll say the rewarding of Negroes, the rewarding of vanquished people, the rewarding of individuals who saw or believed Europeans, the European way to be God or God-like and the way that we're supposed to be when we grow up, the accepting over time due to conditions beyond most of our control, that we did not come from anything and that they represented everything and we needed to be like them in order to be somebody, to be powerful. We have lost sight of who we are. We have lost sight of how we're supposed to be as a people.

We have lost sight of the fact that we are a people, for the most part, so what is going on in a nutshell, and this isn't oversimplification, but what is going on in a nutshell is that we're trying to fit in, and they say you can fit in, we're trying to fit into European culture in such a way that we become a normal part of it, so that we don't become an odd part of it, so that we aren't persecuted because of the color of our skin and because of our heritage and because of the qualities that are innately African in us. So what we have done is we have gone through the process of dismissing from our traditions and doing everything in our power to embrace them, but not only just embrace European traditions, we have taken on that "mentacide" as Bobby E. Wright so aptly coined it, where we not only have allowed our memory and sense of self to be removed, we have allowed ourselves to assimilate and become that which Europeans have defined us as.

Some people look at "mentacide" and they assumed it to say, well Africans are trying to be Europeans. No it's not just simply that. We are trying to be the kind of Europeans that Europeans want us to be. They have not defined us as them; they defined us as sub-us. So when I talk about how us as a sub-integration oriented people, and I mean we are so focused on doing that, in order to do that, we have to raise our children so that they are acceptable to them so that they won't kill our children. We know that they will kill for nothing, so if the idea of being a man, or in fact of being a woman – because a woman in African tradition is not gonna raise her child to be a slave; she's gonna raise her child to be a warrior. She would prefer to have her child dead on the battlefield than to be someone else's slave forever, no matter how many things that person had. But since we have lost that sense of definition of parenthood, since we have lost that definition of manhood and womanhood, we are raising our children to be accepted within this cultural context, within this social context, which is not ours. We are raising them so that they see insanity as their sanity. So that when they're doing all these things that they shouldn't be doing because they're listening to things that we shouldn't be allowing them to listen to, that we shouldn't be promoting and never should have gotten started in the first place, if you will, we are doing what other people want us to do to keep us in the context of the definition that they have given us.

But we see it, I will say, subconsciously as a survival strategy. And when you're looking for a survival strategy because you live in fear and you think that everything is lost, then you rationalize what you see about you is normal. You start looking for anything that will bring joy to your life. To be one of the perfect examples of that entertainment is comedy. Everybody needs laughter in their life; everybody needs some fun in their life, that's balance. But it's almost like the idea that you laugh so much to keep from crying. We have more comedy in our shows in our lives than anybody else, but we have to spend so much time laughing because we really realize deep down inside on a subconscious level, we realize just how bad it is. We realize just how self-hating we are. So to keep from having to look that in the face, then we spend so much time laughing, and of course the entertainment industry, they benefit enormously from that.

Prof. Griff: Right. Exactly. Alright, I've noticed that a lot of the comedians now are moved up in prominent positions on radio and have sitcoms, and they've moved and they're almost as the spokesperson now for the Black community.

Baruti: Oh, absolutely. Anybody who has no sense of consciousness or makes fun of who we are who presents themselves in images that otherwise would be considered buffoonery or really apelike behavior, they are elevated as models of what we're supposed to be, what we're supposed to laugh at, what is funny. And this is entertainment, just like sports, just like anything else, it's political. So you're not gonna find a conscious individual who's spilling forth conscious comedy, if you will, rising to the ranks of being someone that Black folks listen to.

Prof. Griff: Right.

Baruti: You know. That would tell us to approach life in a completely different fashion.

Prof. Griff: Right. So let me ask you something. So Nelson Mandela said you can tell the soul of a nation by how it treats its children. What do you think about that?

Baruti: That is very scary. If I was an alien in a spaceship studying this planet and trying to assess people and I was looking at Black folks – I don't know at what level of, and it's almost an insult to animals, but at what level of animal I would place us because the positions we put our children in, the way we allow other people including those among us who believe in them to mis-educate and dis-educate our children, the way we abuse our children, the way we allow other people to abuse our children's minds, the way we do not protect our children, particularly our daughters, from other people; the way we do not protect our sons from other males, the way that we value things over our children, the numbers of stories of people who have done idiotic things in the face of the children…

It's unbelievable how we've gotten to a point where we will whine about how bad our children are being educated but allow that to happen anyway, the way we are allowing our children to eat, the kind of care that we are not doing for our children – that would tell me that these people absolutely do not care for their children. They essentially are raising them to be slaves for somebody else. Consuming slaves and whatever other kind of slaves these people need, that's what these people are preparing their children for. And it's not out of fear for the children; it's out of fear for self. That's essentially the definition of a slave, someone who doesn't care what you do to everybody else that's connected to him or her as long as you let them live. So we're allowing the world, including other people in our neighborhood who think like other people, to do to our children whatever they want to do to our children, and then we cry afterwards. There's virtually nothing that we are doing that is preparatory in terms of acting in the interest of our children. We're sitting by and watching our children be destroyed…

Prof. Griff: Right.

Baruti: …and we are assisting in many ways.

Prof. Griff: Okay, so you mention on page 21 dealing with the sexual framework in **The Sex Imperative**, you talk about European culture is extreme individualism inducing, and because of its cultural imperialistic orientation, it has literally turned this world upside-down to make humanity fit its sexual idiosyncrasies. Later on in that same chapter you say, "We as adults have failed our children and created walking time bombs whose minds are extremely controlled. We are teaching them or allowing them to be taught that anything is a responsible price for success." With that being said, Franz Fanon said, "each generation out of its own obscurity must discover its mission, fulfill it, or betray it." According to what you wrote in the sexual framework in **The Sex Imperative**, is Franz Fanon, what he's saying in his quote "each generation out of its own obscurity must discover its mission, fulfill it, or betray it," have young people betrayed it, or fulfilled a mission passed down to them by that generation before them?

Baruti: Well, that's a very interesting question, because my first thought is that they have not betrayed it because they don't have a model to look at, and if you've never been taught that you are a warrior, if you don't understand that people are destroying you, in fact if you think that their destruction is your elevation, they you have no reason to pick up that torch and act in a warrior-like fashion and defend yourself. On the other hand, they have picked up this torch. They have out of that relative obscurity that's not – I guess for me, the question is not of whether we have warriors, but where did they come from in many cases, because there isn't a significant sound model for most of them to even understand the fact that we are being destroyed. But they are acting accordingly. Everything around them tells them to act like a warrior, to pick up that torch and defend their people, to defend the future. Everything around them tells them that that's insane – why would you wanna do that? In fact, we're just all a bunch of individuals; we're all human, so why would you even talk about fighting somebody like that. If anyone is the oppressor, it's you and yours. So to have warriors who are coming along, who are doing things that I'm not imagining doing, out of essentially a cowardly people in so many ways, and that's a general statement. We know we have warriors among African people, but in terms of generally speaking, a cowardly people who do not defend their children, leaves individuals to stand up and decide that they want to be warriors in the face of those who came before them in a cowardly fashion and the majority of those around them who are acting in that cowardly tradition says a great deal about their resilience, the strength of our ancestors in our genes.

210

Prof. Griff: Okay. Just a few more questions and we'll be done. I was reading your book, **Homosexuality and the Effeminization of African Males,** and I think I've asked you several times, because I'm constantly asked to become someone's mentor, what is a mentor, and if that's not a correct term, give me the correct term that we should be using to activate that higher consciousness so we can be in line with what the ancestors laid out for us.

Baruti: Absolutely, Griff. It's painful every time I hear it, but I understand. We operate within a European culture and we are operating within the mythology of the European culture, because the mythology defines the people. And the word "mentor" came out of their mythology. The word "mentor" came from the story of **The Odyssey**. In **The Odyssey**, Odysseus, who was the hero who came from Greek society... in Greek society, when a boy reached a certain age, particularly the more privileged boy, but boys in general, when they reached a certain age of beginning to move toward manhood, they were taken out of their homes, if you will, and put in the presence of an individual who gave them the information and the skills and the knowledge that brought them into manhood. This individual also, in exchange for him giving him this information, this knowledge, and this "wisdom," he was allowed access to sodomize them. He was the individual who introduced them to the homosexual lifestyle at a higher level, if you will.

In the story of **The Odyssey**, Odysseus had a son whose name was Telemecus. Telemecus was coming of age. Odysseus came home to get his son and to move him into the presence of someone who was supposed to bring him into this homosexual manhood, and the name of the individual who he turned him over to was Mentor. So when we're saying these things, assuming that our ancestors are correct, and I believe that they are, when we speak something into reality we give it power. We give it force. So every time we say the word "mentor," every time we speak it into reality, we are giving power to the homosexual ideal in terms of raising our boys into "men" within this context. The word that we should be using is a word that was given to us by Wayne Nobles and many others of our warrior scholars who agree with this. It's an Amharic term out of Ethiopia, and the word is **jegna**, and **jegna** has a definition that is enormous. Now, Griff, I have the... I don't know if you wanna use this whole definition. I can give you the definition in a quote, I can e-mail you that.

Prof. Griff: If you don't mind running it down, I don't mind taking it.

Baruti: Okay, so I will send that to you because it's about a little more than a paragraph long. You have the homo book?

Prof. Griff: Yes I have it.

Baruti: Okay, it's on page 149-150, it's a direct quote ... but the definition that he gives makes even what we think about the idea of a mentor in this country ... makes how we think about the idea of "mentor" in this society, how it's defined, it dwarfs it. Because the magnitude of what it's talking about, and just quickly, I'm going to read it: "Jegna, those special people, have (1) been tested in struggle or battle, (2) demonstrated extraordinary and unusual fearlessness, (3) shown determination and courage in protecting her or his people, land and culture, (4) shown diligence and dedication to our people, (5) produced an exceptionally high quality of work, and (6) dedicated themselves to the protection, defense, nurturance, and development of our young by advancing our people, place, and culture." Man, when you think about mentor in the west, especially mentor, and most of the people trying to claim to be mentors are Negroes in many cases, you don't talk about struggle and battle, they don't talk about fearlessness, extraordinary fearlessness in terms of being a quality that the mentor is supposed to have.

Diligence and dedication to our people, our people? And exceptionally high quality of work – any fool in the west can become a "mentor." And dedicated themselves to the protection, defense, nurturance, and development of our youth by advancing who we are and then making sure that they understand that so they act on that, that's not part of the definition of being a mentor in western society. Of course those who do that, and those of us who do that in western society, we're following the western model, and that western equal, we're not even following that western model. Some of us are not exploiting, physically sexually exploiting, if you wanna call it sex, sexually exploiting these young folks, but what they do is so irrelevant to the empowerment of African people – in fact most of the "best mentors" in our community are considered to be those who go and take Black youth and develop in them the mentality to get away from Black folk, to leave the community and go someplace else because that's considered to be progress.

So we need to be very leery of using that word "mentor." We really need to take, those of us who are serious about this need to use the word "jegna." And all of the implications and assumptions that it's supposed to make about you being that. Just a quick note, in my last book **Centered**, I dedicated it to Baba Hannibal Afrique, who is to me one of the greatest warriors on this planet right now. I put on there, you know, Jegna, bla blab bla, and he called me up and he grilled me for a good 15 minutes. I'm not a jegna; I haven't, you know, confronted and enemy or battle, there hasn't been any bloodshed, bla bla bla, you know. When we got finished, I said "this is how I see you in terms of this model, you're as close as I can possibly imagine." But he understood. Even with all that he had done in his humble self, he understood that he didn't come close in any way, shape or fashion to this definition, and most African men, most Black men who I know, and I'm not including you in this, but most of them that I know don't come anywhere close to this model. And he does, and he recognized that he fell short in many areas.

Prof. Griff: Okay. Wow, yeah, that makes me think twice about a lot of things. Alright, I'm trying to figure out my last three questions. I just don't want them to be longwinded, but this one of three is very longwinded on my part because I went through your book three times and I wrote notes because when someone talks about a warrior scholar, I don't want them to mention me. I wanna just **be** it. So when I read the 4th chapter, Another World, when you talk about different things in reference to them colonizing, white people and Europeans colonizing sex, I wrote a note here, basically asking this to myself and to other people... I said, "Have you successfully prepared your child for a world you did not help to create? And evil you refuse to fight and the beast you leave in place to destroy another generation. What have you done to prepare your children?" That's the note I was writing to myself. The African proverb that you put in here says that "no one sends a child on a difficult errand and gets angry if she does not perform it well." So I said to myself, well if I'm understanding that correctly, what mission or what difficult errand did my parents and my spiritual parents and those revolutionary brothas and sistahs that helped mold and shape my consciousness, and did I fail? Or did I deliver?

Baruti: Well, if you're asking me, I can tell you, you have not failed. One of the greatest indicators of not failing is the fact that you are hated so well. Especially by those individuals who don't want this compromise groove to be messed up, to be broken. Part of the problem with that question is that it doesn't allow you to look at yourself relative to other people who are claiming to do this work. There are many people like you, Griff, and I'm serious, many people like you who have gone beyond what they were sent here to do as far as I'm concerned, so the work that you were sent here to do was done.

You were sent here, in my mind, to make people aware of what needed to be done. Some of us are sent here to do the gardening. Some of us are sent here to do the plumbing, if you will. Some of us are sent here to do different things. There are people whose job it is to speak. You were brought here with the gift of gab, you were brought here with an articulate nature, so your job was to explain things to people in a way that they understand. You have done that. Right now, you're just re-explaining, re-explaining, and re-explaining as best you can because you realize that so many people aren't getting the message...

Prof. Griff: Right.

Baruti: But the job, the work that you were sent here to do, has been done. The problem is that so many people don't know what they're here for and definitely don't know what their children were sent here for and what they're supposed to instruct them in. Some of them also, they realize maybe too late, or – a perfect example is an African-centered person who spoils their child. And they raise this child in a spoiled fashion even though they've given them all this understanding of our story and who the enemy is and all the rest of this good stuff, and then when the child comes of some age, they're sending this child off to do tasks that are supposed to be raising the consciousness of African people, defending African people. And this child goes out and acts like a spoiled child who doesn't wanna do anything for anybody but his or herself and doesn't know anything. And then you get upset with this child. You have no business getting upset with this child. You allowed that insanity into his world. You allowed that insanity to penetrate his mind. You allowed that insanity, through your contradictions, to mold that child in a way that moved him or her away from what they were supposed to do, so there's no need to get upset at this child.

213

Prof. Griff: Right. So my second question, and then my last one is gonna be a very simple one. You mention in the book **The African Drummer's Compromise by the European Word**, "Whereas music once informed and elevated our spirit, it now serves only to degrade any higher consciousness and arouse and titillate the biological and material. They have changed our music to vibrate at a sexual frequency, a frequency and beat that creates mental sexual frenzy." Now that's on one page, and then I turn the page, and later on in the book it talks about sex is playin' the western world. How so?

Baruti: Well it's the center, and it's more than just play. In many ways, it's something very serious because the sexual realm in the European mind, freedom is a creation of your ability to control and dominate others. Sex is a way of exercising that domination that control, that power, so your ability to do what you want to do to other people sexually is an exercise of power. It's reaffirming to you, it's gratifying to you, and that tells you that you have power, that you have freedom. So that is where I say it's a very serious thing, but at the level of play, it's like when you are brought into the world and your whole role in that world, in that reality, is supposed to be that of a buffoon, that of someone who does nothing but slaves, that of someone who does nothing but consume, then that becomes a very big part of what you do in terms of being that kind of person. It allows you to feel fulfilled. It allows you believe that you are doing something at the same time that it distracts you from any sense of responsibility or commitment to any higher level thinking. That's where you stay grounded. You don't get above that, you don't get above the physical because your whole world is consumed with the consumption, the need to be more sexual any and everywhere and constantly, so that becomes your all in all. You can't see beyond that. And that becomes your world. You're still a child in a playground, and in this playground you are constantly looking for new toys, new things to play with. Any different variety or amount of sexual world becomes a count, like in a football game or baseball game or basketball game where your score is based upon how many sexual conquests that you have or how many sexual encounters you have, so it does become a play. It might be serious play, you know, for a lot of people in terms of how they define it, but it's still a world of play and it's a child's world because you are, we are under assault. We are at war. People are destroying us, they're destroying our children, they're destroying our communities, and we're sitting here being focused on play. I can't remember who said that, and it's … it was a hip hop group that said, "They're building underground cities and we're busy lookin' at titties" – something like that. And that's the magnitude of the difference in terms of that being play versus that being serious work. When we're so focused on that, you can't build anything 'cause you can't think at a higher level, especially if you think that this is what you should be aspiring to be. Imagine a warrior or would-be warrior in a reality of being destroyed, of his people being at war and the highest level that he can think at is how to take advantage of sisters around him.

Rap music has many detractors. Today, it is often associated with a culture of crass materialistm, sex, violence and irresponsibility. It wasn't always so. In her thorough and entertaining tour of the "golden age" of rap from 1987 to 1996, McQuillar takes us back to a time when the music voiced the social and political concerns of inner-city youth, reflected their hopes and dreams for the future, and strove to inspire positive social change. When Rap Music Had a Conscience gives us the A's - to - Z's of major groups and artists, from Arrested Development to YZ, of this creative and socially conscious age. Broadening its outlook on the culture, the book discusses the interactions of rap music with literature, film and fashion. Finally, it delves into the socio-political dimensions of Hip-Hop in the golden age, exploring the influence of events from the L.A. riots to the unearthing of the oldest human remains in Kenya, to paint a rich and fascinating picture of rap music and its diverse contexts and consequences.

Prof. Griff: Mmm…

Baruti: You know, and that's his play. … But to him, it's something serious; he doesn't in many cases even know that he's even playin'. That's why for some brothers and some sisters, I can't get upset because they don't know. It hasn't been brought to their attention. That's what I'm talkin' about when I say you have done the work that you can, because your job was to bring this to their attention. If they don't wanna pay attention, then, I mean, you can't force people to be who they're supposed to be.

Prof. Griff: Right, exactly. Alright, my last question is probably the one that I think should tie all this together. **The Psychological Covert War on Hip Hop**. First of all, in your mind, from what we've already talked about, you've already stated that there is a war going on. We have to identify the enemy and we have to begin to put together behavior patterns and strategies to counteract racism (white supremacy). And basically I think you're saying if I get it right, that we must conduct ourselves like we're in a war. I've often stated that this is a psychological covert war. Psychology not meaning the study of the mind, but psychology as the study of the soul, which is the psyche, as the ancient, our ancient ancestors has given this to us. If that is true, and I know and understand it is, all of what we talked about for the last 45 minutes should tie into this psychological covert war. My question to you basically is, do you see it, a psychological covert war, not only on hip hop, but on Black youth, and how do we counteract it.

Baruti: Oh, absolutely. Because the music industry has become the teacher. The music industry is the primary means by which our children are educated. The absolute primary means by which our children are educated. So those individuals who are producing this, I'll say music, and I know this is only one aspect of that, but who are producing this music, they are the teachers for our children. So the messages that are coming out of their mouths are forming the priorities of these children. Yes I know that they are being controlled by other people, but they also have a responsibility even if they don't know, 'cause ignorance of the law doesn't mean anything in the universe. The problem there, and the evidence of the covert war, is what we are being instructed to do. We are being instructed to focus on violence. We are being instructed to focus on sex. We're being instructed to focus on conspicuous consumption, on things.   We're being led to focus on domination of other people, being able to control, hurt, and kill other people.

In this book of life lessons culled from hip-hop culture, author Felicia Pride examines a wide range of hip-hop songs and artists, interpreting life through their lenses. Growing up with hip-hop, Pride has come to realize the way it shaped how she thinks, writes, and reacts, making her the person she is today. By incorporating her own experiences and reflections with the rapper's message, she focuses on the positive, motivational influence hip-hop has on its audience.

100 LIFE LESSONS FROM HIP HOP'S GREATEST SONGS
FELICIA PRIDE

That individualism is the important thing that we're supposed to be trained for. And that's what music for young folks, and not just for young folks, for us as a people, the vast majority of the music that comes into our ears is directed toward self-hatred and the destroying of each other and making ourselves not into effective warriors, or Bobby Wright saying the only reason that Black men hadn't went to war against European men is because they had been taught to kill Black men and not white men.

So this music continues that process of us seeing each other as the enemy, and not seeing the Europeans as the enemy or anybody else who is trying to keep us from being ourselves as the enemy. And this music is the primary teacher. That is the main means by which our children are learning who they are and their responsibilities. The schools aren't their teachers, the churches aren't their teachers, and their homes in so many cases are not their teachers. This music is their primary teacher, that's the main thing that they listen to for advice as to what they're supposed to do and what they're supposed to be about. Now I would argue, I wouldn't have argued this nine years ago, but I'm gonna argue this now. I wouldn't have argued it to the degree that I will now.

I'm seeing and hearing so many independent efforts by conscious hip hop artists, young folk all along particularly the east coast – I'm not aware of the west coast, I'm not saying that it's not there – but I'm seeing these artists coming out with lyrics that are trying to change the way those people who listen to them think and act. I'm hearing the lyrics that are explaining to them that they are soldiers that they need to get away from this conspicuous consumption, that we need to respect the Queens that we need to respect the King in us. I'm hearing these things. Now, I don't know the degree to which this is being listened to by our young folks, but I do know that these individuals are able to live their lives and create enough income from that, even though I know it's small, enough income from it to survive, so I know that some folks are listening. I know that from the folks who are buying the books and are talking to me and coming to the lectures, I know that we have in this collection of people who are trying to be warriors and I know that the majority of what they're getting is also coming from the music, even though there's a significant amount of it coming from the lectures and the books also.

So for me, and this is the main means by which our young folks are being educated. We need to get to them through this medium. That's why I say my role isn't to do it; my role is to provide artillery to the folks who are doing this.

That's what I do. And I'm seeing less and less of the young folks doing any kind of serious reading, but the ones who are conveying the message to them are serious readers, they're serious students of who we're supposed to be and what we're supposed to be about, so if I had to put my money into something that would resolve this issue of self-hatred that is coming through in the music, I would put it in the music, but I would put it in those artists, those speakers, those talkers, those hip hop artists who are about the business of producing that insurrection, that African revolutionary music that produces warriors and self-respect among African people, because that is the primary educator in our community.

Prof. Griff: Oh okay, I see what you're saying now. Alright, that was my last question. I think hopefully, if this book is able to reach the good brothers that are locked behind the prison inside a prison, because I believe America 2000 by 3000 is a prison...

Baruti: Yes.

Prof. Griff: I hope there's something that we've said that can reach them so they can come back out in the world and hopefully make a difference. I used to meet them half-way by going to the prison, but if I go now, I think they may keep my ass.

Baruti: Yeah, you have to be very careful because you can disappear.

Prof. Griff: Right, exactly.

Baruti: They know you. Well I'll say, Griff, if there's anything that needs clarification or if you want me to answer something in a different more elaborate way or give a shortened version of something, let me know.

Prof. Griff: Oh, give thanks. I really appreciate you and appreciate your time, and I will send you a copy of this before I actually put it out, alright?

Baruti: Okay. Fair enough, man. Take care of yourself.

Prof. Griff: Yes sir. Alright, hotep brother.

Baruti: Alright, hotep.

Prof. Griff: Okay, this is Professor Griff. That was Mwalimu K. Bomani Baruti, and we were dealing with Homosexuality and the Effeminization of the African Male, and we were also dealing with The Sex Imperative, two books out of his 12 books that he has written, in the context of the Psychological Covert War on Hip Hop as it relates to Pimps, Preachers, Politicians, Pedophiles, and the Pulpit; Money, Madness, Music and Mayhem; and Destroying Hip Hop's Appetite for Self-Destruction. The unconventional proposals were made by the US Air Force US military pondered love not war The US military investigated building a "gay bomb," which would make enemy soldiers "sexually irresistible" to each other, government papers say.

The tool of the Illuminati's agents to turn it into a culture of death

HIP HOP IS NOW OFFICIALLY GAY . . . POPULAR RAPPER THREATENS TO RAPE KANYE WEST . . . IF HE DOESN'T WORK WITH HIM!!! (EVIDENCE)

Hip-Hop Rumors: Lil B Threatens Kanye West With RAPE?

If Kanye West Dosent Acknowledge Me Over Twitter And Work With Me On Music, When i see him im going to fuck him in the ass - Lil B

LILBTHEBASEDGOD

"Hiding in Hip Hop: On the Down low in the Entertainment

we all know that rap and hip hop music hasn't always been friendly to the gays. Now Terrance Dean, a former MTV executive, is about to release his book, "Hiding in Hip Hop: On the Down low in the Entertainment Industry," next month. From the press release: "Hiding In Hip-Hop" uncovers a hidden and well-known unspoken secret. Deep within the confines of Hip-Hop is a prominent gay sub-culture. A world that industry insiders are keenly aware of, but choose to ignore. According to Dean, 'This book is filled with intrigue, sexy celebrity bed partners, abundance of drugs, and of course, the down low/gay men and celebrities in the entertainment industry.'"

GODDESS TALK LIVE BLOGTALK
INTERVIEW WITH UMAR ABDULLAH JOHNSON
AND PROFESSOR GRIFF

Dr. Umar Abdullah Johnson of Philadelphia delivers his presentation. *Photo: Erick Muhammad*
http://www.finalcall.com/artman/publish/ National_News_2/article_7449.shtml

Goddess: Okay, wow, beautiful. Thank you for breaking that down. Because there's the third chakra and below, everybody, is our lower chakra. So when Griff just said it hit him in his heart chakra, that means that his heart chakra was opened up with love for the art form, but Jay-Z and like you talked about the low energy frequency of rap, and thank you for pointing that out because that was really poignant, the low frequency energy of rap when we're talking about money, we're talking about cars, we're talking about clothes. So Bro. Umar, how does that have a direct effect on our young people? Because they glorify and they idolize these rappers...

Bro. Umar: Well, one of the things we have to understand, and this is one of the big shortcomings of Black people, underscoring Prof. Griff's statements and supporting them, is that we tend to be satisfied with simply having our art forms expressed and put out to the world. We are not taking it to the level of ownership, and by virtue of not going all the way to ownership of any art form, you do allow the culture bandits to come in and take it over. See, one of the biggest problems we have with music, with movies, with books, with any art form that you look at, is that most of them are thoroughly dominated financially and corporately by European structures. And the reason why that is, is because Black people coming out of that history of slavery and Jim Crow, coming out of that post-traumatic slavery disorder, coming out of that **mis**-education, we tend to be satisfied just with saying "I created this," but we're not satisfied with saying, "I control this." And as a result of that, more money goes to European corporations within music than actually goes to the arts. In fact, music is America's second leading export industry.

There is only one other industry that brings America more money than music. That's how much it is actually worth to the economy. But we keep very little of that money, and we're able to control very little of the content because we don't control the corporate structures through which these artists pass. See, every artist – whether you rap, whether you write, whether you do poetry, whether you sing, whether you dance – every artist ultimately has to make a decision about the furtherance of their career. They're either gonna decide that they're gonna take cash over control, or profit over power. In other words, if I'm a rapper, if I'm a writer, if I'm a dancer, if I'm an actor, I gotta decide how quickly do I want the world to hear my talent. And if I decided that I want the world to hear my talent too quickly and I don't exercise patience, that means I'm gonna end up giving up a lot of the control over my material to the Jewish-owned corporate structures because they have the distribution networks that allow my music to be heard all across the world. But by doing that, although it increases the amount of people who can hear me, it reduces the control that I have over my product. And ultimately, I become a slave to the same corporations that I made rich.

So we have to deal with control over the cash, the power over the profits. But another issue as it relates to hip hop and rap, and I definitely like the way Prof. Griff separated out the hip hop as being what you are and the rap being what you do – there's also that age-old argument of culture, and whether or not the art imitates the culture or whether the art is directing the culture. And from a psychological standpoint, I would argue that it's bi-directional. Artist's impact culture, but culture can impact artists. And one thing about music that we've always known - and this is true for any people, not just African people – the music of the day is always a good political post of the consciousness of a people.

Wielding her 50-plus radio stations like weapons, Wielding her 50-plus radio stations like weapons, Cathy Hughes gives "Black cover" to corporate, Republican politics while smearing the most progressive members of the Congressional Black Caucus. The presence of Revs. Jesse Jackson and Al Sharpton on her side of the fight over artist royalties is no surprise. How else are they going to stay on the radio?

Listen to the music of any people that which is most predominant on the radio, that which is most predominant in the community and it gives you a pretty good idea of what the level of political consciousness is for that people. And so right now, because so many Black people are so interested in listening to the negative rap, the gansta music, the buffoonery, that also shows how low our political consciousness has gotten. But along with that, another reason why hip hop, that positive creative force is getting lumped in with rap, is because a lot of the positive forces in hip hop, okay, tend not to engage in constructive criticism of those brothers and sisters who are doing the wrong thing.

As products of feverish corporate consolidation unleashed through wholesale deregulation of the industry in 1996, both chains are responsible for the "murder" of local Black radio, as I wrote in a the May 29, 2003 article, "Who Killed Black Radio News?":

"In the process, Black 'stand-alone' stations, typically operated by businesspeople with longstanding roots in the community, have been forced out - or have cashed out. News has most often been jettisoned in favor of 'talk' - the seductive format that ranges from quality syndications that do have value to a national audience but provide little to sustain local struggles, to vapid, 'barber shop'-type offerings, eclectic blocks of time filled with chatter, signifying nothing."

**Black Radio-One Tycoon Runs
Republican Game
by BAR executive editor Glen Ford**

"Cathy Hughes' mission to give greed and right-wing politics a 'Black' angle."
In a letter to station listeners ("my Radio One family"), Hughes claims Rep. Conyers' ("our 80 year old African-American Congressman") bill would "murder" Black-owned radio by putting "many black owned radio stations out of business. And force others to abandon their commitment to provide free music, entertainment, news, information, and money losing formats like gospel and black talk." The message is a wonderment of sheer gall, wild hyperbole, and a kind of audience abuse and blackmail.

219

The relative pittance in artist royalties required by the Performance Rights Act would have virtually no impact on the solvency of Hughes' radio empire, the fifth largest chain in the nation, which recently awarded Hughes' CEO son, Alfred Liggins, a $10 million bonus. The legislation already delays and minimizes the effect on small radio stations (billing less than $5 million a year). Hughes' threat to withhold "free…news" is at once hilarious and profoundly dishonest. Radio One does not do news, just like its main competitor in the Black-formatted radio market, Clear Channel. In this regard and many others, the two corporations are identical.

Black Radio-One Tycoon Runs Republican Game
by BAR executive editor Glen Ford

"Corporate predators like Cathy Hughes now claim to be the champions of small Black broadcasters."

Early in George Bush's first term in office, BET billionaire Bob Johnson ingratiated himself with the new president by convincing 48 other Black business people to endorse the Republican campaign against the Estate Tax. Although less than one-half of 1 percent of African Americans were wealthy enough to pay federal estate taxes, Johnson warned that the levy threatened to wipe out the first generation of Black millionaires, thus stunting the growth of capital in Black America. The claim was nonsense, but it gave "Black" political cover to the Right's ancient jihad against what it called, the "Death Tax." Johnson's attempt to merge general African American interests with those of the rich white Right earned him the gratitude of President Bush, who would later commission Johnson as Black point man in the GOP assault on Social Security. Johnson's anti-"Death Tax" list was top-heavy with on-the-make Black media types, including Radio One founder Cathy Hughes, then a newly-minted member of the Black billionaires club. Hughes is currently running the old Bob Johnson/ Republican game in an attempt to defeat the Performance Rights Act, which would require radio stations to pay royalties to performers of recordings played on the air. The legislation, co-sponsored by Rep. John Conyers (D-MI), is a prime target of the National Association of Broadcasters, the immensely powerful radio and television industry lobby, and the Republican Party, which has countered with its own "Local Radio Freedom Act."

The GOP characterizes the Performance Rights Act as a "tax" on radio, to be resisted like all other taxes – despite the fact that the royalties go to performing artists, not government coffers. But it is Cathy Hughes' mission to give greed and right-wing politics a "Black" angle– just as Bob Johnson did with the Estate Tax and Social Security. In one of the most crude, down-and-dirty campaigns in Black radio history, Hughes charges that the Performance Act threatens to destroy Black radio. Through the megaphone of her 50-plus stations (she once owned 70), Hughes lashes out at Conyers' colleagues on the Congressional Black Caucus who are co-sponsors of the bill ("these black elected officials continue to ignore the imminent danger to black media ownership"), Conyers' wife (who has been indicted for illegal conduct in totally unrelated circumstances), and even Dionne Warrick (who "nobody is playing," anyway, hisses Hughes).

"Hughes wields her broadcasting licenses as weapons to threaten Black congresspersons."

A recent issue of the congressional newspaper The Hill reported that the NAACP has called for a "truce" between Black Caucus members and Cathy Hughes ("Bitter feud between black radio, CBC over royalties," July 27). The headline is somewhat misleading. At its national convention in New York, last month, the NAACP enthusiastically endorsed the Conyers bill, declaring:

"H.R. 848 is the only source of income for many older performers. They didn't write the songs – but they brought them to life. Without the performers, these songs would be nothing but words on a page. And for many of them, radio performances are their only source of potential income. Therefore be it resolved that the NAACP endorses and supports H.R. 848, The Civil Rights for Musicians Act of 2009 and call on the NAACP units and members throughout the country to contact its Congressional members and Senators and the President of the United States to pass this measure into law so America's performers can receive the respect they so long deserve."

In Detroit, where Radio One and Clear Channel battle it out with identical formats and a common non-news policy, local NAACP president Rev. Wendell Anthony called a news conference to demand Hughes "stop [her] dishonest attacks." Rev. Anthony charged that "Conyers and other members of the CBC have been the target of a vicious smear campaign spearheaded by Big Radio corporations and CEOs who refuse to pay royalties to African-American musicians and performers."

The supposed "split" among Black "leaders" over this issue is also an illusion, although one that calls into question the very nature of what passes for "leadership" in Black America. Revs. Jesse Jackson and Al Sharpton have sided with Radio One – or more accurately, with the commercial broadcasting industry and Republicans in Congress. Nothing could be less surprising. Jackson and Sharpton are radio performers whose radio shows exist at the whim of Cathy Hughes or her counterparts at Clear Channel and other corporate chains. The two media reverends have come to more resemble corporate products, captives of broadcast boardrooms, than popular leaders.

"Hughes' message is a wonderment of sheer gall, wild hyperbole, and a kind of audience abuse and blackmail."

It is laughable, and yet also deeply sad, that corporate predators like Cathy Hughes, who grew fat and arrogant by systematically snuffing out and buying up local Black broadcasting, now claim to be the champions of small broadcasters. (As do her Republican allies, with their "Local Radio Freedom Act.") Hughes seems to threaten to pull out of "free" Black broadcasting if she has to pass on a small royalty to performers, as is the law in every other developed country. Folks need to call Hughes' bluff, and dare her to divest her Black radio interests, the source of her fortune. Black radio is a very profitable format, due largely to the unique loyalties of Black audiences. It is this loyalty that Hughes attempts to harness to her corporate, Republican-led campaign against the Performance Rights Act.

With a monopoly on the mass Black media microphone in many cities (literally), Hughes wields her broadcasting licenses as weapons to threaten Black congresspersons elected by citizens in "her" markets. Hughes has targeted Mel Watt (D-NC), Sheila Jackson Lee (D-TX), Bobby Scott (D-VA) and other Black co-sponsors of the Conyers bill. If, as reported, Hughes has run negative commercials attacking Performance Act supporters on her radio stations and refused to sell airtime to proponents of the Act, she is in violation of not only Federal Communications Regulations but also federal restraint of trade laws. Sean Glover, a spokesman for Music First, a coalition of performer royalty advocates, told BAR that legal action is contemplated against Hughes.

http://www.blackagendareport.com/content/black-radio-one-tycoon-runs-republican-game

"Corporate predators like Cathy Hughes now claim to be the champions of small Black broadcasters."

Early in George Bush's first term in office, BET billionaire Bob Johnson ingratiated himself with the new president by convincing 48 other Black business people to endorse the Republican campaign against the Estate Tax. Although less than one-half of 1 percent of African Americans were wealthy enough to pay federal estate taxes, Johnson warned that the levy threatened to wipe out the first generation of Black millionaires, thus stunting the growth of capital in Black America. The claim was nonsense, but it gave "Black" political cover to the Right's ancient jihad against what it called, the "Death Tax." Johnson's attempt to merge general African American interests with those of the rich white Right earned him the gratitude of President Bush, who would later commission Johnson as Black point man in the GOP assault on Social Security.

Johnson's anti-"Death Tax" list was top-heavy with on-the-make Black media types, including Radio One founder Cathy Hughes, then a newly-minted member of the Black billionaires club. Hughes is currently running the old Bob Johnson/Republican game in an attempt to defeat the Performance Rights Act, which would require radio stations to pay royalties to performers of recordings played on the air. The legislation, co-sponsored by Rep. John Conyers (D-MI), is a prime target of the National Association of Broadcasters, the immensely powerful radio and television industry lobby, and the Republican Party, which has countered with its own "Local Radio Freedom Act."

The GOP characterizes the Performance Rights Act as a "tax" on radio, to be resisted like all other taxes – despite the fact that the royalties go to performing artists, not government coffers. But it is Cathy Hughes' mission to give greed and right-wing politics a "Black" angle– just as Bob Johnson did with the Estate Tax and Social Security. In one of the most crude, down-and-dirty campaigns in Black radio history, Hughes charges that the Performance Act threatens to destroy Black radio. Through the megaphone of her 50-plus stations (she once owned 70), Hughes lashes out at Conyers' colleagues on the Congressional Black Caucus who are co-sponsors of the bill ("these black elected officials continue to ignore the imminent danger to black media ownership"), Conyers' wife (who has been indicted for illegal conduct in totally unrelated circumstances), and even Dionne Warrick (who "nobody is playing," anyway, hisses Hughes).

Frankie Crocker

I have many stories to tell about radio personality Frankie Crocker, but this one stands out as the one that began my career.It's not hard to write about a person who I had a crush on. Not the school girl sort of a crush but, an on-the-air "Disk Jockey" I want to be like you when I grow up kind of a crush. That person was Frankie Crocker.The man who put "more dips in your hips, more glide in your stride, Mr. do it to it.

As a teenager in Queens, New York, I grew up listening to the Super 16 - 1600 AM WWRL dj's. Folks like Gregory in the morning, Hank Spann "the soul server," "golden voice" Jerry Bledsoe, and all night Gary Byrd.

For example, those of us who are in the conscious community, if we see something going wrong, we might pull a brother to the side, or we might openly criticize that type of behavior as being anti-African, counter-revolutionary. That same thing is not happening in the hip hop movement. You have Prof. Griff and you have a few other brothers who will openly, opening criticize negative elements that are trying to culture bandit the art form, but a lot of rappers are not doing that, and silence implies consent. So if we really want to widen the gulf between what is rap versus what is hip hop, those positive artists, those true hip hop artists out there, have to start speaking up. They have to stop giving these lame assed, tongue-in-cheek rebukes of what's going on. Because right now we've got a situation in hip hop where the positive artists are doing the right thing but they're too afraid to critique the mainstream artists. And one of the reasons they're too afraid to critique the mainstream artists is because some of these artists have such power given to them by the Europeans – not true power, its false power - but they have such power where they can influence the careers of other artists on much smaller labels.

So if I'm a positive rapper and I'm gonna step out there and criticize Jay-Z, 50 Cent and Lil' Wayne -- Jay-Z, 50 Cent and Lil' Wayne's big connections in the music industry, can have me silenced. They can have my album pushed back. So a lot of positive rappers are afraid of the consequences that's gonna come from criticizing the mainstream. The last thing I'm gonna say and I'm gonna shut up on this point... Rap, gansta rap, negative music alone is not responsible for the destructive consciousness that we see right now in the Black community. Not enough is said about the impact of movies, motion pictures. Halle Berry's buffoonery is just as destructive to the minds of Black people as is Lil' Weezy and Jay-Z. These smut, number-one-selling smut graphic pornography soft-porn novels that our teenagers are reading is just as destructive to the minds of our children as is Lil' Weezy. Our comedians, our comedians with some of their negritude comedic jokes that they make are just as destructive, okay, as Lil' Wayne or

Young Geezy or anybody else, to the consciousness of Black people. So when we talk about art, we have to realize that hip hop, or negative rap, is just one aspect of a negative expression, a negative cultural art form that's sweeping our community. You have to deal with the movies, you have to deal with the comedy, and you also have to deal with these soft-porn novels sweeping our young people.

Bro. Umar: Definitely. Well, what Bro. Griff said, Nicki Minaj is probably gonna be the first of an entire cadre of bisexual, lesbian, and homosexual rappers that are gonna be rolled out to our community in the next five years. Nicki Minaj is a part of the psychosexual war against Black girls which is a deliberate attempt by population control freaks financed by white economic interests and supported by the United States government that is trying to make homosexuality and lesbianism the permanent form of sexual expression in the Black community as a means of population reduction. Whenever you want to enforce a method upon any population, you always want to use the television and the radio to help you do it. Why are the television and the radio more powerful than a gun or a bomb? Because with a gun or a bomb, you can only eliminate life, but with the television and the radio, you can condition the minds of millions of people, thusly converting them into allies in your war, as opposed to having to kill them as enemies.

The television deals with images, and the radio deals with images through sound. Both of them work through the medium of imagination – you can do more with this mind control campaign than you can do with just school alone, than you can do with just newspapers alone, than you can do with just church alone. So whenever you want a people to accept a certain type of indoctrination, you must put it through music. Because music is the language of the unconscious. In fact, our vertebrae in our spine, each note of music, there is a different note of music that corresponds to each of the vertebrae or unconscious in the African psyche. So music is a very, very subliminal and unconscious language and it's being used by the enemy to seduce adults as well as children into the lifestyle of lesbianism.

Nicki Minaj

Nicki Minaj is just the beginning. There's gonna be a whole cadre of homosexuals and lesbians, and this whole hip hop lesbian movement and this whole hip hop homosexual movement is part of a larger societal interest to rid America of Black people. We fail to grasp the essential importance of Marcus Garvey's message. And Mr. Garvey said that if the Negro is not careful, he will drink in all the poisons of western civilization and die from the effects of it. Stated another way, whatever Black people don't control will be used against them. Whatever Black people do not control WILL be USED against them. If you don't control your children, they will be used against you. If you don't control your music, it will be used against you. If you don't control your images, if you don't control your religion, if you don't control your community, it will be used against you. Rap, or the music industry, is just another Black institution that's being used against us because we fail to see the importance of controlling our own corporate structures.

Amber and Wiz Khalifah

223

Goddess: Spirit gave me that! Wow, we're going in tonight, y'all. We may not make it to the end of this show, but that's okay. I've been cut off before. It ain't no big thing. Alright, Bro. Umar, what you got to say, Bro.

Bro. Umar: Number one, I want to go back to the comment that was read before you went to the current topic of discussion. One of your listeners had said, oh boy – here we go again, homophobia. The word homophobia means a fear of homosexuals. Whoever made that comment obviously doesn't know the meaning, and also does not know that I do work with child homosexuals in the Black community. There is no fear of gays, lesbians, transgenders, or anybody else in Umar Johnson. I come in the image of God and I stand on my square. Homophobia – to be afraid of – I fear nobody, no man or woman, whether gay or straight, okay? But the truth of the matter is that homosexuality is a strategy that has been pushed on Black people by the ruling elite in an attempt to reduce our numbers. It is simultaneously being pushed on Black people in America, it is being pushed on Black people in the Caribbean, it is being pushed on Black people in Africa, and it is being pushed on Black people in Asia.

We are under a psychosexual war, and we have to recognize it for what it is. Too many Black people have allowed CNN, C-SPAN, these Negro politicians, and certain religious leaders and the white society at large to convince them that they have to accept homosexuality, just like white people had to accept Black people. I wanna make it crystal clear that who you come out of your mother as, being born as an African is a natural universal phenomenon over which we have no control. All we have to do is look to Michael Jackson, rest in peace, and you'll see someone who tried to make himself look European and could not do it. You cannot change your race. Sexual preference, who you choose to cohabitate with behind closed doors, is a choice. There is absolutely no concrete proof, no research whatsoever that conclusively proves that homosexuals and lesbians are born that way. Furthermore, we have to understand that homosexuality has its roots in Greco-Roman culture, where many of the highly placed and highly educated Greco-Romans were homosexual because they believed that the woman was the foundation of evil; that through the woman, Satan actually did his work. So they stayed away from the woman. They hated the woman, they despised the woman. And whenever they needed to have sex to fulfill their royal oats, they went and had it with men. And not only did they have sex with men, they had sex with boys. Pedophilia and homosexuality goes hand-in-hand. Pedophilia and homosexuality goes hand-in-hand.

Vatican Will Root Out Gay Priests With Sex Tests

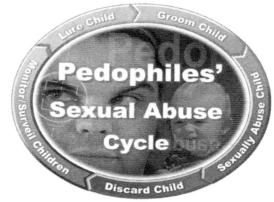

Oct 31. 2008 1:23 AM CDT

224

Furthermore, we have to understand that in the Black community, anybody who is lesbian, anybody who is gay came to that lifestyle because of some unresolved psychological issue that has its root in childhood. Show me a Black homosexual, show me a Black lesbian, and I will show you somebody who was struggling from an unmet psychological need. Homosexuality and lesbianism is a psychopathology. There's nothing natural about it. I do not hate Black homosexuals, I do not hate Black lesbians, and I don't hate **any** Black person. Just like a killer can be rehabilitated, just like a drug addict can be rehabilitated, I also know for a fact that a lesbian and a homosexual can be rehabilitated. So I don't believe in throwing anybody away with the bathwater. Everybody can be saved. But we have to have limits, and we have to be able to constructively criticize behaviors that are detrimental to our community. The bottom line is homosexuality is being pushed by the Rockefeller Population Council, Planned Parenthood International, Bill Gates, the United Nations, and other organizations that are pushing it as an alternative lifestyle to reduce Black numbers.

It is no coincidence that the first documented cases of HIV Aids were uncovered in the early 70's, which is the same time that the American Psychiatric Association decided that homosexuality would no longer be considered a mental disorder in America. Until 1972, 1973, homosexuality was a psychopathology. It changed. Why did they change homosexuality from being abnormal to normal? So it could be used against the Black community. So they could turn Black men gay, give them AIDS, and so those Black men could give AIDS to Black women, and today as we speak, AIDS is the number one killer of Black women on all six continents. (Europe is not a continent.) AIDS is the number one killer of Black women on all six continents, and most of them are getting that AIDS directly from the government – from Black bisexual men who were given AIDS by the government. If you love your people, you cannot be for homosexuality and lesbianism, because homosexuality and lesbianism is the Skull and Bones in the Black community.

Bro. Umar: Well, I totally agree with what Bro. Seville said. The Queen, the Black woman, is the first teacher of the child, as we all know. So anything she believes, consciously or unconsciously, is gonna be taught to that child, verbally or nonverbally. So we have to deal with the sisters. We also have to deal with the fact of; we have to understand that the female energy and the male energy are two opposites of the one whole. It's going to be hard to solve the race focusing on the men without the women and vice versa, by focusing on the women without the men. There is a conscious and the unconscious of African people and African women. There are reasons why so many of our sisters are single, why so many of our sisters have turned to lesbianism, why so many of our sisters keep on attracting the same type of man to them even though they know it's not what they need. The role their father had, or didn't have, in their life and sets them up for certain types of relationship failures. So any Black woman out there are wrestling with why they are in an unsatisfying relationship or why they can't find a satisfactory relationship.

Goddess: Yeah, he was in bed with a white man…

Prof. Griff: Exactly. The Tooth Fairy, or The Tooth Hurts, with – what's the brother's name, Dwayne… this is ridiculous. I'm looking at some of this stuff in front of me. I don't know how anyone can defend this. When we go through the homosexual ritual that's going on in Hollywood, we can talk about Wesley Snipes, Madea now, Ru Paul, Martin Lawrence, I mean we could go on and on. So the only thing we did was ask the question: What is going on in Hollywood that Black men have to go through this ritual where they have to put on a dress and become effeminized. So I went back to do my research and I met with Baruti again and he handed me the book, **Homosexuality and the Effeminization of African Males**. And I started looking into why I am starting to see this homosexual ritual inside of hip hop. So I went back to study these things, and I looked at, what is the character that Jamie Foxx played on In Living Color when he dressed up as a woman?

Prof. Griff: I said wow, this is kind of critical. So I started looking back even further now, and I'm saying, is this just something that they like to do? So in that same lecture, I applauded, what's the comedian's name that gave the $50 million back, Dave Chappelle, who said they tried to set him up, basically…

Prof. Griff: So I started looking back at Eddie Murphy's first single that he put out, **Put It In Your Butt**, and then later on he's dressing up as a woman. And we can go on and on and on. It's almost, now, almost like a ritual, almost like an initiation. And then recently some of the young brothers from B2K came out on Oprah and admitted that they were molested.

Goddess: Yeah, that their manager was sodomizing them and stuff.

Prof. Griff: So we could go on and on and on. So I'm asking the question, when does the buck stop? So I mentioned Quincy Jones and how Quincy Jones set up this sex ring in Hollywood. And Tevin Campbell came through that. Queen Latifah and Fresh Prince came through that. And it's almost like an initiation; it's almost like a ritual. So we have to understand this particular dynamic. And we have to go into racism, white supremacy, and see why this has becoming almost like an initiation and a ritual.

Bro. Umar: It is not just those who are well-placed in entertainment. Even on the entry level, you see people who are asked to make sexual sacrifices in order to be given the opportunity to achieve some sort of stardom. See, one thing we have to realize – the one thing that America fears more than anything else is not the Afghani people, it's not the Iraqis, it's not the conscious. What America fears more than anything else is strong, Black, uncompromising manhood. That's the only thing that could destabilize, okay, the social order. Strong, uncompromising Black manhood. And because it is strong, uncompromising Black manhood, Black men, every Black man, every Black man, has to make or has had to make a decision as to whether they are going to stand up and fight white racism and take it on head on, or whether they are going to accommodate white racism and be used as a tool of the oppressor. Which is why when you look at many Black comedians, when you look at many Black actors, when you look at many Black musicians and rappers, if they have chosen to accommodate and support white supremacy, nearly every last one of them at some point in their career has either had to date a white woman or dress as a woman. Hands down, few exceptions to that rule. You're either gonna date a white woman or dress as a woman. By doing either one of those behaviors, you send a nonverbal message to the white man that "I am okay. I am your boy. I am willing to accept your rule over me."

Because see, at the end of the day, that's the only thing that can resist masculinity is masculinity. So if a Black man decides he's not gonna resist white supremacy which is ran by the white male, and then he's automatically accepting bitchhood to the white man. There is no other way. You are either going to affirm your Black manhood, or you're gonna accept Black male bitchhood. But it can't be both. And that's why they dress up like women, that's why they act like women, that's why they marry these white women, because they have to prove to the white man that "I am …" in order for them not to be emasculated or castrated. And every Black man has to make that decision, and unfortunately a lot of Black mothers, single mothers in particular, because they fear for their son's safety, are raising our boys in a very effeminate way. They are deliberately effeminizing the boys so they pose no threat to white society. And that is exactly why more Black men have to get involved in the lives of Black boys who don't have a father. Because if you leave a Black boy to his Black mother, she may do more damage to him that the white system could ever do, just by virtue of her desire to protect him from the white onslaught of violence. And because so many Black mothers are afraid of what could happen to their sons, they deliberately turn them into women before they even run into a white man.

Goddess: Bro. Umar Abdullah Johnson just said, stop babying our boys. You know, we're afraid because we don't want to turn them in to the world have them be killed or not see them live to be in their right age of manhood, but we also have to stop cradling them and babying them. And Black man, whether you have a son or not, whether he's your boy or not, you gotta get in that boy's life. We got some comments in the chat room. Okay, here's a question from FreeForReal: "If you're so opposed to homosexuality, how do you propose to eradicate it? If you eradicate it, how do you ensure that another woman doesn't bore another homosexual? You're fighting a battle that doesn't need to be fought." Wow. Okay, so what do you guys have to say about that? How do we eradicate homosexuality?

Bro. Umar: Number one, number one, he made an assumption in this question that's incorrect. He said something to the effect that if you eliminate the homosexuals who exist now, how do you prevent a woman from boring another homosexual. That statement assumes that homosexuals are born into this world from nature. That is not true. There is no proof to that whatsoever. So I can't answer the question 'cause there's an assumption in the question that is incorrect. And he's assuming that homosexuals are born from nature to be the way they are. And I'm telling him and everyone else that homosexuals come to that way of life through nurture, not through nature. In fact, just last year, the American Psychological Association revised its official policy statement on homosexuality, and I would recommend that young man go and read the APA's new policy on homosexuality. And they have retraced from their original premise that homosexuality may have been a natural phenomenon.

Goddess Talk Live

"Goddess Talk Live" is a platform and venue where we promote embracing the goddess within. Men are encouraged to listen and to participate. "Goddess Talk Live" is hosted by the "Neo-Soul Nina Simone" Mia Miata and ...

They have since revised their position, and this is white folks, by the way, the American Psychological Association, has now stated that there is no absolute proof that homosexuality is a natural condition. You have to understand as I said before; homosexuality does not have any roots in Africa. There was nowhere in any of the African cultures, we're talking over 200 different ethnicities and languages, and not one of them had a word to describe homosexuality or lesbianism. There was no homosexuality or lesbianism on the continent prior to the arrival of the white man. We don't want to admit it, and it sounds like that brother there, he's so supportive of homosexuals he may be one, and I'm not gonna knock him for that, okay, but we have to be very, very careful that if we are in the business of fighting, okay, for our rightful place in history and our rightful place in the world political structure, then we also have to fight to eradicate any system, any mindset, any strategy, any behavior that hinders the progress of Black people.

I can flip that around on the other side and say look at the fact that only one out of every four Black women will get married in America. Black women have the worst marriage rate, the lowest marriage rate, in America and that's for a lot of reasons. So for every homosexual male cohabitating with a man, that could have been a potential mate for one of my sisters. So if I am about the process, the mission of nation building, how in the hell can I tolerate a man being with a man and a woman being with a woman? Every Black person who is lesbian or homosexual is a lesbian or homosexual because the natural order of things in the household in which they were raised by their mother or father was upset, some emotional need was not filled, some psychological experience unconsciously disturbed them, and the homosexuality and lesbianism is a form of psychopathology. That's all it's ever been, that's all it is, and that's all it ever will be. And for Black people to accept homosexuality and lesbianism as normal means that we have to become insane. For us to accept homosexuality as normal means that we have to become insane.

And the most interesting, the most clever thing that the New World Order folk have done with homosexuality is took it into civil rights mode. That was a very, very powerful move because now, homosexuality is a civil right, so anybody who opposes homosexuality as a behavior, okay, is automatically going to be labeled as a bigot, is automatically going to be labeled as someone who does not believe in equality for all. We gotta be very careful with the way they can use these labels against us. So if you say I'm not for homosexuality, you're automatically, automatically, by definition, someone who does not believe in equality for all people. And I believe all people are people, but I refuse to accept the lifestyle that is anti-African and genocidal. That's just the way it is.

Goddess: Well Bro. Umar, really quickly, FreeForReal says "I am very homosexual and play an important part in my nephews' lives, whose father is nowhere to be found. Do I say to myself, I cannot offer guidance and teach them about responsibility, life, and love because I am a homosexual? No." So to answer your question, yes, he is a homosexual and he defends his lifestyle and says that I can still have a positive impact on the lives of other Black males.

Bro. Umar: I cannot tell him not to play a role in his nephews' lives. And I would trust, and I would like to hope, that he does not attempt to influence his nephews with his own beliefs about gender identity and sexual preference. However, as a psychologist, I am aware that any belief that we hold to be true and all of us have a set of values and core beliefs that our life is based upon, and if you are a homosexual or a lesbian, you have a core belief that homosexuality or lesbianism is a nature form of healthy sexual expression. If you believe that, it is gonna be very hard for him not to impart that message to his nephews verbally or nonverbally. That energy is gonna resonate with that young man. That doesn't mean that his nephew's gonna be homosexual because **he** is, but it definitely means that his nephew may be more accepting of the lifestyle and more willing to explore the lifestyle just by virtue of the fact that he has an uncle who he looks up to who doesn't see a problem with it. So I'm not saying it's wrong for him to be in his nephew's life, but I want them to understand the intentional or unintentional, conscious or unconscious influence he's gonna have on that young man by virtue of him being a homosexual and at the same time serving as his role model.

804: I just wanted to make a brief comment. I do have to respectfully disagree with the guests on a couple of notes. Mainly the key part about there not being any evidence of gays or homosexuality in antiquity. That's just a falsehood. As long as there has been society, there have been gay people. To state that no one in Africa was gay until [recent history] is just ridiculous, simply because when you study the different societies in Africa, first of all, there is not blatant, as much as there is today, there is not separate name calling and different things as that because in antiquity, our societies were different. We didn't cast people aside, we didn't ostracize them, gays were a part of the community, and some societies such as those who recognized the gate keepers who were homosexuals, those were individuals who were actually called upon to keep, so to say, the priests of the community, because it was looked at as they don't have children or wives to take care of, so they were actually the ones who were supposedly blessed to stay spiritual all day while everyone else went and did the business that needed to be done to keep the community running. These were in functioning societies in Africa, that's a fact. You don't find a lot of negative information written because these people were loved and kept as part of the community, therefore they were not separate. So there would be no separate writing about them. They were not ostracized the way that that they are today. Also, this thinking…

804: Yes, this is my last point. What I'm really concerned about is this line of thinking that gay is not African, is not Black, and is less than human. This thought in the conscious community and in the Black family period is the reason why Black women are contracting AIDS at an alarming rate.

Prof. Griff: Can I ask you, where are you getting your facts from?

804: Where am I getting my facts?

Bro. Umar: Yes…

804: The fact that…

Bro. Umar: No, what is your source, Queen?

Prof. Griff: Yeah, what's your source?

Bro. Umar: Where are you getting your information? What sources can you quote? Where are you getting this?

229

804: This is information that can be found widely in books...

Bro. Umar: No, I need a source...

804: You don't even have to go to antiquity to look at this. Look at what's happening to Black women right now

Prof. Griff: We just want to know your facts, where are you getting this from?

Goddess: One at a time, one at a time...

804: I understand that you have rights about people, but what I'm saying is this attitude about being gay or homosexual is not human and is wrong is the reason why we have brothers even in the conscious community grouping together in the form of study groups in temples, getting together in homosexual acts, and then coming back to the women, and the women are being plagued with sickness and disease because rather than having an open discussion about what's natural in nature and what is not, we're ostracizing people and causing the people to keep secrets and lies and bringing things home and disrupting the home. Women are dying because people don't think it's normal to be gay.

Goddess: We may have to go over a little bit, but ...

804: This is information can be researched; this is not secret research into this period. The research ...

Bro. Umar: I wanna know where you got that information, so I'm not gonna research, you put out a certain premise and you are required to defend that premise... If I understand you correctly, you are insinuating that homosexuality was a normal part of African society, and I'm asking...

Prof. Griff: Right.

804: ... society period.

Bro. Umar: No, no, no, no - you were talking about antiquity, though.

804: Everything started in antiquity...

Bro. Umar: Whose antiquity are we talking about? Whose antiquity? If you're talking about Greco-Roman antiquity, you're absolutely right...

Prof. Griff: She's correct, right.

804: No, no, no, no - I find it amazing that we pick and choose what **we** brought here and what we didn't.

Bro. Umar: Okay, so you're saying that **we** brought homosexuality to America. I'm asking you to give me the source of that information. That's all I'm asking.

804: I didn't say we brought it to America. I said ...

Bro. Umar: I wanna check that out. I never heard ...

Prof. Griff: I never heard that either...

804: I didn't say we brought it to America, I said it existed.

Bro. Umar: Okay...

230

Prof. Griff: No, no, no, no, no, like I said, I just wanna know the source. I'm sitting here in my library, I got my finger on my mouse, I got people on my other phone, I got my research team ready, I'm ready. I wanna know where she's getting this information from. 'Cause I'm not just gonna go on somebody's opinion and how they feel 'cause they wanna sleep with somebody that's cute.

Goddess: Well in the chat room it says, "Just Google it man, put 'edu' in the search criteria." Which we all know that everything you find online is not true…

Bro. Umar: No, no, no, no – Google search is not an acceptable form of scholarship. Anything can be put on the internet, okay? So that's not acceptable. And even if you got the information off the internet, you should be able to reference it. So if it's a website, if it was an article, if it was a research journal, if it was a historical document, you should still be able to reference it. But you can't just come on the radio and say that homosexuality was freely practices in Africa and not be able to provide any kind of source material for that information!

Goddess: Alright Bro. Umar, how do we heal…

Bro. Umar: Indeed. Firstly, number one, in order to heal, it must first be accepted that there is a problem. There must be acceptance that there is a problem. One of the biggest issues in the Black community is we don't want to accept that we have problems. We don't want to accept that homosexuality is not healthy. We don't want to accept that boys being raised by single parent mothers are not healthy. We don't want to accept that the violence is not healthy.

You can't solve anything when you've got people trying to defend the illness. We are the only race of people on the face of the earth who will defend our right to destroy ourselves. The **only** people on the face of the earth who will defend the right to destroy ourselves. So we have to accept that there is a problem, and then we have to agree to disagree in coming up on strategies. Now we can disagree on strategy, but we cannot disagree on ideology and policy. There must be a certain set of principles that we are willing to live by and raise our children upon. If we cannot come up with a core set of principles that we are gonna stand on and affirm, we will never be able to have unity in the community because everybody will be raising their child a different way. If anyone needs to reach me, I can be reached at UmarAbdullahJohnson@yahoo.com; you can get me on facebook at umarabdullah-johnson, telephone 215-989-9858. If anybody needs to reach me, any issues regarding your children, special education, ADHD, psychotropic medications, feel free to call on me at any time.

Goddess: Wow, this has been a powerful show, thank you so much for tuning in to Goddess Talk Live. Peace, Kings, thank you so much, to Prof. Griff…

Prof. Griff: Alright, Peace. Peace.

Goddess: Minister of Information, Public Enemy. Love you. Peace and blessings. To Umar Abdullah Johnson, thank you so much for joining us this evening.

This has been another edition of Goddess of Love ………………

nia@goddessoflove.com

US military pondered love not war
The unconventional proposals were made by the US Air Force

The US military investigated building a "gay bomb", which would make enemy soldiers "sexually irresistible" to each other, government papers say.

1. Title: Harassing, Annoying, and "Bad Guy" Identifying Chemicals

2. Type of Effort:S & T

3. Proposed by: Wright Laboratory

4. Capability Sought and Uses to Which It Could Be Put:

   (1) Category #3: Chemicals that effect human behavior so that discipline and morale in enemy units is adversely effected. One distasteful but completely non-lethal example would be strong aphrodisiacs, especially if the chemical also caused homosexual behavior. Another example would be a chemical that made personnel very sensitive to sunlight.

FROM MILITARY DOCUMENTS
UNCOVERED BY THE SUNSHINE PROJECT

Breaking News
LIVE Chinese Military Successfully tests the Gay Bomb

Other weapons that never saw the light of day include one to make soldiers obvious by their bad breath. The US defence department considered various non-lethal chemicals meant to disrupt enemy discipline and morale. The 1994 plans were for a six-year project costing $7.5m, but they were never pursued. The US Air Force Wright Laboratory in Dayton, Ohio, sought Pentagon funding for research into what it called "harassing, annoying and 'bad guy'-identifying chemicals". The plans were obtained under the US Freedom of Information by the Sunshine Project, a group which monitors research into chemical and biological weapons

The Air Force lab responsible for the gay bomb and the fart bomb have nothing on what the DOD has in the works today. Researchers at the Monell Chemical Senses Center in Philadelphia are working with the Department of Defense to develop the baddest smell you ever smelled. We're talking a mixture of vomit, excrement, B.O., burnt hair, and rotting flesh and garbage. Just thinking about it is making me queasy. The important thing to note is the need for a combination of many sources of stench—just vomit or just burnt hair won't do it because our brains can too readily adjust to accommodating one stink. But throw a half dozen at us and we're at the mercy of our gag reflex. Ultimately, the potent cocktail could be used in a "bomb" of sorts for crowd dispersal. It's also being considered for helping soldiers become accustomed to unpleasant environments

9TH DEGREE

© PROFESSOR GRIFF'Z 3RD EYE REFLEXTIONZ

Hustlers of Culture

it's bigger than hip hop, it's beyond beats and rhymes

"There is no reason to accept the doctrines crafted to sustain power and privilege, or to believe that we are constrained by mysterious and unknown social laws. These are simply decisions made within institutions that are subject to human will and that must face the test of legitimacy. And if they do not meet the test, they can be replaced by other institutions that are freer and more just, as has happened often in the past."

-- Noam Chomsky

TAVISTOCK, Tavistock Center - The Best Kept Secret in America

by Dr. John Coleman (February 26, 2004)

The Tavistock Institute - Illuminati Fascists Use Nazi "Mind Control" Techniques

To Destroy America

The Tavistock Institute originated the *mass civilian bombing raids* carried out by Roosevelt and Churchill purely as a clinical experiment in mass terror, keeping records of the results as they watched the guinea pigs reacting under *controlled laboratory conditions*!**Covertmatric.atspace.com**

The Tavistock Institute developed the mass brainwashing techniques which were first **used experimentally on American prisoners of war in Korea**!**Covertmatrix website**

Statue Of Sigmund Freud in
front of the Tavistock Institute
of Human Relations in London

Created at Oxford in 1921 by the Royal Institute for International Affairs, with later funding from the Rockefeller Foundation, the Tavistock Institute of Human Relations is the nerve center for the global manipulation of human consciousness.

Tavistock Institute of Human Relations in London. There I hand in my resignation as a Mindless Robotic Consumer.

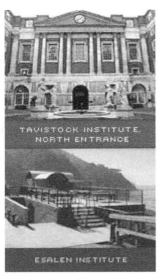

Now let's shift our focus from *Esalen* to *the NTL* and its double headquarters at *Bethel, Maine*; and Washington, D.C. (1201 16th St., N.W.).

Tavistock - The Science of Mass Manipulation through Crisis Creation

An Introduction to the Tavistock Institute of Human Relations

We take a look at the Tavistock Institute of Human Relations, which is described in this video as the nerve center for the global manipulation of human consciousness.

Established in 1921 by the <u>Royal Institute for International Affairs</u> (RIIA), Tavistock has grown into one of the world's biggest and most influential think tanks, working through governments, NGOs, the media, transnational corporations and major universities to manipulate the population of the world into accepting a one world collectivist state.

Tavistock - Systems Psychodynamics - mass brain-washing techniques

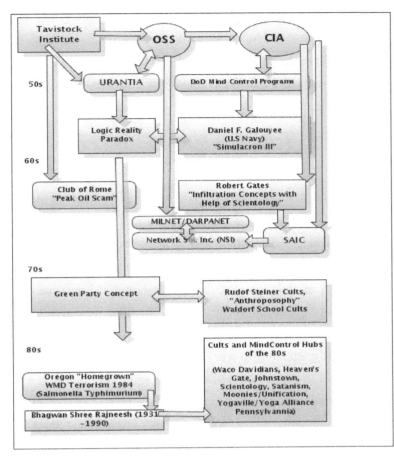

Tavistock Institute developed the mass brain-washing techniques which were first used experimentally on American prisoners of war in Korea. Its experiments in crowd control methods have been widely used on the American public, a surreptitious but nevertheless outrageous assault on human freedom, by modifying individual behavior through topical psychology. A German refugee, Kurt Lewin, became director of Tavistock in 1932. He came to the U.S. in 1933 as a "refugee," the first of many infiltrators. Lewin set up the Harvard Psychology Clinic, which originated the propaganda campaign to turn the American public against Germany and involve us in World War II.

http://educate-yourself.org/nwo/nwotavistockbestkeptsecret.shtml

All Tavistock and American foundation techniques have a single goal -- to break down the psychological strength of the individual and render him helpless to oppose the dictators of the World Order. Any technique which helps to break down the family unit, and family inculcated principles of religion, honor, patriotism and sexual behavior, is used by the Tavistock scientists as weapons of crowd control.

Today the Tavistock Institute operates a $6 Billion a year network of Foundations in the U.S., all of it funded by U.S. taxpayers' money. Ten major institutions are under its direct control, with 400 subsidiaries, and 3000 other study groups and think tanks which originate many types of programs to increase the control of the World Order over the American people. The Stanford Research Institute, adjoining the Hoover Institution, is a $150 million a year operation with 3300 employees. It carries on program surveillance for Bechtel, Kaiser, and 400 other companies, and extensive intelligence operations for the CIA. It is the largest institution on the West Coast promoting mind control and the behavioral sciences.

Systems psychodynamics is an interdisciplinary field that integrates three disciplines — the practice of psychoanalysis, the theories and methods of group relations, and open systems perspectives. Systems psychodynamics is "a term used to refer to the **collective psychological behavior**" (Neumann, 1999, p. 57) within and between groups and organizations. "Systems psychodynamics," therefore, provides a way of thinking about energizing or motivating forces resulting from the interconnection between various groups and sub-units of a social system."(Neumann, 1999, p. 57)

Operation Paperclip was the codename under which the US intelligence and military services extricated scientists from Germany during and after the final stages of World War II. The project was originally called Operation Overcast, and is sometimes also known as Project Paperclip. Of particular interest were scientists specializing in aerodynamics and rocketry (such as those involved in the V-1 and V-2 projects), chemical weapons, chemical reaction technology and medicine. These scientists and their families were secretly brought to the United States, without State Department review and approval; their service for Hitler's Third Reich, NSDAP and SS memberships as well as the classification of many as war criminals or security threats also disqualified them from officially obtaining visas. An aim of the operation was capturing equipment before the Soviets came in. The US Army destroyed some of the German equipment to prevent it from being captured by the advancing Soviet Army. The majority of the scientists, numbering almost 500, were deployed at White Sands Proving Ground, New Mexico, Fort Bliss, Texas and Huntsville, Alabama, to work on guided missile and ballistic missile technology. This, in turn, led to the foundation of NASA and the US ICBM program.

So in the spirit of exploration and discovery, We the team, have dubbed ourselves "Project Paperclip."

In the words of Paul Harvey, "That's the rest of the story . . . . Good Day!"

ALLEN DULLES is shown here in 1962, sitting at center in the presidential limo, between JFK and John McCone, having just been fired as head of the CIA. More than anyone, he affected the shape of modern US intel.

During WWII, he was a top member of the OSS, serving alone at the Berne station where he ran deep cover operations within the Reich and even helped in the failed bomb plot against Hitler. These secret Nazi connections were later exploited by him - along with ANGLETON, HELMS, and others - when secret deals placed Nazis like REINHARD GEHLEN and KLAUS BARBIE in important positions around the world.

In 1953 he became the 2nd DCI. Under his watch, the CIA became the covert action wing of the government, ostensibly under Presidential control. Under Dulles, coups were staged in Guatemala, Iran, Indonesia, Vietnam, and elsewhere. A massive global propaganda machine was created, and called The Mighty Wurlitzer by its commanders. In its darkest shadows, the Agency gave birth to the MK-ULTRA mind control program.

Fired by JFK after the Bay of Pigs disaster, Dulles later helped engineer his assassination and the subsequent cover-up, knowingly hiding key information from the Warren Commission, and quashing important lines of investigation.

Source: **http://subliminal.org/ mugbook/spooks/dulles.html**
http://www.operationpaperclip.info/

Much of the information surrounding Operation Paperclip is still classified

Jim Keith, i*n his 1996 book Mass Control, meticulously lays out the factual and documented ground work for mass mind control through network television and exposes now declassified CIA and Nazi mind control operations such as Project Monarch and Project Paperclip.*

The book also exposes the "culture creation" industry from the minds of the social engineers themselves, from Manchurian candidates and eugenics to secret satanic cults. A must read for anyone interested in the history of social engineering from the mouths of the elite

Experiments Into Remote Mind Control Technology

"The large black top of the Federal Building in San Francisco looks like a giant air-conditioning vent, 50 feet tall, comprising the entire top of the building. It is actually a radar, microwave, and radio transparent shield for an array of communications devices on the roof of the building. Such "blinds" on top of government buildings are nothing unusual, it isn't necessary to visually remind everybody that such buildings also are likenesses of Orwell's Ministry of Information (read, CIA).

-- Jim Keith (1949-1999)

Jay-Z, Diddy, Akon Top Forbes' 2010 "Hip Hop Cash Kings" List

- For the second year in a row, S. Dot Carter tops the Forbes rankings. See what estimated sum your favorite star brought in.Despite the rocky economy of this past year, Hip Hop's elite have still found a way to keep their earnings piling in.

Forbes has put out their 2010 *Forbes* "Hip Hop Cash Kings" list, which includes many returners as well as some rookies. For the second year in a row, Shawn "Jay-Z" Carter tops the list with estimated gross earnings of $63 million, while second- ranked Sean "Diddy" Combs pulled in $30 million.

Mr. Carter's earnings stemmed from the release of his album *Blueprint 3*, the launch of his worldwide tour, his 40/40 nightclub chain, as well as his partial ownership of the New Jersey Nets. Diddy's role in *Get Him To The Greek*, Diago vodka, Ciroc, Diddybeats earbuds, and other miscellaneous roles in television and film, helped him cash in his $30 million.

Lady Gaga, the Konvict Clothing label, and a World Cup soccer ad campaign with Pepsi, assisted Aliuane "Akon" Thiam in his first top five appearance on Hip Hop Cash Kings. Akon ranks number three with $21 million, and right behind him Dwayne "Lil Wayne" Carter lands himself a spot at number four with $20 million. Andre "Dr. Dre" Young rounds out the top five with $17 million from his Beats by Dr. Dre headphone line.

RICHEST MUSIC PRODUCERS:

Dr. Dre and The Neptunes set the bar by charging a $200,000-$250,000 per track but Timbaland took it to another level by charging pop stars $500,000 per track. Earlier this year, Timbaland revealed that hip-hop production fees were much less than they were five years ago. Timbaland followed the money and started producing pop acts: Justin Timberlake, Nelly Furtado, and The Pussycat Dolls. All of their albums went multi-platinum and he's currently working with Madonna. This savvy move netted Timberland $21 million dollars in 2006. Forbes placed him fourth on their "Hip-Hop Rich List," behind Jay-Z ($34 million), 50 Cent ($32 million) and Diddy ($28 million). Music producer Scott Storch (fourth photo) came in 10th place with $17 million.

- **http://panachereport.com/channels/coverstories/jennifer.htm**

Currently Vivendi has a BBB rating and intends to keep it after the merger or purchase. Therefore, Vivendi has to maintain or reduce the consolidated debt when compared to its EBITDA from all its subsidiaries after the acquisition.

Buying Zain Africa for $12bn therefore poses a problem. From financial statements for the Year 2008, Vivendi posted a net EBITDA of about $69bn and net Income of $38bn, while Zain had an EBITDA of $2.78bn and Income of $1.2bn. Let's do simple arithmetic -

Total income for 2008 of both companies will be $38bn + $1.2bn = $39.2bn.
Cost of Zain Africa = $12bn.

Now do you think after spending $12bn for a purchase, we've not calculated net accumulated debts, Vivendi will maintain its BBB rating? Hell NO!!!

Well there you have it folks. One more twist in the ongoing saga. Cheers and have a beautiful day.

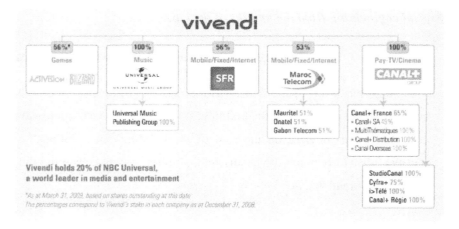

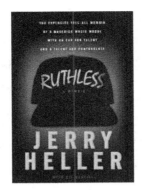

THE LATEST and most fascinating book on the music business, *Ruthless*, written by my friend of 40 years, **Jerry Heller**, is out in stores now. I first met Jerry when he was booking **The Rascals** and **Van Morrison** back in the '60s. Neither of us imagined that later he would make history in partnership with a young visionary from Compton named **Eazy-E**, who was the genius behind N.W.A.

Forming Ruthless Records, they would go on to release one of the all-time greatest rap albums, *Boyz-N-the-Hood*, establish West Coast rap, and launch the careers of **Ice Cube** and **Dr. Dre** (who would then go on to launch the careers of **Snoop Dog**, **Eminem** and **50 Cent**). The book is an insightful look into those early days at Ruthless that even include the beginnings of a young University of Nevada football player turned security guard named **Suge Knigh**, Eazy was a real gentleman and a kid at heart ... I remember Eazy joining Jerry, his wife **Gayle**, and myself for dinner at John Dominis making a grand entrance on a skateboard ...

In Jerry Heller's book, "Ruthless," he gives a tell-all account of a incident involving N.W.A, that inspired the song, "Fuck Tha Police." Eazy, Dre, Yella and Heller were hanging out in front of their recording studio during a break. Heller stood on the sidelines and protested in awe as the police completely excused him from the routine pat-down administered to the other three. He adds, that's what made "F--- tha Police" such a potent and prophetic song. In Related News: It's always been rumored that Eazy-E's widow settled with all of his baby mama's after he died. Allegedly, after the children were proven to be his via DNA, each woman was broken off a nice financial settlement preventing any future financial claims against his estate.

Lara Lavi - The Resurrection Of Death Row

Recently **Lara Lavi**, CEO of WIDEawake Entertainment Group purchased the **Death Row** catalog for 18 million dollars. **Ms. Lavi** is unstoppable! She is an attorney, entrepreneur, CEO, business development specialist, producer, singer/songwriter, pianist, and mother. To say that she is well-rounded is an understatement!

Lara Lavi has big plans for **Death Row**, a label that was home to many unforgettable artists such as **Tupac Shakur**, **Snoop Dogg**, **Tha Dogg Pound**, **Warren G**, and **Lisa "Left Eye" Lopez**. **Ms. Lavi's** aggressive business plan to resurrect **Death Row** includes placing the music in film, television, gaming, and advertising. Additionally, she plans to put out a graphic novel project called *Hustle City*, which you will hear more about below. According to **Ms. Lavi**, **Death Row** music depicts "a militant request for social change" and a "youthful eruption of expression of distrust of the man." She explains that these are the true stories of "the original **Boyz N The Hood** -- some got out, some didn't, some lived, some died." So the story goes...

"Little adapted to reasoning, crowds are quick to act... How powerless they are to hold any opinions other than those which are imposed upon them.... [They are led] by seeking what produces an impression on them and what seduces them."

-- Gustave le Bon, The Crowd: A Study of the Popular Mind, 1899

239

FC: Now, of course, the song that's being talked about, the song "Louis Farrakhan." Take us into your thinking when you laid down the lyrics to that.

Nas being interviewed by The Final Call's Assistant Editor Ashahed M. Muhammad.

He was smart enough to say "I have an army who believe in what I'm saying, that this is the Truth." That "I would die for everyone, every soldier in that army." They believe that and they know that's true. So, you know, how could I not acknowledge that's that; that's what I acknowledge in my life, then, it's going to bleed into the music.

I know a lot of White cats that listen to Farrakhan! I went to a Coldplay concert, and his introduction was Farrakhan's speech! So, I was blown away! I'm sitting next to Gwyneth Paltrow—we're rocking to a Farrakhan speech! So, it made me go: "Damn! If he—why didn't I use that in my music? I've been wanting to!" So I'm just trying to show the love back now.

Nas: Nasty

BOOKING PHOTO/POLICE REPORT

10th DEGREE

Black Music and the Psycho-Analytical Destruction of a Stolen Legacy

"Subliminal persuasion refers to the use of subliminally presented stimuli, or messages presented to individuals beneath their level of conscious awareness, that are intended to influence their attitudes, choices, or actions."

-- What Every Skeptic Should Know About S.P.

Public sentiment is everything. With public sentiment nothing can fail. Without it nothing can succeed. He who molds opinion is greater than he who enacts laws.

-- President Abraham Lincoln

The stated aim was to get young people to vote. The campaign's message, promoted on t-shirts and other things, is "*Vote or Die!*" Many American television **...**

The media is being used to **stir Americans into a revenge frenzy**. Our boys will be over seas when these U.N. troops decide to disarm us, and **when** martial law is declared they will be policing us Americans. Why not send the U.N. troops to round up Bin Laden if he is guilty. Bush has not mentioned using U.N. troops one time. Do you know why? I know why.. The U.N. troops will fire on Americans, our troops will not.

Russell Simmons Launches 'Turn Up the Vote' Campaign

Hip hop heavyweight Russell Simmons launched the "Hip-Hop Team Vote: Turn up the Vote" campaign last week at a rally at the University of Pennsylvania.

"We know that young people answer the call," Simmons said in a statement. "We know that at this critical time our country needs new leadership with new ideas."

The mogul, who announced on March 2 that he's backing presidential candidate Barack Obama, and Hip-Hop Team Vote will hold a hip-hop summit in Philadelphia on April 20, two days before the Pennsylvania primary. The group also plans to target voters in Ohio, Missouri, Texas and Florida.

"No matter how paranoid or conspiracy-minded you are, what the government is actually doing is worse than you imagine."

-- William Blum

Rap Skool: The Notorious B.I.G – Ten Crack Commandments

With Public Enemy compadre Chuck D giving a quick count to ten, Christopher 'Biggie' Wallace introduces his 'Ten Crack Commandments'.

His experience in the drug distribution arena is such that nobody can tell him anything he doesn't already know about this coke, this crack nor weed for that matter. Nevertheless, he would never be so conceited as to let his success get to his head and forget those further down the hierarchy as he.

Christopher gives a quick introduction saying that he is a veteran in his field, being a market leader for years and in the process has become somewhat of a ruthless 'animal'. Consequently, he has decided to write a manual to provide a detailed breakdown on how one should run any successful crack operation, and importantly, to avoid any would-be crack moguls being shot, or get their 'wig pushed back', as he terms it.

The gangsta vocabulary that is often assessed critically for its vulgarity, misogyny, irreverence and feudalistic glorification is what veteran gangsta rapper Ice Cube justifies as "the language of the streets [is] the only language I can use to communicate with the streets. " This vocabulary includes words like ghetto, thug, code of the streets, bitch, ho, prostitute, pimp, nigga, warrior, struggle, shame, hooker, gospel, commandments, drugs, money, escape, pain, and alone—and these words are weaved together to reveal a very disturbing and descriptive tapestry of suffering and isolation indeed. But these words and the behaviors that they sometimes reflect (in visual form in music videos and in the physical reality of the prevalence of domestic violence within the hip-hop milieu) don't exist in a vacuum, as bell hooks points out in her essay "Sexism and Misogyny: Who takes the Rap? Misogyny, gangsta rap, and The Piano." Her analysis includes a critique of the white supremacist capitalist patriarchal (as usual, for bell hooks) mass media that has been quick to demonize black youth culture as it is expressed by some rappers within this one subculture/subgenre, gangsta rap, which is in reality part of a sexist continuum, necessary for the maintenance of patriarchal social order. [...] It is useful to think of misogyny as a field that must be labored in and maintained both to sustain patriarchy but also to serve as an ideological anti-feminist backlash. And what better group to labor on this 'plantation' than young black men. To see gangsta rap as a reflection of dominant values in our culture rather than as an aberrant 'pathological' standpoint does not mean that rigorous feminist critique of the sexism and misogyny expressed in this music is not needed.

Boots Riley   **RZA**   **immortal technique**

'Im trying to empower young people in the hood to make their lives better, like we've been doing for the last 25, 30, 40 years. Not only in Hip Hop, but outside the context of Hip Hop. You can't deny that because we the record, we have the track record, the history of our work. Ask them Brothers that came out of prison that heard Public Enemy music while they were in prison. Ask all of the two million people that went to the Million-Man March. Let me tell you, I'll give you a deeper insight on that, Brother?

DJ: Go ahead, Brother.

Minimalistic - this mural labels US president George W. Bush a "war criminal". One would have thought that Tony Blair (or latterly Gordon Brown) might have been a target closer to home, on the same charge?

PG: Barack Obama got elected President, mainly because young whites galvanized their energy and put him in office along with black people, alright? Let's just look at this now; those young whites, they came up on Hip Hop, they Public Enemy fans, right or wrong?

DJ: That's right.

PG: So really, Hip Hop put Barack Obama in the White House, if you really wanna look at it. Those same whites were the ones listening to quotes from Malcom X and Minister Farrakan and Aba Mahammad and Dr. Khalib Muhammad on Public Enemy albums. Are you following me? They took the vibratory frequency of Hip Hop and the intellect of Hip Hop and energy of Hip Hop and went out and created businesses. They went out and empowered other young whites that kind of grew up on Hip Hop cause if you do your homework and you research, white people buy Hip Hop. They build television shows around it, right or wrong?

DJ: That's right.

PG: They went to the poles, with their energy, their vibratory frequency and that spirit and said, 'You know something? It's about time we put a Brother in the White House so we can change this dynamic here'. So, Lenon Honors I'm sorry, Brother Hip Hop produced some great and powerful men.

DJ: That's what's up, Brother. What do you think of Barack Obama and the job that he has been doing, specifically I would say over the last six or eight months and the type of opposition that he's been getting?

"Beware the leader who bangs the drums of war in order to whip the citizenry into a patriotic fervor, for patriotism is indeed a double-edged sword. It both emboldens the blood, just as it narrows the mind. And when the drums of war have reached a fever pitch and the blood boils with hate and the mind has closed, the leader will have no need in seizing the rights of the citizenry. Rather, the citizenry, infused with fear and blinded by patriotism, will offer up all of their rights unto the leader and gladly so. How do I know? For this is what I have done. And I am Caesar." (Julius Caesar)

Will Hip-Hop Return To Its Activist Roots?

Flavor Flav -- as much of a fool as he presents himself on the mic in Public Enemy -- he was a wise fool," said music writer and critic Toure. "He did 911 is a Joke, talking about the difficulty of getting emergency medical services in the community. That is a political song."

THE ORIGINAL REPORT ON THE EVOLUTION OF HIP-HOP AND POLITICS

Before hip-hop became the multi-billion dollar industry it is today, there was a group of young lyricists who were ahead of their time. Telling unfiltered truths about the struggles of blacks in the late 1960s and early 70s, they called themselves The Last Poets."When we did that first album, I had no idea it was going to catch on like it did," Abiodun Oyewole told theGrio. "We were dealing directly with issues that concerned us."When Oyewole, one of the founding members of The Last Poets, listens to today's hip-hop, he says the music has lost its political edge."It's like hip-hop has taken the backseat to the industry and they're playing with it like you play with Play-Doh or something," Oyewole said. "You don't hear anything that's got any kinda of impact."From the raw sounds of spoken word on street corners, to block parties in the South Bronx, once hip-hop emerged in the late 1960s, it never looked back.But it wasn't until Grandmaster Flash and the Furious Five released The Message in 1982 when the harsh realities of poverty and broken neighborhoods were put front and center by hip-hop artists.The 1980s saw the rise of many emcees and groups who made political protest and social consciousness an integral part of their music. None more than the brash and uncompromising Public Enemy, whose music was as much a movement as it was hip-hop."Public Enemy is forever linked to politics and hip-hop," said Chuck Creekmur, founder of AllHipHop.com. "Songs like Fight the Power, which I think is the ultimate anthem for empowering the youth (and) By the time I get to Arizona — (about when) the MLK holiday which was being in dispute (in that state).""You think about the messages they were putting out, particularly at a time when the murder rates in African-American communities were probably at the highest they had ever been in history — at the time it was something that was absolutely needed," said Fred Mwangaghunga, founder of celebrity website Mediatakeout.com."Flavor Flav — as much as a fool as he presents himself on the mic in Public Enemy — he was a wise fool," said music writer and critic Toure. "He did 911 is a Joke, talking about the difficulty of getting emergency medical services in the community. That is a political song."At the time, other artists, like KRS-One of Boogie Down Productions rallied against black-on-black violence. And female emcees such as Queen Latifah and MC Lyte fought to empower young women."If you're talking about political dialogue in rap, of course Queen Latifah's UNITY is going to come up," Creekmur said. "Even MC Lyte's Georgie Porgie. That was a political statement about a young black man who goes onto die of cancer."Groups like N.W.A. rapped about the horrors of police brutality. Ice T and his heavy metal band Body Count released the single Cop Killer in 1992 — which the L.A. rapper was forced to pull after intense battles over censorship. Later that year, then-presidential candidate Bill Clinton criticized rapper Sister Souljah's comments on the L.A. riots...setting off a storm of controversy and establishing a new political catchprhase.In the late 80s and early 90s, hip-hop and its artists had plenty to say – and more people were listening than ever before.

President Obama Declares June African American Music Appreciation Month

In the US presidential election, YouTube looks as if it will play a key role. The video networking site is already providing what may be the biggest ever audience for a political speech, 13 million and counting.

http://www.telegraph.co.uk/culture/music/3671190/Barack-Obamas-Yes-We-Can-video.html

Obama said black music has helped provide a colorful and unforgettable soundtrack to the lives of tens of millions worldwide. He also cited the transcendent and uplifting properties in the music that helped buoy an oppressed people through an assortment of atrocities throughout the annals of American history.

"African American music has conveyed the hopes and hardships of a people who have struggled, persevered and overcome. Through centuries of injustice, music comforted slaves, fueled a cultural renaissance, and sustained a movement for equality," the President said in an official statement distributed by the White House. Change of tune ... No word yet on whether Obama will duet with Stevie Wonder. Photograph: Stefano Paltera/AP

The song was conceived by Will.i.am of superstar hip-hop trio Black Eyed Peas, and the video was shot by Jesse Dylan, son of rock's original protest superstar, Bob Dylan. The pair claim that it took just a few days from conception to completion. Will.i.am had the idea while watching a televised political debate on January 29, and by Feb 2 it was online, in time for the Super Tuesday polls.

Watch the Will.i.am produced Yes We Can video Yes, he can: Triple win for Obama

PG: Well, I think he's been neutralized by the republicans. That he let the democrats down and now they are coming at his throat and one article I read recently, I don't have it in front of me, pardon me for that. In essence, it said that if Hilary Clinton would give Barack Obama one of her balls, he would would have two. They are really coming at the Brother. They are already calling him a one-term President – let me tell ya'll something man, if we sat for eight years and we watch this idiot Bush, who couldn't even complete a damn sentence – if we went through eight years of that, I'm sure we can have Barack Obama stay there another term to complete the work that republicans are setting up roadblocks in his way, you understand what I'm saying? And making it so difficult for the Brother to complete his mission. Now, I don't agree with everything Barack Obama said and have done, but nonetheless, we love the Brother. I don't want to see anything happen to him – as a matter of fact, I could be so bold to say some of the stuff that Lenon Honors put on his website is very positive and accurate and on point. You can't deny that, if you go over the man's work, you gotta look at it and say, 'Now, wait a minute okay, you know something? He's right about that'. Putting all the ego and other stuff aside, you gotta say, 'Wait a minute man, the Brother's right', you understand what I'm saying? But I think he needs to know that there is a difference between Hip Hop and rap. Hip Hop is something that you are, rap is something that you do, Lenon Honors. And I think what you are doing is you're taking what is going on in rap music today and you treating the entire history of Hip Hop as though it's representative of what these idiots are doing today in this thing called rap music, not Hip Hop. It's called 'shit hop', as Black Dot calls it.

The mind of the enemy and the will of his leaders is a target of far more importance than the bodies of his troops.
-- Brigadier General S.B. Griffith, II, USMC

Rapper Common's White House invite upsets rightwingers

Barack Obama greets Common in 2009. The inclusion of the rapper, at the invitation of Michelle Obama, in a night of poetry at the White House has provoked Republicans including Sarah Palin. Photograph: Charles Dharapak/AP

It should have been a controversy-free event, a night of poetry at the White House. But instead a literary celebration turned into a mini-row over the lyrics of a rapper invited to perform.

Michelle Obama invited a selection of poets and other writers, part of a series highlighting American music and literature.

Republicans Sarah Palin and Karl Rove are among those critical of the inclusion of the lyricist in a music and literature event

http://www.guardian.co.uk/world/2011/may/11/rapper-common-white-house-invite

"He's fresh, you know, he's got good style," Common told CNN. "As far as people in my age group and people that love hip-hop, there's a love for Obama. He represents progress. He represents what hip-hop is about. Hip-hop is about progress, the struggle.""Why is Bush acting like he trying to get Osama?/Why don't we impeach him and elect Obama?" - Common

Common endorsed Obama's presidential candidacy years before the Illinois senator even formed a presidential exploratory committee. This 2004 remix marked the first time Obama was ever namedropped in a rap song. Maybe the Windy City MC knew something we didn't.

Obama Honors Quincy Jones with Arts Medal

Today in the East Room of the White House, President Obama honored music legend Quincy Jones with the nation's most prestigious honor for artists — the National Medal of Arts.

Jones joins the ranks of Aretha Franklin, Maya Anglou and Ella Fitzgerald with this award. According to the National Endowment for the Arts website, the medal is given to artists who "are deserving of special recognition by reason of their outstanding contributions to the excellence, growth, support and availability of the arts in the United States."

Read more: http://www.essence.com/2011/03/02/president-barack-obama-honors-quincy-jones-2010-national-medal-of-arts/#ixzz1bAuiPG8T

LUDACRIS RELEASES RACY
POLITICAL SONG; OBAMA CAMP NOT TOO HAPPY!

Ludacris recently released a song called "Politics: Obama is Here". The lyrics are a bit racy as he called Obama's former Democratic rival Hillary Clinton a "B*tch"! Ludacris also disparages John McCain, President Bush and the Rev. Jesse Jackson.

Check out the lyrics:

Said I handled his biz and I'm one of his favorite rappers
Well give Luda a special pardon if I'm ever in the slammer
Better yet put him in office, make me your vice president
Hillary hated on you, so that b^$&%* is irrelevant
Jesse talking slick and apologizing for what?
if you said it then you meant it how you want it have a gut!
and all you other politicians trying to hate on my man,
watch us win a majority vote in every state on my ma

The Obama Campaign released a statement yesterday saying that they are disgusted by Luda's political song.

"I hope Senator Obama has the presence of mind to denounce and distance himself from Ludacris," wrote Yashar Hedayat, Obama's camp put out the following statement addressing the song:

"As Barack Obama has said many, many times in the past, rap lyrics today too often perpetuate misogyny, materialism, and degrading images that he doesn't want his daughters or any children exposed to. This song is not only outrageously offensive to Senator Clinton, Reverend Jackson, Senator McCain, and President Bush, it is offensive to all of us who are trying to raise our children with the values we hold dear. While Ludacris is a talented individual he should be ashamed of these lyrics."

Rappers speak out against the "War On Terror."
As war with Iraq seems imminent, rappers and hip-hop luminaries have come forward to express their anti-war sentiments. Reverend RunFormer Run-DMC member (Reverend) Run is planning to record an all-star antiwar record Protest recording Hip-Hop's most conscious artists join forces to send a prolific message of peace across the world with the release of a single entitled "Raise Your Hands High... Say Not In Our Name." Read more and get it here.

Lady Gagas Appearance Scares President Obama

President Obama reportedly acknowledged his meeting with pop star Lady Gaga when he spoke to the Human Rights Campaign, which is a gay advocacy organization this past weekend. According to reports, President Obama was apparently intimated by the "Born This Way" singer. He told the audience "I appreciate the chance to join you tonight. I also took a trip out to California last week, where I held some productive bilateral talks with your leader, Lady Gaga."

About his meeting with Lady Gaga, President Obama said "She was wearing 16-inch heels," and then "She was 8 feet tall. It was a little intimidating."

Lady Gaga had previously met the President at a fundraiser lobbying for anti-bullying policies and enforcement after a gay Buffalo teen was bullied and subsequently committed suicide.

"If you're talking about political dialogue in rap, of course Queen Latifah's UNITY is going to come up," Creekmur said. "Even MC Lyte's Georgie Porgie. That was a political statement about a young Black man who goes on to die of cancer."

Hip Hop rapper and businessman Jay-Z who supported President Barack Obama during his 2008 campaign is supporting him yet again. The hip hop artist feels that people should 'bag off' Obama after he took over a devastated America. Nothing like getting a lyrical endorsement from one of the greatest hip-hop artists of all time. Interestingly, Obama once said that he listens to Jay-Z and Beyonce.

Jay-Z and P. Diddy on the Campagin Trail for the Obama and *Now it really starts to makes sense.*

Council of Conservative Citizens

Obama brags about listening to ganster rap music

Responsible black parents were shocked by Obama's repeated endorsements of foul mouthed, violent black hip hop bands. The media and black organizations have been hailing Obama as the pre-einent role model for black people. What message is he really sending?

The Ganster rapper "Nas," wearing a t-shirt that reads "nigger." Obama recently named him as one of his favorite artists. Ludacris. Obama praised Ludicris during the campaign and made an appearance with him. Ludicris responded by writing a pro-Obama rap song in which he calls Hillary an "irrelevant bitch," and suggests Obama will give him a pardon if he breaks the law.Lil Wayne. A thug with multiple felony convictions and prison gang tattoos on his face! Lil Wayne is not a former thug turned rapper. He is serving hard time in prison right now! Obama shocked parents by praising the thug's violent music recently.Obama actually names rapper Jay-Z as his favorite. This thug is most famous for his song "99 problems but a bitch ain't one." Beside being anti-female, the song is also very anti-white. The rapper blames his "real problems" on white people. Jay-Z campaigned for Obama during the election, performing at an anti-Republican rally in Miami.

Groups like N.W.A. rapped about the horrors of police brutality. Ice T and his heavy metal band Body Count released the single Cop Killer in 1992 -- which the L.A. rapper was forced to pull after intense battles over censorship.

"Most of the music, no matter what genre we're talking about from jazz to hip-hop, is actually apolitical," Powell said. "The music becomes political if there's something political happening in the community."

One rapper who isn't shy about speaking out is Kanye West. In 2005, at a telethon to support victims of Katrina, he famously said: "George Bush doesn't care about Black people."

Public Enemy, Poor Righteous Teachers, and X Clan were a big recruitment vehicle for the Nation Of Islam, The 5 Percent Nation Of Gods, etc. KRS ONE unraveled a lot of things I didn't know about and he is actually one of the reasons I started picking up books again after leaving school prematurely.

x-clan

Conscious MC Lakim Shabazz of the 5% Nation of Gods and Earths
"Peace God"

"You think about the messages they were putting out, particularly at a time when the murder rates in African-American communities were probably at the highest they had ever been in history -- at the time it was something that was absolutely needed," *said Fred Mwangaguhunga, founder of celebrity website.* (Mediatakeout.com.)

Blackwards:

Exposin' the Hip Hop Hood Hoax

TRUTH Minista Paul Scott

"Mental pictures, stereotypes and fake history reinforces mystery."☐hy is that☐
-----☐oogie ☐own ☐roduction

From birth, we are taught to believe myths. We start off believing fables about tooth fairies and an old fat dude in a red suit ridin' around the hood in a red sleigh pulled by a red nosed reindeer. As we grow older and enter the mis-educational system, we are indoctrinated by stories about a lost sailor named Chris "discovering" America and an "honest" opportunist named Abe "freeing the slaves." We are also programmed to believe the urban legend that the Hip Hop of today comes out of the hood.

It may come as a shock for some, but the Hip Hop that is played on the radio today owes more to the campus of Harvard than it does the streets of Harlem. Most Hip Hop fans can recite, verbatim, the often parroted propaganda about how Hip Hop started in the parks of the Bronx in the late 70's and went on to become the global enterprise that it is today. Like most myths, there is a shred of truth in this hype; however, the whole truth is hidden from the masses. One flip through the pages of books like "**The Big Payback: The History of the Business of Hip Hop**" by Dan Charnas, and one sees how quickly the focus on Grandmaster Flash spinnin' in the Bronx switches to stories about Maury, the mild mannered accountant thinking of a master plan to have his multi-national company exploit the talents of "ghetto" youth.

Contrary to the popular belief that commercial Hip Hop is the brainchild of mix masters in the 'hood, in reality, much of the credit goes to the masterminds at Ivy League schools. While it is, indeed, true that Hip Hop originated in the Big Apple, the moment that "Rapper's Delight" was played outside of the five boroughs, the corporate takeover of Hip Hop began. Later, as interest in Hip Hop spread throughout the world, the people who were largely responsible for defining what Hip Hop is or is not were not the neighborhood scribes, but Ivy League brainiacs who interpreted the street lingo of the Chocolate cities for the Vanilla suburbs. Although, rap is promoted as being the voice of the streets, it is interesting that the founders of Hip Hop's premier magazine, the Source, Dave Mays and Jon Schechter, as well as early members of "The Mind Squad" formed the magazine while they were students at Harvard during the late '80's.

Also, in 1993, Keith Clinkscales, who received an MBA from Harvard Business School, was named CEO of Vibe Magazine. It was under his watch that the magazine heavily promoted the East Coast/West Coast Beef that resulted in the deaths of Tupac Shakur, Notorious BIG and many others. Which adds to the theory that all the "Hip Hop" beefs are just a part of a diabolical marketing scheme to sell CD's.

Also, although rappers such as Waka Flocka Flame have said in interviews that they purposely dumb down their lyrics to "keep it real" for their homies in the 'hood, according to a 2006 article in New York Magazine, one of the hottest producers at Bad Boy Records was Ryan Leslie who scored 1600 on his SAT, entered Harvard at 15 and graduated at 19 years old.

It must be noted that Harvard's connection to black music did not start with Hip Hop but goes back to the early 70's with "A Study of the Soul Music Environment" aka the Harvard Report. According to Yvonne Bynoe in her essay, **Money, Power and Respect: A Critique of the Business of Rap Music**, "the systematic colonization of Black music began in 1971 when Columbia Records commissioned the Harvard University Business School to conduct an investigation about how they should better benefit from soul music." Later, according to a May 1996 article in the Harvard Gazette, a more Hip Hop version of the study, the "Harvard Report on Urban Music" was compiled by the Harvard Consultation Project.

Besides the money aspect, Hip Hop's influence on the minds of our youth and the strange behavior of some artists cannot be denied.

Ironically, Harvard is also famous for experiments in mind control. Dr. Timothy Leary, a professor in Harvard's Center for Research in Personality, in the early 60's conducted mind control experiments involving psychedelic drugs. According to Alex Constantine in his book **The Covert War Against Rock**, Aldous Huxley, a visiting professor at Harvard, asked Leary to "form a secret society to launch and lead a psychedelic conspiracy to brainwash influential people." Although Harvard has produced some of the most influential African Americans in this country's history including scholar WEB Dubois, who was one of the founders of the NAACP and, of course, President Barack and Michelle Obama, the institution has also been affiliated with some who believed that Black folks are genetically, intellectually inferior to Whites. William Shockley received his PhD from Harvard and Arthur Jensen's "How Much Can We Boost IQ and Scholastic Achievement?" was published in the 1969 Harvard Educational Review.

Also, "The Bell Curve," a 1994 book that also questioned the intelligence of African Americans was co-authored by Harvard professor, Richard Herrnstein. So, is it possible that the current "dumb down" movement in Hip Hop is a self full-filing prophesy orchestrated by those who will stop at nothing to prove a point? That Harvard should produce those who feel that African people are inferior to Europeans should come as no surprise to those who have researched Harvard's dark hidden history. A February 1999, edition of the student newspaper, The Harvard Crimson, reported that buried "deep within the annals of Harvard" there is a file HUD 3502 that reveals information about the Harvard chapter of the Ku Klux Klan that was formed in 1921.

Of course, there are some who will still believe the "Hip Hop hood myth" in the same manner that some people will fight you if you try to tell them that WWE wrestling is fake. No matter what, some Hip Hop heads will still be in denial.

Whether you want to believe it or not, the next hot rapper may not come out of the Marcy Projects in Brooklyn, but from some top secret science project in a lab hidden away deep down in a basement in Harvard.

TRUTH Minista Paul Scott can be reached at info@nowarningshotsfired.com or (919) 451-8283.

Article courtesy of The Militant Mind Militia http://www.militantmindmilitia.com

Today's youth is being conditioned to accept a police presence in their society, ID cards for identification (think Nazi Germany), and thumb printing for the privilege to eat. They're being given incentives to report so-called "suspicious" activity (even to report their own parents!). They're being led on drills where they're herded onto buses with sometimes loaded automatic weapons aimed at their heads.

http://www.fdrs.org/subliminal_persuasion.html

253

About the Author

Professor Griff is an internationally renowned educator, writer, producer, musician, platinum recording/spoken word artist, lecturer and founding member of the pioneering and revolutionary hip hop group **Public Enemy**. Author of the popular music business guide: **Musick Bizness R.I.P. (Resource Information Publication)**, Griff stands as a highly acclaimed, seasoned entertainment industry veteran and sought-after resource on all aspects of the music business. An activist within both the conscious and hip hop communities, Griff currently stands as a permanent fixture on the international lecture circuit with his riveting and powerful discourse/book, **The Psychological Covert War on Hip Hop**. An energetic and passionate educator, Griff skillfully customizes this extensively documented lecture to suit the needs of all audiences.Armed with an exemplary life of service and an impressive twenty-year musical career, Griff captivates audiences with his universal call for social responsibility within both the hip hop community and larger culture.

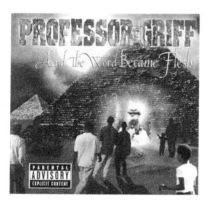

254

As perhaps a testament to his firm commitment to raise the level of consciousness of today's entire hip hop generation, Griff effortlessly draws upon his own extensive entertainment industry experience and a vast reservoir of historical scholarship and research to deliver this poignant message. Reared in Long Island, New York and a current resident of Atlanta, Georgia, Griff maintains a coveted role as Minista of Information for Public Enemy and is currently celebrating an unprecedented sixty world tours and 20th Year Anniversary, with the group. A well-rounded music enthusiast, Griff is also a member of the hip hop/metal band **7th Octave**, and has created an empowering youth hip hop curriculum entitled **Kidhoppaz**, designed to fuse education and entertainment into a positive, effective instructional module.

Musically, Griff has recorded nine albums with his group Public Enemy; however, he has long distinguished himself as a talented and acclaimed solo artist as well. Namely, while signed to Luke Records, Griff wrote, produced and recorded three powerful and thought-provoking albums entitled: **Pawns in the Game** (1990), **Kaoz II Wiz-7-Dome** (1991) and **Disturb N Tha Peace** (1992). Also, in 1998, Griff released **Blood of the Profit** on Lethal Records. With his group Confrontation Camp Griff recorded the album **Objects in the Mirror May be Closer than they Appear** (2000) and **The Word Became Flesh** (2001); with his group 7th Octave he recorded the album **The Seventh Degree** (2004). Griff has appeared in the following films: **Turntables** and **The Chip Factor**, in addition he spearheaded the production of the informative documentary entitled **Turn off Channel Zero**.

Griff holds a Bachelor of Science degree in Education, is a licensed personal security defense instructor, and is an accomplished martial artist. An avid lecturer, known for his innate ability to impart life-changing ideas, concepts and techniques for the spiritual/personal growth and development of all who attend his lectures, Professor Griff is uniquely equipped to meet the needs of an international wide-ranging audience. Remaining true to his title as Minista of Information, Professor Griff has continued his vigilance by providing information for the masses. Most recently, he has published the **Atlanta Musick Bizness Resource Information Publication (R.I.P.)** providing invaluable industry information for those interested in breaking into the business of MuSick. Griff s current projects include: **7th Octave- God Damage Album, Psychological Covert War on Hip-Hop** (book & lecture), **Metaphysical Goddestry of the Soul of Hip-Hop** (book & lecture), and more in the works.

Griff at Yoshi's in San francisco 2011

About the book from one who has benefited from the work and the word before the physical book was ever completed.

The Psychological Covert War on Hip Hop is written with heart and intensity, as Professor Griff takes on the difficult task of speaking truth to power. Griff's writing style is as the man himself, brave and assertive. A true soldier...who uses his insight and ability to educate and captivate his readers and audiences.

The Psychological Covert War on hip hop provides the reader with a look into the Illuminati's takeover of hip hop. It may be shocking for some and eye-opening for most. But for those of you who are upheld by keeping in line with being Politically Correct, it will make you think twice as you realize you to may be carrying out the Luciferian agenda.

The Psychological Covert War on Hip Hop is fearless, audacious and brilliantly written. The author exhibits insightful judgment as he speaks up and out, revealing the Truths behind the diabolical scheme of brainwashing millions, if not billions, who listen to Hip Hop music.

As hip hop is faced with being at the cultural crossroads, the cultural genocidal program aimed at hip hop led by the culture bandits and some behind the scene insiders of the music industry have their hands full. Take a look into the Illuminati's destruction of the soul of hip hop via "The Psychological Covert War on Hip Hop."

----------**Tyra Coles 2008**

What will be your reward in regards to the destruction of the devil?
Peace and happiness. I will give all I have and all within my power to see this day for which I have waited – 379 years. ———THE MOST HONORABLE ELIJAH. MUHAMMAD

The Psychological Covert War on Hip Hop --- $25.00
Analytixz --- $20.00

To place an order online through PayPal:
PCW --- PCWHipHop@gmail.com
Analytixz --- 7thoctave@gmail.com

QTY	DESCRIPTION	UNIT PRICE	TOTAL

PAYABLE TO HEIRZ TO THE SHAH --- MAIL PAYMENTS TO:

KAVON SHAH
P.O.BOX 11902
ATLANTA, GA 30355

Please print clearly, so we may get the book to the correct address

SUBTOTAL	
SHIPPING AND HANDLING	$4.95
TOTAL	

Your Name: _____

Address: _____

City: _____ State: _____

Please allow 2 weeks for Domestic shipping and
3 weeks for International shipping.
To check on orders please call 678 557 2919 or email professorgriffpe@gmail.com

CPSIA information can be obtained
at www.ICGtesting.com
Printed in the USA
LVOW04s1515190917
549275LV00026B/425/P

9 780977 124299